I0824107

THE 5 LOVE LANGUAGES® COACHING

HANDBOOK

A Practical Guide for Coaches, Counselors, and Leaders to Help Others

Gary Chapman and
Les & Leslie Parrott

#1 *NEW YORK TIMES* BESTSELLING AUTHORS

NORTHFIELD PUBLISHING
CHICAGO

Edited by Connor Sterchi
Interior design: Puckett Smartt
Cover design: Kaylee Lockenour Dunn

ISBN: 978-0-8024-4053-2

We hope you enjoy this book from Northfield Publishing. Our goal is to provide high-quality, thought-provoking books and products that connect truth to your real needs and challenges. For more information on other books and products that will help you with all your important relationships, go to northfieldpublishing.com or write to:

Northfield Publishing
820 N. LaSalle Boulevard
Chicago, IL 60610

1 3 5 7 9 10 8 6 4 2

Printed in Colombia

Contents

The 5 Love Languages® Coaching Network Qualifications

This handbook is designed to equip, inspire, and guide you in the art and practice of relationship coaching using the 5 Love Languages® framework. Whether you are a counselor, pastor, ministry leader, or coach, the insights and tools in these pages can strengthen your ability to help others love well.

However, it's important to be clear: Reading this handbook alone does not qualify someone to represent themselves as a *Certified Love Language™ Coach.*

Certification as an official Love Language Coach requires the successful completion of the authorized online certification program, along with maintaining active status through annual renewal. This process ensures that every certified coach has received consistent training, understands the ethical and practical application of the framework, and is equipped to serve others with integrity and excellence.

Those who complete certification and remain in good standing are granted the right to identify themselves as a *Certified Love Language™ Coach* and to display the official certification indicium in their professional materials. This designation signals to clients, organizations, and the broader public that you have met the standards established by the 5 Love Languages® Coaching Network.

If you have not yet completed certification, this handbook will serve as a valuable foundation—and an invitation. The certification process will help you deepen your skills, expand your impact, and confidently step into the role of a trusted guide for others.

To learn more or begin the certification process, visit:

Coaching.5LoveLanguages.com

The Coaching Landscape Today

Not long ago, the only option for relational support was therapy. Now, relationship coaching is filling a critical gap: helping people who aren't in crisis but are stuck. People want more than advice—they want a guide. Someone to help them see their patterns, clarify their needs, and practice love in ways that stick. They're not looking for a diagnosis. They're looking for direction.

The Rise of Coaching

The coaching movement began taking shape in the 1980s and 1990s, emerging from a blend of business consulting, personal development, and humanistic psychology. Executive coaching took the lead, but it wasn't long before niches began to form—health coaching, financial coaching, spiritual coaching, and eventually, relationship coaching (Williams, 2017).

Unlike therapy, which is often retrospective and focused on healing, coaching is proactive and forward-thinking. It's rooted in growth, clarity, and action. Coaches don't excavate trauma or explore childhood wounds. They help people take ownership of their present and align their behavior with their goals (Stober & Grant, 2006). That difference, while subtle, is often profound.

Relationship coaching gained traction as more and more people realized they needed a sounding board. A relational mirror. A coach who could walk with them through the complexities of love—someone who wouldn't pathologize their struggles but would help them build new patterns.

By the early 2000s, the International Coach Federation (ICF) recognized relationship coaching as a specialty in its own right. Today, it's one of the fastest-growing areas in the coaching field, fueled by cultural shifts in how we pursue love, how we communicate, and how we seek support (ICF, 2023).

What's Driving the Growth?

Several factors are accelerating the demand for relationship coaching:

- **Accessibility:** Coaching is often more affordable, flexible, and approachable than therapy. It's not clinical—it's conversational.
- **Relational Stress:** The pressures of modern life—from career overload to digital distraction—are fraying emotional connection.
- **Desire for Practical Tools:** People want more than theory. They want language, structure, and steps they can actually use.
- **Preventative Mindset:** More people are seeking help *before* things fall apart. They don't want to fix what's broken—they want to strengthen what's working.

And while coaching isn't therapy, it can be deeply transformative. Coaches often become the first safe person a client has ever processed with. The first one to name what's missing. The first one to help them not just understand love but practice it.

Why This Handbook?

We created this handbook to accompany the online Love Language™ coaching certification program and equip you with everything you need to become a confident, effective Love Language™ Coach. It's designed to meet you wherever you are.

You don't need to have it all figured out. But you do need a road map.

That's what this book offers. A proven framework. Tools you can use immediately. Stories you'll recognize. And a deeper understanding of how people grow in love—not just by theory but also by practice.

Welcome to the work.

Why This Handbook?

You're here because you care. You care about relationships. You care about helping people thrive. And you believe love—real, enduring love—can be learned, practiced, and lived.

But caring isn't enough. Not today.

People are overwhelmed. They're bombarded with content—videos, blogs, reels, and relationship "hacks." Yet they're still struggling. Despite unprecedented access to advice, people are more confused, more disconnected, and more discouraged than ever (Stanley, Rhoades, & Markman, 2006). They don't need another hot take on Instagram. They need someone who knows how to guide them.

That's where you come in.

Whether you're a counselor, pastor, small group facilitator, ministry leader, or simply someone others turn to for wisdom, this handbook is your guide to becoming a confident and effective relationship coach—one who knows how to help people not just understand love but also practice it.

Coaching Is Rising—And for Good Reason

Coaching has grown rapidly in recent years, especially in areas where people are hungry for growth but not in crisis (Williams, 2017). Relationship coaching offers something distinct from therapy: a forward-looking, action-oriented approach that's supportive without being clinical.

Many people are seeking help not because their relationship is in ruins but because they're bewildered. They want clarity, language, and direction. A coach can provide all three. You help them make sense of what's happening, name what's missing, and take meaningful steps toward connection.

The shift is real: We're moving from reactionary relationship care to proactive relational guidance.

Why the 5 Love Languages Work So Well

The 5 Love Languages® framework is one of the most accessible, transformative tools available to a relationship coach (Pett, Lozano, & Varga, 2022). Developed by Dr. Gary Chapman, it gives people a shared language for expressing and receiving love—and perhaps more importantly, for understanding emotional disconnection.

Millions have read *The 5 Love Languages*. But few know how to coach others in living it out.

That's what this handbook is for. You'll learn how to help clients translate insight into action. You'll walk them through the frustrations, the mismatches, the breakthroughs. And you'll help them personalize their journey—not just recite a concept.

Research confirms that personalized emotional expression plays a vital role in long-term relationship satisfaction (Gottman & Silver, 2015). The Love Languages help partners decode each other's needs in ways that feel intuitive and intimate.

But a concept only becomes transformational when someone walks with you as you live it out. That's your role.

Coaching Is About Who You Are, Not Just What You Know

Techniques matter. But presence matters more.

Relationship coaching isn't just about tools—it's about trust. It's about showing up with empathy, emotional safety, and wisdom. The kind of coach who changes lives is the kind of person who is emotionally attuned, spiritually grounded, and relationally present.

This handbook will help you with both: the skill set and the soul-work. You'll learn how to guide people through miscommunication, unmet needs, and reactivity. But just as importantly, you'll learn how to become a calming, catalytic presence.

What to Expect from This Handbook

Each chapter in this book is designed to give you a deep dive into the art of Love Language coaching. You'll explore:

- The psychology behind the model.
- The practical tools for guiding people.
- The soft skills that turn insight into impact.
- The ethics and boundaries of coaching.
- The invitation to deepen your own emotional intelligence and spiritual awareness.

Whether you're considering certification as a Love Language Coach or simply want to sharpen your natural gifting, you'll find actionable wisdom here. And if you choose to pursue our Love Language coaching certification, this handbook will be your essential guide.

Your Next Step

If this work resonates with you—if you find yourself eager not just to understand these principles but to help others live them out—then your next step is clear. Becoming a Certified Love Language Coach equips you with more than knowledge. It gives you a proven pathway, practical tools, and a trusted framework for guiding people toward lasting connection.

At the heart of this certification is the 5 Love Languages Premium Assessment. As a certified coach, you'll receive exclusive access to this powerful tool—designed to uncover not only a person's primary Love Language but also the unique dialects and nuances that shape how they give and receive love. You'll be trained to interpret assessment results with clarity and confidence, helping individuals and couples gain insight that goes far beyond surface-level understanding.

Our certification process is designed to help you grow in both competence and credibility. You'll receive structured training, hands-on coaching guidance, and access to resources that enable you to use the Premium Assessment effectively in real coaching conversations. More than that, you'll join a global community of certified coaches who share your commitment to helping people experience love in ways that truly transform their relationships.

If you're ready to take this step, we invite you to learn more and begin your certification journey today at:

Coaching.5LoveLanguages.com

The need has never been greater. People are searching for clarity, insight, and someone who can help them love well. With the right training—and the right tools—that someone can be you.

Helping others love well is one of the most meaningful things you'll ever do. So take a breath. Lean in. And let's begin the journey. You bring the heart. We'll equip you with the insight.

Dr. Gary Chapman

Drs. Les and Leslie Parrott

PART 1

THE FOUNDATIONS OF RELATIONSHIP COACHING

"We cannot teach people anything; we can only help them discover it within themselves."

—GALILEO GALILEI

Before you can help others rewrite the way they love, you need to sharpen how you show up. This opening section lays the groundwork—not just with techniques, but with the kind of self-awareness and emotional presence that make transformation possible. You'll discover how to build trust that disarms defenses, ask questions that cut through the noise, and guide people with clarity and courage. From understanding your role as a coach to navigating the deeper dynamics of connection, these chapters help you coach not just from your skill set—but from your soul. If you're serious about doing this work well, this is where it begins.

Chapter 1

The Role of a Relationship Coach

Relationship coaching is more than a conversation. At its best, it's a catalyst. It's what happens when a coach sits across from someone—not to analyze them, not to fix them, but to hold up a mirror and say, "Let's take a look at how love is showing up in your lives—and how it could grow." It's focused, it's intentional, and it's profoundly personal.

That's the role of a relationship coach.

Not a lecturer. Not a referee. Not a therapist. A relationship coach is a translator of emotional needs, a trainer in love's daily practice, and a guide through the fog of disconnection. In a world where love is too often assumed, miscommunicated, or misunderstood, coaches step in to help people speak clearly—and act deliberately.

And there's never been a greater need. Studies consistently show that while people value emotional connection, they often lack the tools to sustain it—especially under modern stressors like digital distraction, overwork, and relational ambiguity (Gottman & Silver, 2015; Stanley, Rhoades, & Markman, 2006). Even couples who report high commitment struggle to express love in ways that land—especially when emotional needs go unrecognized or unarticulated (Lavner, Karney, & Bradbury, 2016).

When you coach with the 5 Love Languages in your toolkit, you're not just offering insight. You're giving people a framework they can hold on to, return to, and live out. Research on emotional expression supports this: Couples who learn to communicate affection in a way their partner receives it report higher satisfaction and lower conflict over time (Gottman et al., 2002; Chapman, 2024).

This chapter will unpack what makes this role so unique—and why it matters so much. We'll explore how coaching differs from other helping professions, what qualifies someone to take on this work, and the core traits that define an exceptional Love Language coach.

What Is Relationship Coaching?

Relationship coaching is a collaborative process that helps individuals or couples build stronger, more intentional relationships. It's rooted in the present, focused on the future, and structured around actionable growth—not clinical treatment or crisis management.

While therapy often explores the past and seeks to heal psychological wounds, coaching helps people clarify goals, develop relational skills, and practice new habits that move them toward greater connection and satisfaction (Grant, 2006; Stober & Grant, 2006; Gollwitzer, 1999).

A relationship coach isn't there to diagnose, interpret dreams, or resolve trauma. They're there to help couples *tune in* to each other, *translate* emotional needs into action, and *train* love as a practice, not just a feeling.

And unlike informal "mentoring" or advice-giving, coaching is structured. It has a beginning, middle, and end. It operates with clear boundaries, defined goals, and measurable progress. Research has shown that coaching, when grounded in evidence-based frameworks, improves client outcomes in both individual and relational domains (Green, Oades, & Grant, 2006; Hudson & McLean, 2012).

Relationship coaching is not a replacement for therapy, but for many people who are not in crisis, it's the support system they didn't know they needed. It's preventative. It's empowering. And in many cases, it's what helps a good relationship grow stronger before it becomes strained.

Who Can Become a Relationship Coach?

Coaching democratizes relational support—no graduate degree required. But solid training and ethical grounding are essential.

Many relationship coaches begin as trusted mentors—people who are already walking alongside couples informally. With training, structure, and clarity of role, this natural mentorship can evolve into an intentional coaching relationship (Parrott & Parrott, 2005).

Some relationship coaches are licensed counselors or seasoned pastors. Others are teachers, mentors, small group leaders, marriage mentors, or simply people who have walked through relational challenges, been helped by the 5 Love Languages, and want to help others. The beauty of coaching is that it's accessible. If you have a heart to serve, a willingness to learn, and the humility to stay within your scope, you can become a powerful force for change in people's relationships.

But accessibility doesn't mean anything goes. Great coaches know how to guide without controlling, listen without fixing, and create a space where people can grow without shame.

Though not legally required, certification through a reputable program (such as the 5 Love Languages® Coaching Network) provides the structure, tools, and ethical foundation necessary for impactful coaching. These programs equip you with:

- **Evidence-based techniques** rooted in positive psychology and adult learning theory (Passmore, 2015; Norcross & Wampold, 2011).
- **Structured session formats** that create focus and momentum.
- **Ethical clarity** around boundaries, confidentiality, and referral (ICF, 2021).
- **Confidence** to coach people from diverse backgrounds and in various relationship stages.

Coaches aren't expected to know everything—but they are expected to know what they can offer, and when to refer out. Knowing when to refer is not a limitation of coaching; it's a commitment to the wellbeing of the people you serve. Professional counseling offers the clinical training and therapeutic depth that certain situations rightly require.

Personal Qualities of Effective Coaches

Coaching isn't about having all the answers. It's about presence and character. Skills can be trained and tools can be learned—but lasting impact starts with presence. The best relationship coaches lead not with credentials but with character. They carry a kind of emotional posture—open, grounded, curious, and safe—that makes it easier for others to be honest, try new things, and confront what's not working.

In this section, we explore four core qualities that consistently show up in effective relationship coaches. These aren't checkboxes to complete; they are traits to cultivate over time—and they matter just as much as any framework or technique you'll ever use.

1. Emotional Intelligence (EQ)

Emotional intelligence is the cornerstone of relational work. It includes the ability to manage your own emotions, recognize the emotions of others, and respond with empathy and attunement (Goleman, 1995). Research shows that coaches high in EQ are more effective in building trust, navigating tension, and helping clients feel understood (Boyatzis, Smith, & Beveridge, 2013).

In coaching, EQ looks like knowing when to pause rather than press, sensing when a client is pulling back, and staying regulated when a conversation becomes emotionally complex. It creates the safety people need to take relational risks.

2. Nonjudgmental Curiosity

Great coaches don't rush to fix—they stay curious. Carl Rogers (1951) referred to this as "unconditional positive regard," a foundational belief that people are worthy of empathy, even in their mess. Coaches who embody this stance avoid moralizing or pathologizing. Instead, they ask, "What's behind that reaction?" or "What need might that behavior be pointing to?"

This kind of curiosity invites exploration without shame. It lowers defenses and helps clients see their patterns with more clarity and less self-condemnation—opening the door for real change.

3. Growth Mindset

Coaching is about possibility. A growth mindset—the belief that people can change and relationships can improve—creates the environment where that belief becomes reality (Dweck, 2006).

Coaches with a growth mindset normalize setbacks and celebrate progress. They don't expect perfection; they expect learning. And because they expect it, they help clients move through frustration with hope rather than resignation.

In the context of love, this mindset says, "You can get better at this. Love is a skill—not just a feeling." That message alone can reframe a person's entire outlook.

4. Ethical Behavior

Good intentions aren't enough in coaching. Without ethical clarity, even well-meaning efforts can cause harm. Effective coaches understand and respect their limits. They protect confidentiality, avoid dual relationships, and know when to refer a client to a licensed mental health professional (International Coach Federation [ICF], 2021; American Psychological Association [APA], 2017).

Ethical awareness also means being mindful of power dynamics, cultural sensitivity, and the unique vulnerabilities that arise in relationship conversations. Coaches who hold this awareness create a space that is not only effective—but deeply respectful.

These four traits—emotional intelligence, nonjudgmental curiosity, growth mindset, and ethical behavior—form the inner scaffolding of great coaching. You won't always embody them perfectly. But the more you cultivate them, the more relational safety and transformation your clients will experience.

The Ethics of Relationship Coaching

Let's take a deeper dive into ethics. If emotional intelligence forms the heart of coaching, ethical clarity forms the backbone.

Unlike therapy, coaching isn't regulated by state licensure boards. That means it's the responsibility of the coach to uphold professional standards—often guided by organizations like the International Coach Federation (ICF) or outlined in resources like the American Psychological Association's ethics code. The goal is not to police every conversation, but to create a coaching relationship that's built on integrity and mutual respect.

Here are four pillars of ethical coaching practice every relationship coach should honor:

1. Informed Consent & Coaching Agreements

Every coaching relationship should begin with clear communication about what coaching is—and what it isn't. This is often formalized through a coaching agreement or written consent form. You'll find an example of one of these you can use in the Appendix. Being upfront about your process builds credibility and empowers your clients to participate with full understanding (ICF, 2021).

2. Confidentiality (With Limits)

Coaches must hold client disclosures in confidence unless a risk of harm is present—such as suicidal intent, abuse, or threat of violence. In these cases, ethical responsibility outweighs confidentiality, and the coach should have a clear plan for how to respond appropriately and refer out to a professional therapist when necessary (APA, 2017).

It's wise to state these exceptions clearly at the beginning of your work together—not after an emergency arises.

3. Avoiding Dual Relationships

In relationship coaching, blurred boundaries can happen fast. You may know a person or couple from church, from a small group, or from past ministry interactions. While some overlap is inevitable, dual relationships—where the coach has another role that may interfere with objectivity—should be approached with caution or avoided altogether (ICF, 2021).

If you're unsure whether a relationship could compromise your role, ask yourself: *"Can I coach this person without bias, and without expectations outside the coaching space?"* When in doubt, consult a supervisor or refer to another coach.

4. Cultural Humility & Inclusion

Relationship coaching must be culturally attuned. Expressions of love, emotional vulnerability, and gender roles can look very different across cultural, ethnic, or religious contexts. Ethical coaches don't assume sameness—they ask thoughtful questions, listen deeply, and adapt without judgment (Arredondo et al., 1996). Ethical practice isn't static—it's responsive, curious, and committed to protecting the wellbeing of the people you're serving.

Boundaries aren't meant to restrict connection; they are intended to deepen connection. When clients feel safe and respected, they're more likely to open up, reflect honestly, and take relational risks that lead to real growth.

When to Refer

One of the most important things a relationship coach can do is know when *not* to coach.

Coaching works best when clients are emotionally stable, open to feedback, and capable of practicing new skills. But sometimes, clients carry wounds that are too deep, or relational dynamics that are too volatile for coaching alone to address. In those cases, the most loving and ethical thing a coach can do is pause the process and refer to a licensed professional.

Referring isn't a failure. It's responsible. It protects your clients, your credibility, and the integrity of the coaching relationship (Linehan, 1993).

Here are some common indicators that it's time to refer:

Red Flag	Referral Reason
Mental health symptoms such as depression, panic attacks, disordered eating, or suicidal thoughts	These require clinical assessment and possible treatment (APA, 2017).
Active trauma response or PTSD symptoms (e.g., dissociation, flashbacks)	These can overwhelm the coaching container and often need trauma-informed therapy.
Addiction or substance misuse that affects relational functioning	Couples cannot practice new relational habits while one or both are impaired.
Abuse or coercive control (physical, emotional, sexual, or spiritual)	Coaching can unintentionally reinforce imbalance unless safety is restored first.
One or both clients unwilling to engage (e.g., shut down, contemptuous, or resistant)	Coaching requires participation. Severe relational gridlock may need therapeutic mediation.

If you're unsure, always err on the side of caution. Consult a supervisor or mentor if something feels off but you can't fully name it.

How you refer is just as important as when you refer. A referral should never feel like rejection. Instead, it should communicate care and confidence that another form of help will be more appropriate for their current needs.

Here's a simple script to adapt: "Based on what you've shared, it sounds like a therapist would be the best support for you right now. Coaching works best when clients are in a place where they can focus on growth and skills. I can recommend a few trusted professionals who specialize in what you're navigating. Once that process is underway and you feel ready, we can revisit whether coaching might be helpful in augmenting the therapy or even later on down the line."

If possible, offer a short list of therapists you know and trust and encouragement to start soon, while momentum is still strong. Some coaches build a network of local or online therapists with specialties in trauma, couples work, faith integration, or addiction. The stronger your referral network, the more confidence you'll have when these moments arise.

Relationship coaching can change lives. But it can't do everything. When clients need a deeper level of care, the most powerful coaching move you can make is to step back—so healing can step in.

A Note for Dual-Trained Practitioners

Many coaches who use *The 5 Love Languages* are also licensed counselors or therapists. If that's you, it's critical to clarify which hat you're wearing—and to communicate that clearly to your clients. Mixing the two can be confusing at best, and unethical at worst.

If you're practicing as a coach, follow coaching standards. If you're offering therapy, follow the clinical and legal guidelines of your licensure. Transparency is one of the greatest forms of care.

Summary

The role of a relationship coach is unique. You're not stepping in to diagnose or to rescue—but to walk alongside people with wisdom, structure, and emotional presence. You help them build something better, not by telling them what to do, but by guiding them to discover it together.

At the heart of this role are two essential commitments:

Clarity—about what coaching is and isn't, what your role involves, and where your boundaries lie.

Care—for the emotional safety of your clients, the ethical integrity of your practice, and the quiet strength you bring into every conversation.

Coaching is most effective when it's grounded in emotional intelligence, guided by clear ethics, and practiced with a growth-oriented mindset. And it's most trusted when you know when to refer, when to pause, and when to point toward deeper care.

You don't have to be perfect to do this well. But you do have to be present. The kind of presence that says: *"You're safe here. Let's grow together."*

QUESTIONS TO PONDER

1. Why am I drawn to relationship coaching?
2. How do I typically respond when others are in relational distress?
3. Which core quality—emotional intelligence, nonjudgmental curiosity, growth mindset, or ethical behavior—comes most naturally to me? Which one might I need to grow in?
4. Have I clarified my own boundaries yet?
5. Do I have a list of trusted referral sources? If not, how can I begin to build one?
6. What does "success" look like in a coaching relationship for me?

Chapter 2

Building Trust and Connection with Clients

The moment you step onto a commercial airplane, something remarkable happens—whether you realize it or not. You surrender control. You don't stop at the cockpit to quiz the pilot about their training or ask when they last passed a flight simulation. You don't review the maintenance logs for the plane or double-check the weather radar. You sit down, stow your bag, fasten your seat belt, and trust.

You trust the plane will stay in the air. You trust the crew knows what they're doing. You trust that someone, somewhere, is paying attention to the details you can't see or even understand. Trust isn't optional on an airplane—it's the invisible force that makes the entire experience possible. And when it's missing, even the smoothest flight can feel like a white-knuckled ordeal.

Coaching is no different. Your clients may not consciously realize how much they're trusting you when they show up, but make no mistake: they are. To let someone into your inner world—your hurts, fears, longings, and dreams—takes incredible courage. And it only happens when the other person feels steady, safe, and attuned with you. You may be equipped with brilliant insights and transformational tools involving the 5 Love Languages and more, but your coaching will never get off the ground if you don't learn how to engender trust and connection with your clients.

This chapter is all about that foundation. Not technique. Not advice-giving. Not clever questions. But the relational posture that makes all of it work.

We'll explore the elements that build trust: emotional safety, empathy, attunement, and a nonjudgmental presence. And we'll also look honestly at the things that can quietly erode trust—sometimes without us even noticing. Because trust isn't just the prerequisite for good coaching—it is good coaching.

Why Trust Is the Bedrock of Coaching

You've probably heard the phrase, *"People don't care how much you know until they know how much you care."* In coaching, this isn't just a warm sentiment—it's a foundational truth. Coaching isn't built on credentials or cleverness. It's built on trust. Without it, clients might show up, nod politely, and even go through the motions. But they won't open up. They won't take risks. And they certainly won't experience lasting transformation.

Trust is the bedrock because it does more than make people feel comfortable—it allows them to be vulnerable. And that's where the real work begins.

What Is Trust, Really?

Trust in a coaching relationship isn't blind faith. It's not "I believe you're perfect." It's "I believe I'm safe with you—even in my imperfection." It's the sense that you, the coach, will listen well, hold confidence, show care, and stay steady even when things get messy. Trust is a deeply felt sense of safety that develops when three qualities are consistently present:

1. **Reliability**—You show up on time. You follow through. You do what you say you'll do.
2. **Warmth**—Your presence feels welcoming, nonthreatening, and emotionally available.
3. **Respect**—You treat your client's story with dignity. You honor their pace and perspective, even when it's messy or unformed.

The best coaches communicate all three without ever having to say them outright. They're felt in tone, in consistency, in the way silence is held and pain is received.

The Psychology of Trust

Carl Rogers, one of the most influential figures in the development of therapeutic psychology, identified a "core condition" that foster real growth in a helping relationship: **unconditional positive regard** (Rogers, 1957). It says, "*You are worthy of care no matter what.*" It invites your client to exhale a little deeper. To stop performing. To stop protecting. To risk being known.

Modern research supports Rogers' intuition. Studies on **psychological safety**, for example, show that people thrive—emotionally, mentally, even physiologically—when they are in relationships where they don't fear humiliation or rejection (Edmondson, 1999). While that term is often used in workplace culture, it translates seamlessly to coaching: your clients grow best when they feel safe enough to be honest.

The Paradox of Trust

One of the paradoxes of trust is that it's both **earned slowly** and **given quickly**. You might only get one shot to make a trustworthy first impression. At the same time, lasting trust is built over time through a thousand micro-moments: the way you respond to emotion, the way you stay present during silence, the way you handle disagreement or redirect a session that's veering off course.

Every one of those moments is a brick in the foundation. Your job isn't to construct the whole house at once. It's to lay those bricks, one by one, with consistency and care.

The Role of Emotional Attunement

If trust is the foundation of coaching, emotional attunement is how you build on it. It's not about having the right answers—it's about tuning into the right frequency.

Emotional attunement is your ability to sense what your client is feeling—sometimes even before they say it—and respond in a way that makes them feel deeply seen. It's what transforms a conversation from transactional to transformational. When a coach is emotionally attuned, the client feels not just heard, but *felt.*

Think of a parent gently adjusting to their baby's cry—not just reacting but discerning what kind of cry it is and responding accordingly. Or a musician in a duet who listens so carefully that their timing and tone shift in real time to match their partner. That's attunement. And in coaching, it's what helps your client feel safe enough to go deeper.

Empathic Accuracy and Emotional Intelligence

Psychologist William Ickes coined the term **empathic accuracy** to describe the ability to accurately infer the thoughts and feelings of others (Ickes, 1997). In coaching, this means you're not just listening to *what* a person says, but picking up on what's underneath—the hesitations, the tone, the energy, the emotion behind the words.

This doesn't require mind-reading. It requires presence.

Daniel Goleman's model of emotional intelligence (1995) provides helpful scaffolding here. Two of its key components—social awareness and relationship management—are particularly relevant:

- **Social awareness** allows you to recognize emotional cues in others.
- **Relationship management** helps you respond with empathy, diplomacy, and care.

When you're emotionally attuned, you're not reacting—you're *responding*. And that difference matters.

Signs You're Attuned (or Not)

You'll know you're attuned when your client...

- Feels increasingly open and relaxed over time
- Uses phrases like, *"I've never said that out loud before"*
- Shifts from guarded or scripted language to honest reflection

And you'll know you're missing it when...

- They seem distant, distracted, or disengaged
- They keep the conversation on surface-level topics
- They smile while telling you something that clearly hurts

Being attuned doesn't mean you always *get it right*. But it does mean you're paying close attention—and willing to adjust when you don't.

Attunement Requires Self-Awareness

Here's the kicker: you can't attune to someone else if you're not attuned to yourself. If you're distracted, anxious, or preoccupied with your own internal noise, you'll miss the signals your client is sending (Hill, Knox, & Pinto-Coelho, 2008).

That's why emotional attunement starts with **self-regulation**—learning to notice your own emotional state and consciously choose to be present. It's a skill that grows with practice. And the payoff is profound.

Try This: Practicing Emotional Echoes

Next time you sense a strong emotion from your client—sadness, shame, relief—try naming it gently:

"That sounds painful."

"I can see that meant a lot to you."

"I'm wondering if that left you feeling really alone."

Then pause. Watch what happens. Often, this small gesture of attunement will open a door that logic alone never could.

Creating a Safe Coaching Environment

Imagine walking into a stranger's office (or jumping online with them) and being asked to talk about your deepest fears, unresolved wounds, and private relationships—all within sixty minutes. For most people, that's not just uncomfortable, it's unthinkable.

That's why the first—and most sacred—task of a coach is to create safety.

Psychological safety isn't a soft skill. It's a relational necessity. When clients feel emotionally protected, they don't just talk more—they think more clearly, feel more deeply, and become more open to growth. Safety calms the nervous system. It lowers defenses. It invites the kind of inner honesty that real coaching depends on.

Safety Starts Before the First Session

Long before your client starts talking, they're picking up cues about whether you're safe:

- How do you greet them?
- What does your tone communicate?

- Are your boundaries clear and respectful?
- Do you seem rushed—or fully present?

Even subtle details matter. A warm environment. An uncluttered space. Clear communication about confidentiality and expectations. These seemingly small things send a powerful message: *You're safe here.*

Safety Isn't Agreement—It's Attunement

A common misconception is that creating safety means always agreeing or affirming. But safety isn't the same as appeasement. It's not about nodding to everything a client says. It's about being present without panic, responsive without overreaction, and curious without control.

Safety means a client can be honest—even messy—and know they won't be punished with shame, silence, or sermonizing. They can say, *"I don't know if I love my spouse anymore"* or *"I'm afraid I'm broken,"* and not have to immediately clean it up.

This doesn't mean you don't appropriately challenge your clients. But challenge without safety feels like criticism. Challenge *within* safety feels like care.

The Science of Feeling Safe

Research on attachment and interpersonal neurobiology confirms what wise coaches intuitively know: people flourish when they feel emotionally secure. According to Cozolino (2014), our brains are literally wired for connection—and the presence of a calm, attuned, and accepting person can help regulate emotional distress and foster resilience. In short, safety isn't just felt; it's *neurologically experienced*: "The right hemisphere of the brain is specialized for detecting threat and nonverbal cues, which makes safety in the relationship a biological prerequisite for processing emotion and experience" (Cozolino, 2014, p. 50).

In coaching, this means your tone of voice, facial expression, posture, and pacing all speak volumes—whether you intend them to or not.

Try This: Your Presence Audit

Before your next session, pause for 60 seconds. Ask yourself:

- *Am I fully present?*

- *Is anything distracting me—internally or externally?*
- *What would it feel like to sit across from me right now?*

Just a moment of intentional grounding can make a profound difference in how safe your client feels when they walk in the door.

The Power of Relational Warmth

Ask people to describe the best mentor, teacher, or coach they've ever had, and one trait almost always rises to the top: warmth. Not brilliance. Not credentials. Not strategy. But something far more human: the ability to make them feel cared for.

Warmth is deceptively powerful. It's not flashy or loud. But it creates the conditions where transformation can take root. When a coach exudes warmth, clients lean in. They let their guard down. They feel worthy—not just of insight, but of kindness. And that changes everything.

More Than a Smile

Relational warmth isn't just about friendliness or cheerfulness. It's about presence. It's communicated in the small but potent cues that say, *"I see you. I'm with you. I care."*

Warmth shows up in:

- Eye contact that feels engaged, not invasive
- A voice tone that's calm and responsive
- Gentle, appropriate humor that puts people at ease
- A posture that's open, relaxed, and receptive
- A way of speaking that honors emotion without trying to fix it

You can't fake warmth—not for long. Clients can sense when it's performative. But when it's genuine, it makes you the kind of person people *want* to be open with.

First Impressions Matter

Social psychology confirms that people form judgments about warmth and competence in *milliseconds*—and of the two, warmth matters more. In a groundbreaking study, Ambady and Rosenthal (1993) found that participants could accurately rate a teacher's warmth after viewing just thirty seconds of silent video—and those ratings strongly predicted student evaluations at the end of the semester.

As it turns out, people don't need a long time to decide if you're emotionally safe. Which means that the way you show up *before* the conversation begins can have a bigger impact than what you say once it does.

The Warmth-Competence Balance

Of course, warmth alone isn't enough. In coaching, it needs to be paired with clarity, strength, and direction. But many coaches overemphasize authority or "expertise" too early—especially when they feel uncertain themselves. Ironically, this erodes trust rather than strengthening it.

Clients aren't looking for perfect coaches. They're looking for *real* ones. The kind who can gently hold space for their story while also helping them move forward. The kind who makes you feel less alone just by the way they listen.

Warmth creates that atmosphere.

Try This: The One-Minute Check-In

Before each session, ask yourself:

- *What would it feel like to be coached by me today?*
- *What energy am I bringing into the room?*
- *Does my face, tone, and posture communicate openness?*

Small adjustments—a softened expression, an unhurried pace—can radically shift the relational tone of a session.

Listening That Builds Trust

There's a kind of listening that goes beyond technique. It doesn't just track what someone is saying—it holds space for who they are. It's the kind of listening that makes people feel *safe enough to keep talking*, even when the words are hard to say.

In coaching, this kind of listening isn't optional. It's essential. Because your listening is your presence—and presence builds trust.

From Active to Transformational Listening

Most coaches have heard of active listening—skills like summarizing, paraphrasing, and reflecting feelings. These are important. But on their own, they're not enough. Because listening isn't just a set of techniques—it's a posture of the heart.

Transformational listening means you're not waiting for your turn to speak. You're not steering the conversation toward your agenda. You're listening with no other goal than to understand—and to make sure the client knows they've been understood.

This kind of listening communicates:

- *"I'm not in a hurry."*
- *"You don't need to impress me."*
- *"This space is for you."*

It's the opposite of performance. It's invitation.

Listening as Ministry

In many ways, good listening is a sacred act. It's a ministry of attention. When someone feels deeply listened to, it's not just emotionally healing—it's spiritually grounding. They begin to believe they matter. That their story is worth telling. That their inner world isn't too much for someone else to hold.

One of the most powerful things you can say in a coaching session isn't a clever insight. It's a simple, quiet: *"I'm really glad you said that."*

Techniques That Support Deeper Listening

While heart posture is central, certain skills help structure and support that depth:

- **Reflection:** Repeat the client's words in distilled form to confirm understanding.
- **Clarification:** Gently ask questions to better grasp the emotional nuance: *"Can you say more about that feeling of being stuck?"*
- **Validation:** Affirm the client's experience without needing to agree: *"It makes sense that you'd feel overwhelmed."*
- **Silence:** Sometimes, the most powerful response is no response at all—when it's productive and the client's wheels are turning. Silence gives space for truth to surface.

Why Listening Works

Research supports what every seasoned coach knows intuitively: high-quality listening significantly increases a client's sense of support, clarity, and openness (Itzchakov & Kluger, 2018). In fact, the act of being deeply listened to can reduce defensiveness, improve self-awareness, and even lead clients to discover insights they didn't know they had.

And it all begins with presence.

Try This: Three-Minute Mirror

During your next session, take three full minutes to listen without interrupting, reframing, or redirecting. Just listen. Nod. Make eye contact. Let the client feel your presence. Afterward, reflect on what you heard. You may be surprised how much trust deepens in just 180 seconds.

Developing Empathy and a Nonjudgmental Presence

You can be the most insightful coach in the world, but if you lack empathy, your words won't land. Empathy is what allows a client to feel understood at a heart level. It softens defenses. It builds connection. And it creates the kind of relationship where people dare to be real.

Without empathy, clients stay guarded. With empathy, they begin to unfold.

What Empathy Is—And Isn't

Empathy isn't about fixing. It's not about agreeing. It's not even about knowing exactly how someone feels. It's about communicating, *"I'm with you in this. I see you. I feel the weight of what you're carrying."*

Psychologist Carl Rogers (1957) defined empathy as the ability to perceive another's experience and communicate that understanding back to them. It's an act of presence, not persuasion.

Empathy is not the same as **sympathy**. Sympathy looks down and says, *"That sounds hard."* Empathy comes alongside and says, *"You're not alone."* Empathy honors the story as it's told, without adding commentary, solutions, or a moral at the end.

The Power of a Nonjudgmental Stance

Empathy with judgment becomes *hindering*. Empathy without judgment becomes *healing*.

Clients are often more self-critical than they appear. If they even *sense* disapproval in your tone, posture, or silence, they'll begin to edit themselves. They'll minimize. They'll steer away from their real emotions. And the coaching relationship will become an exercise in polite distance.

That's why one of the greatest gifts you can offer as a coach is nonjudgmental presence—a space where someone can be raw, unfinished, inconsistent, and still accepted.

This doesn't mean you affirm everything. But it means you suspend evaluation long enough to let the story be fully told. When people feel safe from judgment, they begin to judge themselves less harshly too.

Empathy as Emotional Discipline

Empathy requires you to stay grounded. You can't offer it well if you're triggered, distracted, or emotionally flooded. That's why self-regulation is a core part of your preparation as a coach.

When a client shares something difficult—an affair, a past trauma, an explosive conflict—you may feel a wave of emotion yourself. That's normal. But your job isn't to match their intensity. It's to be the calm in the storm. To stay emotionally present without being emotionally overwhelmed.

This is where spiritual maturity, emotional intelligence, and your own healing journey all converge.

Empathy can be thought of as the ability to temporarily switch roles—to "trade places" emotionally with another person, even if just for a moment (Parrott & Parrott, 2008). This kind of intentional perspective-taking isn't about agreeing—it's about *understanding*. When coaches adopt this stance, even momentarily, they create a relational bridge strong enough to carry difficult truths.

The Neuroscience of Empathy

Functional MRI studies have shown that when we observe others in pain, the same neural networks light up in our own brains (Singer et al., 2004). In other words, we are literally wired for empathy. But the *skill* of empathy—especially in professional relationships—requires intention. It's not about emotional contagion. It's about conscious connection.

Try This: Empathic Echo

After a client shares something vulnerable, pause and say: *"Can I reflect what I think I'm hearing?"*

Then paraphrase not just the content, but the feeling beneath it: *"It sounds like you've been carrying a lot of that alone—and it's worn you down."* Or *"You're torn, because you love them—but you also feel like you're losing yourself."*

When done well, this kind of reflection doesn't just show that you're listening—it makes the client feel *held*.

Pitfalls That Undermine Trust

Trust is fragile. It's earned slowly but can be damaged in an instant—and sometimes by things the coach doesn't even notice. You don't have to be unethical or unkind to erode trust. Often, it's the subtle missteps that leave clients feeling uncertain or unseen.

And when trust begins to fray, so does the client's willingness to go deeper.

The Trust-Eroding Behaviors Coaches Rarely Intend

1. **Premature Advice-Giving**

   It can be tempting to help a client "solve" something right away—especially if you spot the issue clearly. But moving too quickly to advice shuts down vulnerability. It bypasses empathy. Clients feel like a problem to be fixed, not a person to be known.

2. **Over-Talking or Interrupting**

   Even with good intentions, talking too much—especially in emotionally charged moments—can feel like emotional crowding. It communicates, *"My insight is more important than your process."*

3. **Inconsistent Presence**

   Running late, rescheduling frequently, or seeming distracted in session can send the message that the client's story isn't a priority. Over time, these small lapses can wear down a client's sense of psychological safety.

4. **Judgmental Micro-Expressions**

   A subtle eye-roll. A long pause. A pursed lip. These tiny, often unconscious cues can say more than words. They may communicate disapproval even if you never speak it.

5. **Failing to Repair**

   Every coach will occasionally miss a cue, misread a moment, or say something that lands wrong. But failing to acknowledge or repair those moments can do lasting damage. What could have been an opportunity for relational depth becomes a point of disconnection.

What Clients Won't Say—But Will Feel

Most clients won't say, *"I'm starting to trust you less."*

They'll just become more guarded. They'll share less. Sessions will feel more "polite" and less personal. Progress slows. Vulnerability dries up. They may even ghost you altogether.

That's why awareness is essential. You're not aiming for perfection but for responsiveness—a willingness to notice when something's off and to name it gently when needed.

"Hey—I might've jumped in a little too fast there. Can we go back?"

A sentence like that can do more for trust than a dozen good insights.

The Research on Rupture and Repair

Research in therapeutic relationships consistently shows that ruptures in connection are inevitable, but when handled well, they can actually *strengthen* trust (Safran & Muran, 2000). Clients don't need a perfect coach. They need a present one—someone who is humble enough to acknowledge missteps and steady enough to stay when things get real.

Try This: Rupture Radar

In your next session, watch for these signs of subtle disconnect:

- The client's tone goes flat or guarded
- They stop making eye contact

- They begin deflecting with humor or vague responses
- The conversation suddenly shifts topics

If you sense any of these, don't panic. Slow down. Ask a curious, open-ended question. Or just say: *"I want to check in. I'm sensing a shift. Are we still tracking?"* That single moment of attunement may restore more trust than you realize.

Summary

Trust and connection aren't just the backdrop to coaching—they are the coaching. Every insight, breakthrough, and forward step depends on the relational safety you cultivate. And that safety doesn't come from strategy or skill alone. It comes from who you are in the room.

Throughout this chapter, we've explored why trust is the foundation of all effective coaching, and how emotional attunement invites vulnerability and deepens rapport. We've looked at the importance of creating an emotionally safe environment—beginning with your own grounded presence—and the quiet power of relational warmth and nonverbal connection. We've seen how transformational listening builds more than just understanding; it builds relationship. Empathy and nonjudgment, far from being accessories to coaching, are essential tools that allow real growth to take root. And we've acknowledged the subtle ways trust can be eroded, along with how to repair it through humility, curiosity, and care.

When trust is present, clients take emotional risks. They share honestly. They reflect more deeply. They grow. But when trust is absent, even the best coaching tools fall flat.

QUESTIONS TO PONDER

1. What helps you feel safe enough to be vulnerable? How might that inform the environment you create for clients?
2. How attuned are you to your own emotional state before and during a session?
3. What rituals or habits help you stay grounded?
4. What part of your coaching presence (tone, pace, posture) most clearly communicates warmth? What might need attention?
5. When was the last time you noticed a rupture in a conversation—big or small? How did you respond? Would you do anything differently now?
6. Do you tend to lean more toward empathy or problem-solving? What might shift if you paused longer in the presence of emotion?

Chapter 3

Effective Communication Techniques for Coaches

A master sculptor doesn't force the stone into shape. They study it. Walk around it. Look for its contours. And then, when the moment is right, they begin to reveal what was already hidden inside.

That's what great coaching does. It doesn't impose form. It reveals it. Not by applying pressure, but by asking the right questions. Listening well. Observing carefully. And making small, skillful movements at just the right time.

This chapter is about those small, skillful movements—the tools of the trade. You'll learn the art of shaping a session with structure and flexibility. You'll explore how to co-create meaningful goals, ask powerful questions, follow emotional threads, reflect what you're hearing, and name what others may overlook. These aren't mechanical tricks. They're relational practices that build momentum and invite transformation.

If chapter 2 focused on *who you are* in the room, this chapter focuses on *what you do* once trust begins to form.

And just like a sculptor works with a different touch depending on the material, coaches must adapt to the uniqueness of each client. Nowhere is this more apparent than in how clients give and receive love—which brings us to the 5 Love Languages.

As you'll discover in Part 2 of this handbook, the Love Languages offer a powerful lens for understanding how people connect. But even this trusted framework is nuanced. What "Words of Affirmation" means to one person may feel quite different to someone else. Personality, past experience, and emotional wiring all shape how love is expressed and received, not to mention Love Language dialects. The same is true in coaching. One client's silence might signal thoughtfulness. Another's might signal withdrawal. One might light up when asked a direct question. Another might shut down.

Your job as a coach is not to rely on formulas. It's to bring skillful presence. To know when to ask, when to pause, when to follow, and when to gently guide.

And that's what this chapter is all about. Not gimmicks. Not guesswork. But real tools, applied with discernment. Because even the most beautiful coaching posture—empathy, warmth, attunement—needs tools to give it shape. The sculptor may love the stone. But it's the chisel that helps it come to life.

Structuring a Session with Flexibility

One of the most common questions new coaches ask is some version of: *"What do I actually do in a session?"* And it's a good question. Because while coaching is dynamic and relational, it's also purposeful. There's a difference between a meaningful conversation and a meandering one. Coaching isn't casual talk—it's structured discovery.

Here's the paradox: The best sessions have a *shape*, but not a script.

Coaching requires a rhythm—an underlying structure that offers containment without control. Without structure, the session drifts. Without flexibility, it becomes rigid. Your job is to strike the balance.

A Loose but Reliable Framework

Think of a coaching session as having three natural movements:

1. **Opening**—This is where rapport is renewed, the emotional tone is set, and focus is clarified. Good openings feel both welcoming and intentional. They might begin with a simple check-in (*"What's been on your mind since our last session?"*) or a revisit of previous progress. This phase establishes the emotional and cognitive ground for the conversation to follow.
2. **Exploration**—This is the heart of the session. It's where curiosity leads, emotion deepens, and the client gains insight. You're asking thoughtful questions, reflecting what you hear, and occasionally helping to name what's emerging. The key here is responsiveness.

3. **Closing**—The last few minutes are often overlooked, but they're critical. This is the time to consolidate insights, identify next steps, and emotionally anchor the session. Clients may leave with an action step or simply with more clarity. Either way, the session ends with intention.

Think of these three movements like a gentle arc: *orient, deepen, anchor.*

Why Structure Builds Safety

Even though every session is unique, clients feel safer when they sense the coach knows where they're going, even if the path meanders. Structure offers containment, which is especially important when the content becomes emotionally charged. It reassures the client that they won't get lost or left in the lurch.

Research in therapy and coaching supports this: Clients tend to feel more secure and more engaged when they understand the general flow of a helping relationship (Grant, 2014). While the work itself is nonlinear, the sense of movement matters.

When to Flex the Framework

Structure is a guide, not a grid. Sometimes, a client will arrive with something heavy that needs to be processed right away. Other times, the real issue won't surface until minute forty. Being a good coach means sensing when to stick with the plan and when to pivot.

Here are a few scenarios that call for flexibility:

- A client begins with a topic you didn't expect—but their energy says *follow it*
- They seem scattered or anxious—so you slow down and use grounding questions
- They hit an emotional nerve—and you drop your agenda to sit with the feeling
- They finish early—and you don't stretch the session just to "fill time"

The point isn't to rigidly follow steps—it's to offer a framework the client can *relax* into.

Common Mistakes in Session Structure

- **Starting too strong.** Jumping in with an intense question before establishing rapport can leave clients disoriented or defensive.
- **Losing the thread.** It's easy to get pulled into side stories or intellectual rabbit holes. Anchor to what matters.
- **Ending abruptly.** When a session ends without reflection or closure, it can feel jarring—and the client may walk away ungrounded.

Tip: Reserve at least 5–7 minutes at the end to "land the plane." Ask questions like, *"What are you taking from today?"* or *"Is there anything you want to sit with this week?"*

Setting Goals That Guide and Grow

Most clients come to coaching because they want something to be different. But they don't always know what that something is—or how to articulate it. They may start with vague hopes: *"I want to communicate better." "I want to feel more connected." "I don't want to keep having the same fight." "My wife says I need to learn her Love Language."*

That's where goal-setting becomes an essential coaching skill.

But here's the key: Coaching goals aren't imposed—they're co-created. They aren't fixed—they're flexible. And they're not just about outcomes—they're about movement.

Why Goals Matter

A well-formed coaching goal gives the client a sense of agency and the session a sense of direction. Without a goal, the conversation may feel meaningful but unanchored. With a goal, even a single insight can feel like progress.

Research in coaching psychology supports this: Goal-oriented coaching tends to produce more measurable change, especially when clients are involved in shaping the direction (Grant, 2014). It's not just about having a target—it's about owning the aim.

Coaching vs. Therapeutic Goals

In therapy, goals often focus on healing or symptom reduction. In coaching, goals tend to center on growth, clarity, and action. They're not about "fixing" the client but about helping them move toward something they value.

Coaching goals often emerge from moments where love feels misfired, misunderstood, or missing. And while clients might not use the language of *The 5 Love Languages* right away, their struggles almost always circle around connection, meaning, and emotional safety.

That means coaching goals can be:

- **Behavioral:**
  "I want to listen without interrupting when we argue—especially when my partner is trying to express appreciation and I shut it down." (This might relate to struggles with receiving *Words of Affirmation*.)
- **Emotional:**
  "I want to feel more confident in how I handle conflict so I don't withdraw every time things get tense." (Possibly tied to discomfort with *Physical Touch* or *Quality Time* during difficult conversations.)
- **Relational:**
  "I want to understand what respect looks like to my partner—not just what it means to me." (This may surface when *Acts of Service* or *Receiving Gifts* are misunderstood or undervalued.)
- **Exploratory:**
  "I want to figure out what's really behind my frustration when I don't feel appreciated." (Often connected to unmet needs in a primary Love Language.)

These types of goals don't just clarify direction—they reveal the emotional and relational terrain that coaching will explore. And as we'll examine more deeply in Part 2, even within the same Love Language, no two clients experience love the same way. Dialects, personality traits, attachment history, and emotional needs all shape how that language is spoken—and how it lands.

Helping clients set goals around love, respect, and emotional clarity not only gives shape to the coaching process—it gives *depth to the work.*

Outcome Goals vs. Process Goals

Outcome goals describe what the client wants to *achieve.*

Process goals describe how they want to *grow.*

Both matter—but process goals often lead to the most lasting change.

Outcome: *"I want fewer arguments."*

Process: *"I want to stay calm when I feel criticized."*

Outcome goals are measurable. Process goals are transformational.

Using SMART Goals Wisely

You've probably heard of the popular SMART goal framework (Specific, Measurable, Achievable, Relevant, Time Bound). It can be helpful—especially for clients who are pragmatic or task-oriented. But be careful not to force every goal into a spreadsheet. Some of the most powerful goals in coaching are less tidy, more human:

- *"I want to stop walking on eggshells."*
- *"I want to enjoy my marriage again."*
- *"I want to trust that I'm not too much."*

These are harder to quantify—but often easier to feel. They reveal what matters most.

Evolving the Goal Over Time

Goals in coaching aren't set in stone. Often, what begins as one goal evolves as the client gains clarity. For example:

Start: *"I want to communicate better."*

Three sessions in: *"Actually, I want to understand why I shut down when I feel hurt."*

That's not a failure of goal-setting. That's the fruit of good coaching.

A rigid coach will push the client back to the original goal. A wise coach will say, *"That sounds important. Let's follow it."*

Try This: The "Why Now?" Prompt

To figure out coaching goals early in the process, try asking:

- *"What made you decide to reach out now?"*
- *"If coaching helps, what will be different in your life?"*
- *"What would make this worth your time and energy?"*

These questions honor the client's motivation and begin to shape their sense of direction—without boxing them in.

The Power of Questions

Coaching isn't about having the right answers. It's about asking the right questions.

Questions are the coach's primary tool—not to control the conversation, but to unlock it. Done well, a question isn't just an invitation to think—it's an invitation to *feel*, *explore*, and *discover*. Questions don't just collect information; they create transformation.

In fact, the best questions are the ones your client remembers long after the session ends—not because they were clever, but because they helped them hear their own truth.

Why Questions Work

Psychologically, questions activate curiosity and promote **self-generated insight**—a key driver of behavior change (Deci & Ryan, 2000; Grant, 2011). When a client discovers something on their own, it has greater emotional weight and cognitive "stickiness" than if they were simply told.

Good coaching questions bypass the inner critic and awaken the part of the brain wired for reflection. They invite ownership instead of compliance. Exploration instead of explanation.

What Makes a Question Powerful?

A powerful question doesn't need to be long or poetic. It simply needs to be:

- **Open-Ended**—It invites more than a yes/no. (*"What felt most important to you about that?"*)
- **Short**—Longwinded questions confuse more than clarify.

- **Client-Centered**—Focused on their experience, not your curiosity.
- **Evocative**—It touches emotion or reveals meaning.
- **Present-Tense**—Orients the client in the here and now. (*"What's most stressful for you right now?"*)

Sometimes a powerful question can be as simple as:
"What's the real issue here? What would it look like to let go?"

The Questions to Avoid

Some questions sound helpful but subtly undermine trust or autonomy:

- **Stacked questions**—"So, do you think it's more about how you were raised, or is it more about how your partner reacts, or maybe both?" (The client doesn't know where to start.)
- **Leading questions**—"Don't you think you're being too hard on yourself?" (That's more of a disguised opinion than a legitimate question.)
- **Fix-It questions**—"Have you tried journaling about it?" (That's a suggestion in question form—and likely premature.)

Even well-meaning questions can miss the moment. Coaching is not an interview—it's an emotional and relational exchange. Clients don't need to be prodded. They need to be invited.

When a Question Lands

You'll know when a question lands by the pause. The breath. The shift in body language. The moment they say, *"Wow. I hadn't thought about that."*

That's when you lean back. Let the moment breathe. Don't rush to the next question. Stay in the space you just opened.

Try This: Your Top 5

Every coach eventually develops a few "go-to" questions—ones that reliably open space. Here are five worth trying:

1. *"What feels most important to talk about today?"*
2. *"What do you wish your partner understood about you right now?"*

3. *"What are you learning about yourself through this?"*
4. *"What's the story you're telling yourself—and is it true?"*
5. *"If nothing changed, what would that cost you?"*

You don't need a script. You just need presence—and practice.

The Power of the Follow-Up Question

Most of us go through life surrounded by questions that skim the surface. Small talk. Efficiency. Politeness. But how often does someone really linger with us in a conversation? How often does someone say, *"Wait—tell me more about that part."*

That's why follow-up questions can feel so profound. They don't just dig deeper into the topic. They illuminate the person. They say, *"You're not a data point. You're a story. You're worth staying with."*

In *How to Know a Person*, David Brooks describes the art of truly seeing someone—not as a problem to solve, but as a human being to discover. He writes, "What artists do with paint and clay, good questioners do with attention and curiosity" (Brooks, 2023, p. 67). The follow-up question, then, becomes a kind of relational art form. It shapes space for someone's humanity to be revealed, not just explained.

And in coaching, this is sacred work.

Anyone can ask, *"How did that go?"*

The coach asks, *"What did that mean to you?"*—and waits to find out.

If a good coaching question opens a door, a follow-up question invites the client to walk through it.

The follow-up is where coaching often shifts from surface to substance. It's not just about gathering more information—it's about helping clients pause, examine, and illuminate what's underneath their initial response. Many clients are so used to functioning on autopilot that they don't always know what they really think or feel until someone helps them slow down and stay with the moment.

That's what a well-timed follow-up does.

First question: *"How did that conversation go?"*

Follow-up: *"What part of it stayed with you afterward?"*

The first answer reports *facts*. The second reveals *meaning*.

What Follow-Up Questions Do

- **Slow the pace** so insight can catch up with emotion
- **Highlight patterns** the client may not notice
- **Deepen ownership** of the discovery process
- **Show presence**—you're not just following a script; you're *with* them

This is especially important when you're working with clients around love and connection. For example, a client might say:

"I told her I appreciated her, but she didn't really respond."

Instead of moving on, a simple follow-up could open something deeper:

"What did you hope she would do in response?"

"What does appreciation look like to you?"

"Have you two ever talked about what love feels like when it lands?"

Without using the phrase "Love Languages," you're already coaching toward it—helping your client reflect on how their emotional expression may not match their partner's emotional reception. And that gap is where miscommunication—and transformation—lives.

Simple but Mighty Follow-Ups

Here are a few go-to follow-ups that are small in size but rich in potential:

- *"Can you say more about that?"*
- *"What else do you notice?"*
- *"Where do you feel that in your body?"*
- *"What surprised you about that?"*
- *"Why do you think that mattered so much?"*

These aren't interrogations—they're invitations. They help the client explore not just what happened, but what it meant.

Observing and Reflecting

Great coaches don't just listen to what's being said. They notice what's not. The tone. The tension. The tiny turn of phrase. They pick up on patterns and energy shifts—and then gently hold them up for the client to see.

That's the art of observing and reflecting. It's not analysis. It's not interpretation.

It's offering the client a clearer mirror so they can recognize themselves more honestly—and with more compassion.

Reflection says: *"Here's what I'm hearing."*

Observation adds: *"And here's something I'm noticing."*

Both are powerful. Used well, they deepen insight, foster self-awareness, and often lead to those moments where a client says, *"I've never said that out loud before."*

Types of Reflection

Reflection can take many forms. Each has a different purpose and effect:

- **Content Reflection**—Restating what the client said to clarify or confirm: *"So you told your partner you needed space, but inside you were hoping they'd pursue you—did I get that right?"*
- **Feeling Reflection**—Naming the emotional undercurrent, even if the client didn't:

  "That sounds like it really stung."

  "I'm hearing a lot of pride in your voice right now—does that feel true?"
- **Pattern Reflection**—Noticing repetition or emotional themes over time:

  "This seems to be the third time your desire for connection gets tangled up in a fear of rejection."
- **Metaphorical Reflection**—Offering imagery that encapsulates the client's experience:

  "It sounds like you're constantly patching the roof in a storm."

Not every reflection will land. But even the attempt often builds trust, because it shows you're listening with care—not just for facts, but for meaning (Lichtenberg, Lachmann, & Fosshage, 2002).

The Value of Noticing

Observation doesn't mean diagnosing. It means attuning. It might sound like:

"You smiled just now, but your voice softened—what's happening there?"

"You said that quickly—like you've had to defend it before."

"I've noticed that you keep using the word 'should' when talking about your relationship."

When said with curiosity, not judgment, these small observations can open big doors.

You're not telling the client what's true.

You're holding space for them to explore what *might be* true.

And that's often where transformation begins.

Love Languages and Misaligned Meaning

This skill becomes particularly helpful when clients are misfiring in how they give and receive love. A client might say, *"I tell him I love him all the time, but he still doesn't believe it."* A coach might gently offer:

"I wonder if he's listening for love in a different dialect."

A single sentence like that can unlock an entirely new conversation—not just about communication, but about emotional fluency and mutual understanding.

A client might describe how they cleaned the entire house for their spouse only to be met with indifference. The pain isn't just about the chore—it's about the perceived disconnect: *"Didn't you see what I was trying to say?"*

A coach might reflect:

"You were speaking love through Acts of Service—but it sounds like what you longed for in return was simply to be noticed."

This kind of reflection brings dignity to the client's effort and clarity to the emotional gap. It helps them articulate their need without shame—and that's where healing starts.

Why Reflection Matters

Research in client-centered therapy and interpersonal neurobiology supports the idea that accurate reflection helps individuals integrate emotion and develop insight (Siegel, 2010; Rogers, 1961). When someone hears their experience reflected back with empathy, it activates a deeper level of processing—both emotionally and neurologically.

And sometimes, it's the first time they feel truly seen.

Summary

Coaching isn't magic. But it can feel magical when it's done well—when structure meets soul, and skill meets presence. In this chapter, we've explored the practical tools that give coaching its shape and power. These tools aren't flashy. They're subtle. They require attentiveness, restraint, courage, and care.

- A well-structured session creates containment and flow—with enough flexibility to follow what matters most.
- Goal-setting invites the client into ownership and direction, whether the goals are outcome-based, process-driven, or emotionally exploratory.
- Powerful questions unlock insight—but the real depth often comes through the quiet courage of the follow-up.
- Reflection and observation help clients hear themselves more clearly—to make meaning, not just share stories.
- Naming what's in the room, done with humility and trust, allows the client to see what they've been skirting, and possibly, to step into it.

The best coaches don't use these tools rigidly. They use them like a sculptor handles a chisel: gently, skillfully, and with reverence for what's taking shape.

QUESTIONS TO PONDER

1. As you reflect on your own coaching sessions, how naturally do you balance structure and flexibility? When do you tend to rely too heavily on one or the other?
2. Think about a time when a client's goal shifted during coaching. How did you respond, and what did that experience teach you about co-creating goals rather than directing them?
3. Which types of questions do you find yourself asking most often? How might you become more intentional about using open-ended, evocative questions that invite deeper reflection?
4. Recall a moment when a follow-up question helped a client move from surface-level reporting to deeper personal insight. What made that moment effective?
5. How comfortable are you observing and reflecting emotional patterns back to clients? What helps you decide when to speak a reflection aloud—and when to simply hold the observation quietly?

Chapter 4

Understanding Relationship Dynamics

A relationship coach stands in a space that few people ever hold for others. You're not a therapist. You're not a pastor. You're not a best friend. You're not a problem-solver with all the answers. And yet, somehow, your presence carries the weight of all those roles—without becoming any one of them.

You hold a sacred middle space.

You're a guide without agenda. A mirror without judgment. A steady hand that helps people see what's real and move toward what's possible.

In the chapters leading up to this one, we've explored the *role* of a relationship coach (chapter 1), the *posture* you bring to the work (chapter 2), and the *practices* that give it shape (chapter 3). But this chapter is different. This one is about *you*—not the function you fulfill, but the person you become in the process. It's about the heart behind the role, and the deeper motivations that make this work sustainable and sacred.

Because no matter how good your questions are, no matter how well you manage the session or structure the process, your presence is what your client will remember. The tone of your voice. The space between your sentences. The look in your eyes when they risk telling the truth.

People don't just change because they learn something new. They change because they feel safe enough to see themselves more clearly. And that only happens when someone holds the space with courage, humility, and grace.

This is the unteachable part of coaching. And yet it can be cultivated.

In this final chapter of Part 1, we'll explore what lies beneath the skills:

- The motivations that keep you grounded—or pull you off course
- The emotional maturity required to stay steady in the storm
- The quiet courage to hold tension without needing to fix it
- The humility to let the client—not your insight—be the hero
- The inner work that keeps you soft, present, and real

Because in relationship coaching, you have to have the right motivation, mindset, and maturity in order to cultivate positive growth in others.

The Coach's Core Motivations

Behind every coaching relationship is an invisible force: the coach's motivation. Why you do this work—what drives you, what sustains you, and what you hope to offer—shapes the space more than any single skill.

Coaching, by its nature, draws people who care. People who want to help. Who want to make a difference. Some coaches are drawn to the work because they love insight. Others because they've lived through relational pain and want to help others avoid it. Still others come from ministry, therapy, or caregiving spaces and see coaching as a new channel for supporting people's growth. These motivations are common—and often compassionate. But if left unexamined, they can become entangled with ego, identity, or unresolved need.

None of these motivations are wrong. But they can become unbalanced—especially when the coach subtly starts needing something *from* the client: admiration, validation, gratitude, or proof that they're doing a good job. This is where burnout, role confusion, or compassion fatigue begins to take root (Figley, 2002).

When your coaching becomes more about being insightful than being helpful, it's time to step back. When you're more energized by the spotlight than the stillness, it's time to reflect.

Sustainable coaching is rooted in self-determined motivation—driven by a sense of autonomy, purpose, and genuine relational care (Deci & Ryan, 2000). When your "why" is grounded in curiosity and service rather than validation, your presence becomes both lighter and more powerful.

Curiosity Over Control

At the heart of sustainable coaching is *curiosity*. Not curiosity as strategy, but curiosity as a way of being—an open posture that says:

"I don't need to shape your story. I want to understand it."

This is where coaching diverges from consulting or teaching. You're not transferring knowledge. You're helping your client uncover it. That requires restraint—and deep respect for their process.

Self-determination theory tells us that people thrive when they feel autonomous, competent, and connected (Deci & Ryan, 2000). Coaching aligns beautifully with this framework, because good coaching respects the client's autonomy. It doesn't coerce or correct. It invites.

Motivation rooted in control—no matter how subtle—will eventually erode trust.

But motivation rooted in *honor* will deepen it.

When the Ego Slips In

Every coach will feel it at some point—the subtle thrill of being the one with the question that landed, the observation that unlocked something. That's okay. You're human. But it's worth noticing what happens next.

Do you let the moment return to the client's experience—or do you take just a little more airtime?

Good coaching is client-centered. Great coaching is *client-anchored*—even when your insight shines. Client-centered coaching keeps the focus on the client's needs, goals, and experiences. Client-anchored coaching goes a step further: It continually returns the conversation to the client's values, agency, and growth, rather than the coach's expertise or perspective.

When your motivation is grounded in service rather than performance, the client feels it. They relax. They risk. They go further. And that's the whole point.

Emotional Maturity and Self-Awareness

You can only take a client as far as you're willing to go yourself.

That's not a slogan—it's a reality. In relationship coaching, your emotional maturity isn't just background noise. It's part of the atmosphere. Clients may not consciously name it, but they *feel* whether you're grounded. They notice how you respond to silence, emotion, resistance, or raw pain.

A coach with high emotional maturity doesn't need to prove, perform, or protect. They're present. Not perfectly, but consistently.

Emotional maturity is the difference between a coach who reacts and a coach who responds. It's what allows you to stay steady when your client isn't.

Becoming a Non-Anxious Presence

Edwin Friedman, in his work on leadership and systems theory, describes the power of being a *non-anxious presence*. Not emotionless. Not detached. But calm, clear, and courageous—especially when others are swirling.

As a coach, this means:

- You don't mirror your client's panic.
- You don't rush to rescue.
- You don't shrink from tension.
- You stay available—even when the conversation is uncomfortable.

In *A Failure of Nerve*, Friedman (2007) argues that the greatest leaders don't fix—they *differentiate*. They remain connected but not entangled. In coaching, this is crucial. When a client brings their anxiety, grief, or confusion into the session, your job is to hold space, not absorb it.

That takes practice. And it starts with knowing your own emotional patterns.

Know Your Triggers, Tendencies, and Temptations

Every coach carries a personal story. And that story—your attachment style, past wounds, relational habits—will inevitably show up in your coaching.

Do you tend to overfunction when things get messy?

Do you crave affirmation from clients?

Do you feel compelled to give advice when silence stretches?

These aren't flaws. They're signals—opportunities for reflection. When you're aware of your internal landscape, you're far less likely to unconsciously act it out in the coaching space.

Self-awareness is the foundation of ethical and effective coaching. You can't regulate what you don't recognize.

The best coaches have done—and are doing—their own work. They're not perfect. But they're honest. And that honesty creates safety.

Courage, Humility, and Staying in the Tension

Most of the meaningful moments in coaching don't happen when things are easy. They happen when things get *uncomfortable.* A client faces a painful truth. Emotions rise. A relationship pattern is named. Insight knocks—but the door isn't open yet.

These are the moments that ask something more from the coach—not more strategy, but more *courage and humility.*

The Courage to Stay

Coaching takes courage. Not just for the client, but for you.

It takes courage to:

- Ask the hard questions, even when you're afraid it might make things awkward
- Let silence stretch longer than your comfort
- Name the moment that feels emotionally charged
- Stay with a client's pain instead of steering toward relief

This kind of courage isn't loud. It doesn't push. It doesn't come from ego. It comes from trust—trust in the process, trust in the client's strength, and trust that growth often happens just on the other side of discomfort.

The Humility to Step Back

Courage alone isn't enough. Coaching also requires humility—the kind that allows you to loosen your grip on outcomes.

That means:

- Resisting the urge to "solve" something the client hasn't asked you to fix
- Being okay when your brilliant question doesn't land
- Not needing to be the most insightful person in the room
- Allowing space for the client to be confused, contradictory, or stuck—without rushing in to clean it up

Humility says: "*This is not about me.*" Even when the client is grateful. Even when the breakthrough seems connected to your words. You don't need to deflect the credit—but you do need to hold it loosely.

Holding the Space Without Closing the Gap

One of the hardest things for new coaches is learning how to sit with tension—to stay present when there's no clear answer yet. We're wired to want resolution. But sometimes, the most powerful thing you can do is simply *hold the space.*

When a client is wrestling with ambivalence

When they feel shame but aren't ready to name it

When something is surfacing emotionally, but words haven't come

In those moments, don't rush. Don't overreach. Let the silence work. Let the discomfort speak.

As Parker Palmer writes, "*The human soul doesn't want to be fixed or saved. It simply wants to be witnessed—exactly as it is.*" That's your job as a coach. To witness. To walk alongside. To hold space without having to fill it. And that requires both courage and humility in equal measure.

The Coach's Inner Work

The best coaches do their own internal work. Not because they have to be flawless—but because they know they're not. They recognize that their presence in the coaching space is shaped by their inner life, not just their training. And they take that seriously.

Relationship coaching, more than many other forms of helping, has a way of pressing on your personal story. You will be triggered. You'll have moments where your client's struggle mirrors your own. You may feel jealous of their growth. You may feel helpless in their stuckness.

This doesn't disqualify you. It *qualifies* you—if you're willing to stay awake to it. The inner work of a coach is not about mastery. It's about integrity.

Staying Curious About Your Own Story

Coaches who lead with curiosity are usually living with curiosity. They ask questions of themselves—not just their clients:

- Why did that session leave me so drained?
- Why did I feel the urge to steer the conversation?
- What fear or hope showed up in *me* just now?

When you stay attentive to your own emotional patterns, needs, and blind spots, you're far less likely to unconsciously act them out in a session. You create more room for the client to do *their* work—because you've already taken responsibility for yours.

Seeking Feedback, Not Just Validation

One of the gifts of healthy coaching community is honest feedback. Not just affirmation (though that's important), but thoughtful reflection on how your presence lands.

Ask your peers:

- What do you notice about my coaching posture?
- Where might I be unintentionally rushing, rescuing, or avoiding?
- What do you hear me repeating in client conversations?

Supervision, peer consultation, and even informal check-ins with fellow coaches can help you stay honest—and growing.

Letting Your Love Language Shape, Not Sabotage

As you'll explore in Part 2, everyone gives and receives love differently. That includes coaches.

Your primary Love Language will subtly shape how you coach:

- If you're high in **Words of Affirmation**, you may default to verbal encouragement—but need to guard against over-validating.
- If your language is **Acts of Service**, you may love giving clients tools—but need to watch for doing too much for them.
- If you value **Quality Time**, you might naturally hold space well—but may feel especially frustrated when a client disengages.
- If **Physical Touch** or **Receiving Gifts** speaks deeply to you, you may resonate with emotional expressions of connection—but be mindful of boundaries in coaching relationships.

The point isn't to suppress your wiring. It's to understand it—so it enhances, rather than complicates, the coaching relationship. Good coaching flows from skill. Great coaching flows from *wholeness*—or at least the pursuit of it.

Practices That Shape the Coach

There's no certification or degree that makes you fully ready for the relational complexity of coaching. What prepares you—what *shapes* you—is the quiet, consistent rhythm of tending to your own life with intention.

You can't offer what you haven't received. And you can't walk someone else into emotional clarity if you're avoiding your own. That's not a call to perfection—it's a call to practice.

Here are a few rhythms and habits that help shape not just your coaching, but your character.

Spiritual Practices That Center You

The work of relationship coaching draws deeply on your inner life. Make time—daily, if possible—for spiritual grounding. Not just productivity-fueled prayer, but stillness.

- **Silence and solitude**—Even five minutes of quiet can shift your presence for the day.
- **Breath prayers or centering practice**—Help you return to the present moment before or between sessions.
- **Scripture engagement**—Not for content, but for formation. Read slowly. Ask: *"What is being formed in me through this?"*

Reflective Practices That Build Awareness

Build the habit of pausing after sessions—not to evaluate the client's growth, but your own presence.

- What stirred in me today?
- Where did I feel most connected or most distracted?
- Did I overfunction? Did I withdraw?
- What patterns in me surfaced—and what might they be pointing to?

Journaling even a few bullet points after sessions can reveal subtle growth over time.

Embodied Awareness

Pay attention to what your body is telling you—especially in session.

- Did you lean in or pull back?
- Did your breath quicken or your shoulders tighten?
- Were you exhausted afterward—or energized?

Your body often knows things before your mind can name them. Use that wisdom as a coaching tool—not just for your clients, but for yourself.

Feedback Loops You Can Trust

Make it normal to seek feedback—not just applause.

- Schedule regular peer consultation or coaching supervision—even quarterly. Reach out to a fellow coach you respect and ask, "*Would you be open to swapping sessions or doing a reflective debrief together?*"
- If available, join a coaching cohort or small group of practitioners who meet monthly for honest, growth-focused dialogue.
- Record a session (with permission) and reflect: "*What's my tone here? Am I listening or performing?*"
- Ask a trusted peer: "*What do you notice about how I show up when I'm trying too hard?*"

Feedback doesn't need to be formal to be transformative—it just needs to be honest.

Boundaries and Sabbath

You are not your client's hope. You are not their hero. You are not your calendar.

- Practice intentional Sabbath—time set apart that reminds you that your worth is not measured by output.
- Build in margin between sessions, even if it costs you a little.
- Protect the version of you that exists *outside of coaching.*

You coach best when you're not overextended.

Stay on Your Own Journey

If you coach others toward healing, clarity, and growth—then pursue those things yourself.

- Work with your own coach.
- Seek therapy when needed.
- Talk to mentors who see *you*, not just your work.

Don't try to be the kind of coach who doesn't need anything.

Be the kind who *gets what you need*, so you can offer from overflow—not depletion.

Summary

There's no shortcut to becoming the kind of coach people trust with their real selves.

You can learn the tools. You can practice the posture. But at the heart of it all is *who you are*—the presence you bring into the room. Relationship coaching is soul work, not just skill work. And the transformation begins with you.

This chapter has reminded us that great coaching flows from:

- The **motivation** to serve, not impress
- The **maturity** to remain calm, curious, and clear
- The **courage and humility** to hold space without control
- The **inner work** of emotional and spiritual growth
- The **habits and rhythms** that keep you grounded, whole, and real

These aren't optional extras. They're the heart of sustainable, relationally intelligent coaching. And they are what give your skills the soul they need to truly matter.

QUESTIONS TO PONDER

1. What most motivates you to do this work—and what tends to pull you off center?
2. Where in your coaching do you feel most alive? Where do you feel most unsure?
3. Which practice (spiritual, reflective, relational) would most nourish your inner life right now?
4. How do you want to grow—not just as a coach but as a person?

Chapter 5

The Science and Psychology Behind the 5 Love Languages

"Why does this matter so much to you?"

That's what one coach asked a tearful client after she described how her husband vacuumed the entire house without being asked.

She paused, collected herself, then said, *"Because for once, I didn't have to ask. And that meant—he saw me."*

Moments like that are common in coaching sessions that touch on the 5 Love Languages. What looks like a simple act of service or a kind word can carry the emotional weight of being known, cherished, and emotionally safe. That's the power of personalized love: it speaks directly to the heart.

But why do some acts of love land—and others fall flat?

Why does receiving flowers feel romantic to one client but irrelevant to another?

Why can two people sincerely love each other but still miss the mark again and again?

That's where the science comes in.

The 5 Love Languages didn't begin as a scientific framework. I (Gary) distilled the concept from years of pastoral counseling—not laboratory research. Since its publication in 1992, the model has endured (and become one of the bestselling books of all time) not because it's perfect, but because it resonates. And now, decades later, research in psychology, neurobiology, communication, and attachment theory offers us the scaffolding to understand *why* it works—and *how* to coach it well.

As a coach, you don't need to become a psychologist. But you *do* need to know what's happening under the surface of this model. Because when you help clients explore how they give and receive love, you're not just tweaking behaviors. You're stepping into their attachment patterns, unmet needs, past pain, and deepest longings for connection.

In this chapter, we'll explore the emotional and scientific foundations that make the Love Languages more than a pop-psych quiz. We'll show how the model aligns with what we know about human needs, secure relationships, behavioral reinforcement, and brain chemistry. And we'll introduce the essential idea that the Love Languages are not fixed types but adaptive emotional strategies, shaped by story, personality, and experience.

The better you understand the psychological layers beneath the Love Languages, the more equipped you'll be to coach with wisdom, empathy, and lasting impact.

Let's start at the root: What do humans need, emotionally, in order to thrive?

Emotional Needs Theory: Why the Love Languages Resonate

At the heart of every coaching conversation is an unspoken question:

What do I need in order to feel loved—and what's getting in the way?

The 5 Love Languages gained traction because they offer a simple answer to that question. But beneath that simplicity is something more profound: the idea that humans have core emotional needs—and we're constantly navigating how to meet them in our closest relationships.

Psychologists have long recognized that emotional wellbeing is not a luxury—it's foundational. While Abraham Maslow's (1943) hierarchy of needs famously positioned *love and belonging* just above safety and physiological survival, this concept is far from theoretical. Dozens of empirical studies confirm that human beings are hardwired for relational connection, and that emotional isolation has measurable consequences for mental and physical health.

For instance, research on social pain demonstrates that rejection and disconnection activate the same neural pathways as physical pain (Eisenberger &

Lieberman, 2004). In fact, loneliness has been associated with increased inflammation, higher mortality rates, and impaired immune function (Burleson, 2003; Cacioppo et al., 2015; Holt-Lunstad et al., 2010). These aren't just emotional inconveniences—they're existential threats to our flourishing.

From infancy onward, the need for attuned connection is biologically encoded. Bowlby's (1969) attachment theory, and decades of follow-up research (Mikulincer & Shaver, 2007), demonstrate that safe, consistent emotional bonds are a prerequisite for psychological security. Adults, like children, need to feel seen, soothed, and safe in order to thrive (Guerrero, Andersen, & Afifi, 2017).

Modern neuroscience confirms what ancient Scripture hinted at: "It is not good that the man should be alone" (Genesis 2:18 KJV). This declaration wasn't just about romantic companionship—it was a statement of fundamental design. To be human is to be relational. Love, when expressed in ways that resonate, isn't sentimental fluff—it's soul-level oxygen.

The 5 Love Languages tap directly into that. Each language is a behavioral shorthand for meeting the deeper need to be:

- **Seen**—noticed and acknowledged, not invisible
- **Safe**—emotionally secure and accepted without fear
- **Valued**—affirmed for one's worth and contributions
- **Desired**—wanted, pursued, cherished
- **Chosen**—prioritized above other distractions or demands

When a client lights up because their partner brought them coffee or sent an encouraging text, it's not about the beverage or the words. It's about feeling *chosen*. It's about feeling *loved in a way that actually lands*.

This is why the Love Languages model resonates across cultures, ages, and stages of life. It offers a framework to help people interpret how love is translated from intention into impact.

Integrating Choice Theory and Self-Determination Theory

Dr. William Glasser's *Choice Theory* (1998) proposes that all human behavior is an attempt to satisfy five basic needs: survival, love/belonging, power, freedom, and fun. Of these, love and belonging are often the most emotionally loaded—and the least well-articulated.

The 5 Love Languages express how people attempt to satisfy that need. They also help couples or individuals move from guesswork to clarity.

Similarly, Self-Determination Theory (Deci & Ryan, 2000) posits that human beings thrive when three psychological needs are met:

- **Relatedness** (connection to others)
- **Competence** (feeling effective)
- **Autonomy** (having choice and volition)

Love Language fluency supports all three. When someone knows how to love their partner in a way that's felt, they feel *competent*. When they choose to act in love, rather than passively waiting, they express *autonomy*. And when their gestures are received and reciprocated, they experience *relatedness*.

In coaching, connecting the dots between emotional needs and relational habits is one of your most powerful interventions. You're helping clients discover not just what they want—but why it matters.

Attachment and the Need for Connection

If emotional needs are the *why*, attachment theory helps explain *how* we seek to meet those needs—and how we respond when they're not met. From infancy through adulthood, we form emotional bonds as a way of navigating vulnerability, connection, and security (Hazan & Shaver, 1987).

At its core, attachment theory is about connection under stress. Originally developed by John Bowlby (1969) to understand the bond between infants and caregivers, attachment theory has since expanded into adult relationships, showing that the desire for secure, dependable connection is lifelong. Whether we're six months old or sixty years old, we all long to know: *Will someone come for me when I'm hurting? Will anyone stay when I'm struggling?*

The 5 Love Languages, though not framed as such, are relational practices that offer secure signals—they're ways of saying: *I'm here, I see you, and you matter to me.*

When partners speak each other's Love Language fluently, they're reinforcing secure attachment bonds (Keely & Malouff, 2022). When they continually miss, dismiss, or resist each other's Love Language, they create emotional distance and sometimes even activate attachment injuries, which are relational wounds formed when a partner feels unsafe, unseen, or abandoned in moments of emotional need. So when a client gets emotional about a "small" thing—like a missed hug or a forgotten note—they're not reacting to the event. They're reacting to the meaning: *I don't matter*. The Love Languages don't just signal care; they signal emotional safety.

Attachment Styles and Love Language Preferences

Research shows that our attachment style—secure, anxious, avoidant, or disorganized—often shapes how we both express and interpret love. For example:

- **Securely attached individuals** tend to express their needs clearly and receive love openly across multiple languages.
- **Anxiously attached clients** may crave frequent Words of Affirmation or Physical Touch as reassurance of their partner's presence.
- **Avoidantly attached clients** may prefer Acts of Service because it allows closeness without intense emotional vulnerability.
- **Disorganized attachment** can result in an unpredictable push-pull dynamic, where love is both desperately desired and deeply distrusted.

As a coach, recognizing these patterns is essential. And it will lead you to not just ask *what* a client wants from their partner but also *why* it matters. What fear does it soothe? What story does it rewrite? What longing does it answer?

The point is that you're not just helping clients communicate more clearly; you're helping them create emotional safety, which is the foundation of any growth-oriented relationship (Simpson & Rholes, 2012).

Emotional Responsiveness: The Heartbeat of Secure Love

Dr. Sue Johnson, the founder of Emotionally Focused Therapy (EFT), notes that the central question in attachment is: *Are you there for me?* Her model emphasizes three key components of secure bonding:

1. **Accessibility**—Can I reach you?
2. **Responsiveness**—Will you tune in when I need you?
3. **Engagement**—Will you value and stay close to me?

The Love Languages, when attuned and consistent, reinforce all three. They are daily rituals of responsiveness, creating emotional feedback loops that build trust over time. Love, at its best, is a form of relational resilience. And secure connection isn't just about comfort—it's what allows people to take risks, grow, and flourish.

Communication and Perception: Why Love Gets Lost in Translation

If attachment theory explains how we reach for connection, then communication explains how those attempts succeed—or get lost in translation. Even the most heartfelt gestures can miss their mark if they're sent in the wrong language or received through the wrong filter.

Here's the through line for love:

- **Emotional Needs:** *What we long for*
- **Attachment:** *How we instinctively seek what we long for*
- **Communication:** *How we try to express and receive what we long for*

At the heart of the 5 Love Languages model is the insight that love must be expressed in a way that's actually perceived as love. And this is where things often break down—not for lack of care, but because of mismatched delivery systems (Chaplin & Aldao, 2013). A partner who offers Acts of Service may feel they are showing love clearly, but if their spouse craves Quality Time or Words of Affirmation, that love may never register.

Communication theory reminds us that sending a message isn't enough—it must also be received, decoded, and interpreted. That's why you can speak fluently in your own language and still be emotionally unintelligible to your partner.

The Basics of Relational Communication

Communication scholars emphasize that every message has two levels:

1. **Content**—the literal information ("I cleaned the kitchen")
2. **Relational meaning**—the emotional subtext ("I care about our shared space" or "I want to help you feel less overwhelmed")

Love Languages live mostly in the second layer. They are symbolic actions that carry emotional meaning, not just practical value. And if the emotional intent doesn't match the partner's receptive channel, the message can be missed entirely.

Missed Bids for Connection

John Gottman's (1999) concept of "emotional bids" is particularly relevant here. A bid is any attempt to connect—a look, a touch, a comment, a favor. The health of a relationship often hinges on how frequently and meaningfully those bids are received.

Love Languages, in many cases, are those bids. When ignored or misread, they can lead to erosion of trust and intimacy—not because the love isn't there, but because it isn't registering.

As a coach, you'll often encounter clients who feel unloved not because their partner doesn't care—but because they're speaking a different language. Your job is to help them slow the exchange down, identify the missed bids, and begin matching intention with perception.

Nonverbal Expression and the Power of Interpretation

Many of the Love Languages rely on nonverbal cues: a hand on the back, the timing of a favor, the tone of a compliment. But perception of those cues is deeply shaped by:

- Cultural background
- Personality traits (e.g., sensitivity, neurodivergence)
- Past experiences, including trauma or neglect

A hug may feel comforting to one client and intrusive to another. A compliment may feel affirming—or patronizing. Coaches must help clients move from simply *doing* a Love Language to *learning their partner's dialect* and checking for impact (more to come on this in later chapters).

The message you're helping your client to receive is this: Love isn't just what you give. It's what the other person feels.

To help you client become more aware of "Intention vs. Impact," you might ask your client to reflect on questions like these:

- What's one thing I've done recently to show love?
- How did I hope it would be received?
- How do I think it was actually received?
- What could I do differently next time to bridge that gap?

These simple questions often open the door to deeper awareness—and deeper humility. They shift the conversation from *"Am I loving well?"* to *"Is my love landing where it's needed most?"* That's the work of a coach: not just helping clients express love but helping them translate it.

Psychological Complexity: Personality Traits

While the 5 Love Languages provide a practical and accessible framework for understanding how people express and receive love, the psychology beneath those expressions is rarely one-size-fits-all. In fact, individual differences—especially personality traits—play a crucial role in shaping how love is interpreted, expressed, and experienced.

One of the most widely accepted models in personality psychology is the Five-Factor Model, often referred to as the "Big Five": openness, conscientiousness, extraversion, agreeableness, and neuroticism (McCrae & Costa, 1997). These traits correlate meaningfully with variations in how people both give and interpret relational gestures.

- **Extraverted** individuals may gravitate toward expressions of Physical Touch and Words of Affirmation, thriving on social engagement and verbal feedback (Asendorpf & Wilpers, 1998).
- Those high in **agreeableness** tend to be responsive to emotional needs and are more likely to initiate loving acts—especially service-oriented ones (Jensen-Campbell & Graziano, 2001).
- Highly **conscientious** people may favor Acts of Service, showing love through responsibility, reliability, and attention to shared goals.
- Individuals high in **openness to experience** may be more flexible in their emotional expression, trying new ways to connect or explore unfamiliar relational habits (McCrae & Costa, 1997).
- **Neuroticism**, by contrast, is linked to relational insecurity and emotional volatility. Clients high in this trait may second-guess their partner's expressions of love or require higher frequency and reassurance through their preferred language (Robins, Caspi, & Moffitt, 2002; Finkel et al., 2014).

Other personality constructs offer additional insight. For instance, highly sensitive persons (HSPs) are more reactive to both positive and negative relational input and may experience loving gestures—like touch or tone—more intensely than others (Aron & Aron, 1997). Similarly, individuals with attachment-related anxiety may prioritize certain Love Languages (e.g., constant affirmation) as a buffer against relational fear (Mikulincer & Shaver, 2007).

For coaches, understanding the intersection between Love Language preferences and personality traits is essential (and we make it easy with the 5 Love Languages Premium Assessment; more to come on that later). It prevents oversimplification and enables more tailored, attuned relational strategies. While the 5 Love Languages model offers categories, personality provides the texture—and it's often the texture that determines whether love is actually felt.

Love, Behavior, and Neurobiology

The 5 Love Languages don't just feel good—they do something to the brain, the body, and the behavioral patterns of a relationship. That's part of their staying power: Consistent expressions of love create both emotional connection and neural reinforcement.

From a behavioral perspective, loving acts function as positive reinforcers. When a partner offers a gesture in the other's preferred language and it's well received, both individuals experience emotional reward. This mirrors classical and operant conditioning theory, where behaviors followed by satisfying consequences are likely to be repeated (Skinner, 1953). Over time, this builds relational habits—small rituals of connection that reinforce intimacy.

But the science goes even deeper. Neurobiological research shows that loving connection activates a range of hormonal and neural systems linked to trust, safety, pleasure, and memory. When clients report feeling "safe," "calm," or "lit up" after a moment of connection, that's not just metaphor—it's measurable.

Expressions of love—especially when aligned with a person's Love Language—can trigger:

- **Oxytocin**, known as the "bonding hormone," which is associated with emotional closeness and stress reduction (Insel & Young, 2001)
- **Dopamine**, linked to reward, anticipation, and motivation

- **Endorphins**, which provide a sense of wellbeing and pain relief
- **Deactivation of the amygdala**, reducing the brain's threat response during safe emotional contact (Coan et al., 2006)

These biochemical responses help explain why a small gesture—like holding hands or receiving a kind note—can significantly reduce stress or shift the emotional climate of a relationship.

Just like a workout strengthens muscles, consistent expressions of love in a person's native language build emotional security. Repeated actions carve neural pathways—what neuroscience calls experience-dependent plasticity (Perry et al., 1995). In practical terms, this means that loving behavior creates *emotional memory over time. Partners begin to expect goodness from one another, not as a surprise, but as a pattern.* In this way, Love Languages aren't just emotional preferences. They're behavioral and biological tools for reinforcing safety and connection.

Interestingly, when loving behavior is offered in a non-preferred language—or delivered inconsistently—it may fail to activate the same neural reward systems. In coaching, this explains why one partner might say, *"I'm doing all these things for them, but nothing seems to work,"* while the other says, *"I don't feel loved."*

This isn't ingratitude. It's mismatch of input and interpretation—and a missed opportunity for neurobiological reward.

Summary

The 5 Love Languages model may look simple on the surface, but beneath it lies a deep reservoir of psychological insight. This chapter explored the emotional needs that drive connection, the attachment patterns that shape how we seek it, the communication dynamics that help (or hinder) love from being received, the personality traits that filter expression, and the neurobiological processes that reinforce relational habits.

As a coach, understanding this complexity doesn't mean becoming a therapist or neuroscientist—it means coaching with **greater precision and empathy**. Knowing *why* a client clings to one expression of love or rejects another helps you look beneath behavior to motive. It helps you ask better questions, spot deeper patterns, and guide clients toward more meaningful and sustainable connection.

The 5 Love Languages are not static labels. They're emotional strategies, shaped by story, shaped by wiring, shaped by need. And when they're spoken with awareness and intention, they become a kind of emotional fluency—helping people translate love not just clearly, but courageously.

QUESTIONS TO PONDER

1. Which psychological insights from this chapter most expanded your view of the Love Languages?
2. How might your own personality traits influence the way you coach Love Language discovery or expression?
3. In your coaching experience, where have you seen a mismatch between a client's intended expression of love and how it was received?
4. How comfortable are you navigating conversations about attachment, personality, or emotional need with clients?
5. What might you need to keep learning in order to coach this framework with increasing depth and confidence?

PART 2

COACHING THROUGH THE 5 LOVE LANGUAGES

"The single biggest problem in communication is the illusion that it has taken place."

—ATTRIBUTED TO GEORGE BERNARD SHAW

This is where the framework comes to life. In Part 2, you'll learn how to coach people through the 5 Love Languages with insight, nuance, and emotional fluency. It's not enough to know the model—your clients need your help turning it into muscle memory. Whether you're helping someone find their primary language, navigating a mismatch between partners, or guiding a couple through years of missed signals, this section gives you the tools to make love tangible. You'll move from theory to real-world practice as you learn to coach each language with sensitivity, creativity, and precision. Because when love is expressed in the right language, everything changes.

Chapter 6

Helping Clients Discover Their Primary Love Language

Most people love discovering something true about themselves. Even the skeptics—the ones who shrug off personality quizzes or roll their eyes at emotional vocabulary—light up a little when a description lands. When something finally expresses what they've always felt but couldn't quite articulate.

That's what discovering your Love Language does.

It doesn't tell you everything about yourself, but it does reveal something important. Something tender. It gives you a handle on your heart.

For many clients, this kind of clarity feels like a gift. They've known the ache of misconnection. They've tried to explain what they need in a relationship but struggled to find the words. And suddenly—here's a language that helps them name it.

As a coach, you get to facilitate that discovery. Not by handing them a label, but by walking with them into the deeper work of self-understanding. You get to ask the right questions, notice what lights them up, and reflect what they may not have seen in themselves.

Discovery is sacred. It opens the door to empathy, communication, and healing—and ultimately love—not just between couples, but within the individual. And it reminds the client that their needs aren't too much or too mysterious. They just need to be named.

In this chapter, we'll explore how to guide clients through that naming process.

You'll learn to listen for patterns, create space for emotional clarity, and gently challenge assumptions when needed. You'll also learn how to help people discover their languages together in ways that deepen empathy—not defensiveness.

Because when someone sees themselves more clearly, they're more equipped to be seen—and to love well in return.

Why Discovery Matters

Discovering your Love Language is more than finding a category—it's uncovering a key to your emotional landscape.

When clients learn how they most naturally receive love, something often shifts. They begin to name needs that may have long gone unspoken or misunderstood. They recognize why certain gestures feel deeply meaningful while others fall flat. And perhaps most importantly, they start to give themselves permission to care about what they need—not as a selfish act, but as an act of clarity and connection.

That's why discovery matters. It moves love from guesswork to understanding. From generic to personal. From invisible to seen.

This process is not only emotionally clarifying—it's psychologically transformative. Research on self-concept clarity shows that when individuals gain insight into their own preferences, needs, and values, they tend to experience stronger relationship satisfaction and lower levels of anxiety and emotional reactivity (Campbell et al., 2003). In other words, knowing yourself—even in one focused area like relational needs—can improve how you show up with others.

Similarly, studies on emotional intelligence suggest that people who can name and understand their own emotional patterns are better equipped to engage in secure, mutually satisfying relationships (Mikulincer & Shaver, 2007; Schutte et al., 2001). Discovery creates language—and language creates access. When a client can finally say, *"This is what love looks like to me,"* they're not just finding a preference—they're finding their voice.

That's why helping a client discover their Love Language—or explore what they've already identified—isn't a surface-level step in the coaching process. It's a gateway to lasting relational growth.

The Many Paths to Discovery

One of the reasons the 5 Love Languages model has endured is its simplicity. Many people "get it" almost immediately. They take a quick quiz online, hear a podcast, or read the original book and instinctively think, *"Oh—that's me."* And often, they're not wrong.

Clients frequently arrive in coaching having already self-identified their Love Language. Sometimes they've taken the free online tool. Sometimes they've just guessed based on past experiences or how they express love to others. This can be a helpful starting point—but it's rarely the full picture.

As a coach, it's important to affirm the accessibility of the model while also inviting clients to move beyond surface-level insight. Because while self-diagnosis may feel satisfying, true discovery often happens in layers—through stories, patterns, and reflection.

There are several pathways coaches can use to help clients deepen or confirm their Love Language awareness:

1. **Self-Reporting and Personal Reflection**

   Start with what the client believes to be true. Ask open-ended questions like:

   - "Which of these languages do you most naturally gravitate toward?"
   - "Can you remember a moment when you felt deeply loved? What was happening?"
   - "What do you complain about or long for most in your relationships?"

Clients often know more than they think—they just need help connecting the emotional dots.

2. **Observation of How They Give Love**

   People often express love in the way they most hope to receive it. Watching what someone does—how they initiate, serve, or speak—can offer valuable clues. But this isn't foolproof. Sometimes clients love others through a learned behavior rather than a natural expression. So be curious about the difference between what a client does and what they deeply desire.

3. **Noticing Emotional Reactions**
   Which gestures light them up? Which ones do they barely register? Emotional resonance is a strong indicator. Encourage clients to pay attention to their **internal responses**, not just their assumptions.
4. **Looking at Patterns in Conflict**
   Where there is pain or disappointment, there is often a buried need. What a client complains about ("You never say anything nice," "You're always on your phone") can be a stronger signal than what they request. As Gottman and Silver (1999) noted, emotional bids for connection often come wrapped in frustration or sarcasm.
5. **The Free Quiz vs. The Premium Assessment**
   While the original online quiz is a helpful entry point, it is not a comprehensive diagnostic tool. It offers a small snapshot, not a full portrait. Clients may anchor to its result prematurely—and sometimes, inaccurately.

As a coach, you can honor the accessibility of the free tool while introducing the **5 Love Languages Premium Assessment** (covered in depth in Part 3) as a more nuanced, coach-supported instrument. This tool not only confirms preferences with greater precision but also explores dialects, blends, and shifts over time, giving both you and the client a deeper foundation for change.

There are many entry points into Love Language discovery. Your job is to welcome whatever insight your client brings, and then gently walk with them into greater clarity, depth, and emotional resonance. The goal isn't to contradict what they believe—it's to expand it.

Coaching Through Resistance or Confusion

Not every client arrives with clarity about how they feel loved. In fact, some show up unsure, hesitant, or emotionally foggy—not because they're unmotivated, but because naming personal needs can feel risky. For some, the idea of having a Love Language is intuitive and affirming. For others, it's disorienting or even triggering.

A client might say, *"I don't think I have a Love Language."*

Or, *"None of these really apply to me."*

Or, *"Honestly, I think I have all five."*

Or, more subtly, *"I don't really need much. I just want my partner to be okay."*

Each of these responses deserves attention to explore what's underneath. The person who says they have all five may, in fact, be open-hearted and expressive—or they may be uncertain, conflict-avoidant, or so accustomed to adapting to others that they've lost contact with what they themselves truly need.

In those moments, the coach's role is not to diagnose or redirect—it's to stay grounded in curiosity. Resistance is rarely just resistance. More often, it's a protective reflex: a way to guard against disappointment, vulnerability, or exposure.

Many clients have lived in emotional environments where their needs were overlooked, minimized, or even shamed. Others have spent years suppressing their preferences to care for others, to keep the peace, or simply to avoid the pain of unmet longing. And for some—especially those who've experienced relational trauma or chronic misattunement—the very act of identifying a Love Language can stir up grief, fear, or self-doubt.

Research in trauma-informed neuroscience confirms this dynamic. When love is inconsistently received or unsafe, the brain adapts. It becomes harder to access or trust emotional signals (Perry et al., 1995; Siegel, 2012). In other words, the client isn't being evasive—they're being adaptive. And that adaptation deserves respect.

In these moments, coaching must slow down. Discovery can't be rushed. Instead of trying to "figure out" a client's language, you're helping them build emotional permission—the permission to want, to feel, and to be loved in a way that resonates.

Gentle prompts can help surface what words alone may not:

- *"Is there a kind of love you've always longed for but rarely received?"*
- *"Which of these gestures feels awkward to receive—and why?"*
- *"What have you learned to dismiss or downplay that might actually matter?"*
- *"When was the last time you felt deeply known or cherished, even briefly?"*

These conversations are not always tidy. But they're sacred. When a client starts reconnecting with what feels good, comforting, safe, or wanted, they're not just identifying a Love Language—they're reclaiming their emotional landscape. They're learning it's okay to have a preference. To have needs. To matter.

This is where the power of coaching is so evident. Not in offering answers, but in staying present—calm, curious, and compassionate—as a client slowly steps out of emotional autopilot and into emotional awareness. Love Language discovery doesn't always begin with clarity. Sometimes it begins with courage.

Sample Coaching Dialogue

Discovery doesn't happen in a vacuum—it happens in dialogue. And while no two coaching conversations are exactly the same, it helps to have a feel for how a session might unfold when you're helping a client personalize their Love Language.

Here's a brief sample from a discovery-focused coaching conversation. The goal here isn't to lead or correct but to guide the client into their own insight with open-ended questions and gentle reflection.

Coach: When you think about times you've felt most loved or emotionally full—what comes to mind?

Client: Probably when someone goes out of their way to help me with something. Like, my friend just took my car to get washed because I've been slammed with work. That meant a lot.

Coach: What do you think that gesture communicated to you?

Client: That I'm not alone. That I don't have to carry everything myself.

Coach: How did it feel—beyond just being convenient?

Client: Honestly, I felt seen. And kind of . . . cared for without having to ask.

Coach: That sounds like a pretty meaningful moment. If you had to guess, would you say that kind of care—when someone does something practical but thoughtful—is a pattern in what fills your tank?

Client: Yeah. I never thought about it that way, but it definitely is. My mom used to do little things like that, and I always felt loved by it. I think that's why Acts of Service might be so important to me.

Coach: It sounds like it's not just the act itself—but the intention behind it, and the timing. That's helpful to notice.

Client: Right. It only feels good when it's not out of obligation—when it feels like someone *wants* to help, not like they *have* to.

In this short exchange, the coach didn't assign a label or rush to define the client's Love Language. Instead, they slowed the process down—drawing out the emotion behind the memory, linking it to a pattern, and helping the client notice the *why* beneath the *what*. This is the heart of effective discovery: creating space for a client to name what resonates in their own words, at their own pace, with insight that feels earned rather than imposed.

Primary, Secondary, and Situational Preferences

One of the most helpful insights a coach can offer during the discovery process is that Love Languages are not rigid categories. While many people identify a strong primary preference, most experience a blend of emotional cues that feel meaningful—some more central, others more contextual.

Clients often describe this blend with hesitation, unsure if they're "doing it wrong" because they resonate with more than one language. One might say, *"I think I'm Quality Time, but I also really love thoughtful surprises."* Another might note that Words of Affirmation feel essential most of the time, but during periods of high stress, nothing means more than someone stepping in to help with tasks. These are not contradictions—they're expressions of nuance and relational depth.

In fact, research by Keely and Malouff (2022) found that relationship satisfaction was positively associated not only with alignment in primary Love Languages, but also in secondary expressions—suggesting that Love Language fluency involves more than just getting one "type" right. Helping clients reflect on both their core emotional channel and their situational responses creates more clarity, not less.

It's often helpful to think of preferences in three overlapping zones: primary, secondary, and situational. A client's primary language is the one that, when consistently spoken, tends to create the deepest emotional resonance. Their secondary language may feel nearly as strong or show up more clearly in certain dynamics or relationships. And then there are situational shifts, where context—such as life stage, grief, burnout, distance, or parenting—reshapes what feels most loving in the moment.

Situational preferences often emerge in response to changing emotional demands or relational environments. For example, a client who typically thrives on Physical Touch may find that during seasons of parenting young children—when they're constantly "touched out"—they crave Words of Affirmation or a moment of quiet Quality Time instead. Someone recovering from illness or burnout may not be looking for passionate connection but instead find deep comfort in Acts of Service—meals prepared, chores handled, details managed. Long-distance couples may find that Receiving Gifts takes on new weight, not because material things matter most, but because they function as tangible proxies for presence.

These shifts don't negate the client's core Love Language—they expand it, showing how emotional need and relational context shape receptivity. Helping clients notice these patterns allows them to communicate more clearly about what they need *right now, without assuming their preferences have permanently changed.*

This kind of emotional adaptability is not a weakness; it's a mark of relational maturity. When clients begin to recognize how their needs flex across time and circumstance, they become more intentional in both asking for love and offering it. You might invite them to reflect on what mattered most to them during a past season of their life, and how that compares to what matters now. This awareness can be especially useful when a client feels stuck, misunderstood, or unsure why a once-effective relational rhythm no longer satisfies.

Helping clients articulate both their core needs and their contextual sensitivities allows for a more accurate, compassionate understanding of their emotional landscape. It also builds trust with themselves: they learn they're allowed to shift, grow, and reevaluate.

As the 5 Love Languages Premium Assessment (explored fully in Part 3) reveals, effective discovery is rarely a one-time moment. It's an evolving awareness. Preferences may stay steady, or they may stretch. But when clients are encouraged to pay attention with curiosity, they gain a language for connection that grows with them.

Personality and the Discovery Process

Love Language discovery doesn't happen in a vacuum. Clients bring their entire psychological makeup to the process—including their personality traits, communication style, comfort with vulnerability, and emotional wiring. What feels natural to one person might feel awkward or even overwhelming to another—not because they don't value love, but because their personality shapes how they experience it.

An introverted client may prefer Quality Time that involves quiet, side-by-side presence (e.g., reading together or taking a slow walk) while their extroverted partner interprets Quality Time as constant interaction or lively conversation. A highly conscientious client might default to Acts of Service, valuing responsibility and structure, while someone high in openness might experiment with varied expressions across all five languages. Those high in agreeableness may be more attuned to what their partner needs and more likely to adapt, even at the cost of their own preferences (Jensen-Campbell & Graziano, 2001). Understanding these patterns helps coaches interpret what clients say *and* what they struggle to say.

In some cases, personality traits may obscure discovery altogether. A client high in emotional restraint (or "neuroticism" in the language of the Big Five) may hesitate to express needs for fear of being misunderstood or dismissed. Another might dismiss their preferences as unimportant—especially if they've spent years believing that needing love makes them needy. For highly sensitive people (HSPs), subtle variations in tone, timing, or setting can dramatically affect whether an expression of love feels nourishing or overwhelming (Aron & Aron, 1997).

You'll see exactly how personality informs a person's Love Language when you begin using the Premium Assessment. It will help you gently surface these dynamics by noticing where a client seems energized and where they seem uncomfortable. Asking questions like *"Does that feel like something you'd enjoy, or something you'd endure?"* or *"Have you ever dismissed something as not your style but wondered later if it just felt unfamiliar?"* helps clients move past default responses and into deeper emotional awareness.

Integrating personality awareness into Love Language discovery doesn't complicate the process—it deepens it. It reminds the client that they don't have to fit into a relational mold. Their way of receiving and offering love is not only valid—it's valuable. The key is to honor how they're wired while stretching gently into new relational understanding.

The Role of the Coach: Curator, Not Authority

It's tempting, especially in a structured model like the 5 Love Languages, to want to bring clarity fast. But discovery is not a diagnostic process—and the coach's role is not to declare a client's Love Language from the outside. Instead, great coaching creates a curated space for exploration, where insight emerges not because it's delivered, but because it's discovered.

Coaches are most effective in this process not when they act as experts, but when they serve as attuned companions—noticing, naming, and inviting reflection. That means resisting the urge to label or guide the client too quickly toward a conclusion. Even if you have a strong sense of what their primary language might be, it's far more powerful for the client to come to that awareness themselves (even if they're reading it for the first time on the Premium Assessment report).

This posture takes both discipline and trust: the discipline to hold back when you think you know, and the trust that your client's inner wisdom will surface with time. Discovery is a living process, not a one-time answer (Feeney & Collins, 2015).

This is especially important in couples work, where one partner may feel compelled to "correct" or define the other's Love Language based on their observations. A skilled coach gently redirects that dynamic:

"That's helpful input—let's also see how your partner experiences it internally."

This reminds everyone in the room that love isn't just about what's offered—it's about what's received.

When a coach models curiosity, patience, and respect for nuance, clients often follow suit. They become less anxious about "getting it right" and more open to asking deeper questions of themselves and their relationships.

Coaching discovery, then, is less about narrowing a person down and more about helping them unfold. And when that happens, clients often find that what they needed most wasn't just a label—it was permission. Permission to want, to ask, to feel, and to be known.

Summary

Discovering a Love Language is not a formula—it's an invitation. It invites the client to pay attention to what stirs them, comforts them, and draws them closer in relationship. And while quizzes and categories definitely help, deeper discovery happens in conversation: when a person feels safe enough to name their needs without apology.

As a coach, you serve as a guide in that process. You don't assign the answer—you cultivate the space where the answer can surface. Whether a client arrives with clarity or confusion, with confidence or hesitation, your role is to be patient, curious, and attuned. Because discovering one's Love Language isn't about labeling—it's about listening. And once a client begins to listen to their own heart, they're more equipped to let someone else in.

QUESTIONS TO PONDER

1. How comfortable are you sitting in the ambiguity of a client's "I'm not sure"?
2. When are you most tempted to name a client's Love Language for them?
3. What questions have helped your clients move from instinct to insight?
4. In what ways does your own personality affect how you coach Love Language discovery?
5. How do you respond when a client's Love Language seems to shift—or defy the model?
6. Are you inviting clients to not only identify their language but explore how it's shaped by context, history, and personality?

Chapter 7

Coaching Words of Affirmation

Tasha sat quietly for a moment before answering.

"I mean . . . I say nice things. I try to encourage him. But he says it feels forced."

She shrugged, her voice tightening. *"I'm not fake—I just wasn't raised in a house where we said that kind of stuff all the time."*

Tasha had been married for eight years. She loved her husband deeply. She showed it through planning special weekends, texting reminders when he had a big meeting, and never missing his mom's birthday. But when he said what he needed most was to hear that he mattered, Tasha felt backed into a corner.

"It's not that I don't feel it," she told her coach. *"It just feels awkward to say it out loud. I don't want it to sound cheesy or rehearsed. And when I do try, he doesn't seem to believe me."*

On the other side of the same conversation, Tasha struggled to receive words, too. Compliments made her squirm. Affirmation felt suspect. Even encouragement sometimes stirred guilt instead of warmth.

For Tasha, Words of Affirmation felt like the most unnatural Love Language to speak—and the hardest one to believe.

Her coach could see the real issue; it wasn't just about learning to say kind words. It was about helping Tasha understand why affirming or receiving verbal love felt so vulnerable—and how to step into a new way of connecting that could deepen her relationship, not dilute it.

Tasha's struggle isn't rare. Words of Affirmation is one of the most emotionally direct Love Languages—and for that reason, it can feel both powerful and perilous. For some clients, it's second nature: they speak encouragement, appreciation, and affection with ease. For others, like Tasha, it can feel clumsy or exposed. When love is expressed through words, there's nowhere to hide. That's what makes this language so meaningful—and so often misunderstood.

In this chapter, we'll explore the emotional core of Words of Affirmation, break down the dialects identified in the 5 Love Languages Premium Assessment, and equip you as a coach to help clients give and receive this language with authenticity. Whether a client craves this form of connection or wrestles to express it, your role is to guide them toward clarity, courage, and connection—one word at a time.

Understanding the Heart of Words of Affirmation

At its core, Words of Affirmation is about being seen, valued, and emotionally validated through language. For clients who resonate with this Love Language, words are not just nice—they are necessary. They serve as relational oxygen, affirming worth, reinforcing connection, and offering emotional clarity. A kind word at the right moment can soothe insecurity, energize commitment, or diffuse distance. But when this language is absent—or spoken poorly—it can leave clients feeling invisible or emotionally malnourished.

Psychologically, this language taps into the need for positive regard and relational mirroring—the experience of having someone reflect back your value in a way that feels specific, sincere, and earned. Carl Rogers (1951) emphasized the foundational power of unconditional positive regard in creating emotional growth. For many clients, especially those with attachment-related sensitivities, affirmation helps solidify a sense of relational security (Mikulincer & Shaver, 2007). It's not just about flattery. It's about reassurance: *I see you. I know you. I delight in you.*

From a developmental standpoint, verbal affirmation can function as a corrective experience for those who grew up in emotionally reserved or critical environments. Clients may find that, although they hunger for affirmation, they also distrust it—waiting for the "real" message behind the compliment. This ambivalence often reflects early relational learning, where praise was conditional or emotionally inconsistent (Siegel, 2012). Coaches should expect some clients to wrestle with both a desire for affirmation and an inability to fully receive it.

For others, giving this Love Language can feel equally fraught. While research in communication theory consistently shows that verbal affirmation strengthens trust, satisfaction, and relational resilience (Burleson, 2003; Guerrero et al., 2017), some clients feel unnatural speaking it. Whether due to cultural norms, family dynamics, or personality style, they may view verbal praise as unnecessary or uncomfortable. For these clients, learning to speak this language is not about becoming eloquent—it's about becoming emotionally available.

In coaching, Words of Affirmation presents a unique opportunity to help clients develop emotional vocabulary, increase interpersonal attunement, and practice intentional expression. For couples, this often becomes a tipping point: Once one partner learns to affirm the other in a way that feels specific and sincere, it can create emotional momentum that reshapes the entire relational tone.

But the flip side is equally important. When words are misused—through harsh sarcasm, criticism, passive-aggression, or even silence—they can damage trust far more than a missed gesture. Research shows that negative interactions carry more emotional weight than positive ones—with some studies suggesting it takes five or more positive expressions to offset a single negative one in close relationships (Gottman & Levenson, 1992). For clients who speak this Love Language, a cutting word can feel like relational betrayal.

As a coach, it's essential to help clients recognize that this language is about more than compliments. It's about emotional truth delivered with care. Whether it's a word of appreciation, a note of encouragement, or a moment of honest affirmation, the power lies not just in what is said but also in the attunement behind the saying.

The Dialects of Words of Affirmation

Not all affirming words are created equal. For clients who resonate with Words of Affirmation, the form, tone, and context of verbal expression matter just as much as the content. That's where dialects come in. In the 5 Love Languages Premium Assessment, each Love Language is broken into distinct dialects—variations in how the language is spoken and received. Understanding these dialects is crucial for coaching precision. It's the difference between speaking the right language and actually being understood.

For clients whose primary Love Language is Words of Affirmation, identifying their preferred dialect (or blend) can unlock clarity—not just in what they need but *how* they need it expressed. It also helps reduce frustration between partners who are trying to be affirming but feel like their efforts are missing the mark.

Here are the core dialects of Words of Affirmation (the same ones you'll see in the Premium Assessment) with coaching applications for each:

1. **Encouragement**

   Encouraging words affirm potential. They reflect a deep emotional belief in the other person's abilities, intentions, or growth—even when the outcome isn't yet visible. For clients who favor this dialect, love sounds like support: *"I believe in you—even when you don't."*

   Encouragement is especially powerful during moments of stress, change, risk, or self-doubt. It helps the recipient feel emotionally backed, like they're not facing life alone.

   Examples of encouraging words:

   - *"You've handled so much already—I know you've got this."*
   - *"I believe in the direction you're headed, even if it's hard right now."*
   - *"What you're doing takes courage. I hope you're proud of yourself."*
   - *"Keep going. I can see how much this matters to you."*

   This dialect isn't about hype or pep talks. It's about emotional presence. Coaches may notice clients who seem energized when someone expresses belief in them—or devastated when that belief is withheld.

2. **Appreciation**

   This dialect centers on recognizing effort, especially in the unseen or taken-for-granted parts of life. It's not praise for being impressive, it's gratitude for showing up. Clients who crave appreciation often don't want to be applauded—they want to be noticed.

   Words of appreciation speak to labor, reliability, thoughtfulness, and sacrifice. In relationships, this may include parenting tasks, household responsibilities, work stress, or relational investments that go unspoken.

Examples of appreciative words:

- *"Thank you for always making sure everything runs smoothly behind the scenes."*
- *"I see how much effort you put into today. It didn't go unnoticed."*
- *"I appreciate you doing that—it made my day so much easier."*
- *"You're the glue that holds so much together, and I don't take that for granted."*

When this dialect is neglected, clients may feel resentful, not because they weren't praised, but because their everyday devotion wasn't acknowledged.

3. **Compliments**

   Compliments are the most recognizable form of this Love Language, offering direct praise for appearance, character, skill, or personality. For clients who value this dialect, love is heard in words that reflect who they are—and how they show up in the world.

   The key to effective compliments is *sincerity and specificity*. Vague affirmations often fall flat or feel disingenuous.

Examples of meaningful compliments:

- *You have such a calming presence. I love that about you."*
- *"You're such a gifted problem-solver. I admire how your mind works."*
- *"You look incredible in that—it suits your confidence."*
- *"You're one of the most thoughtful people I know."*

This dialect is less about boosting ego and more about reinforcing identity. When clients who favor this dialect receive targeted, genuine compliments, they often feel deeply seen.

As a coach, having clients articulate which of these three dialects resonates most will help them cultivate greater emotional precision and impact.

Coaching Clients Who Want to Learn to Give Words of Affirmation

Many clients who want to speak this Love Language—usually for someone they deeply care about—find that it doesn't come naturally. In fact, one of the most common coaching challenges with Words of Affirmation is helping clients who are trying to learn how to give it—awkwardly, inconsistently, and often under emotional pressure.

They've usually heard it from a partner:

"I just need to hear that you love me."

"You never say what you're thinking."

"I feel invisible to you."

For clients who didn't grow up in an affirming environment—or who are uncomfortable with verbal expression—these requests can feel overwhelming. They may try to offer kind words but feel fake, cheesy, or scripted. And when their efforts are met with doubt or disappointment from a partner, it reinforces the belief: *"This just isn't me."*

This is where coaching matters most. Your role is to normalize the discomfort of learning a non-native Love Language while affirming the courage it takes to try. Clients don't need to become eloquent or emotionally fluent overnight. They need support in building a new skill set—one that may challenge long-held emotional habits or cultural expectations.

Clients who resist giving Words of Affirmation often fall into a few common patterns:

- They associate verbal praise with performance rather than connection.
- They fear saying the "wrong thing," so they say nothing at all.
- They believe their action should "speak for itself."
- They feel emotionally vulnerable when offering praise, especially if it hasn't been modeled for them.

From a psychological standpoint, this discomfort often relates to a low tolerance for emotional exposure (Brown, 2012), or to internalized family dynamics where love was assumed but rarely named (Siegel, 2012). For men in particular, studies show that some experience gendered inhibition around verbal affection, especially in cultures where emotional restraint is linked with strength (Chaplin & Aldao, 2013). These barriers are real but not insurmountable.

Start by helping the client understand that Words of Affirmation is about emotional presence, not poetic delivery. The goal is not to impress. It's to connect. You can help reframe the task by asking:

- *"If your partner were to feel completely seen by you, what would they need to hear?"*
- *"What's one thing you appreciate about them that you've never said out loud?"*
- *"What do you hope they know but maybe haven't heard from you directly?"*

You can also explore resistance more directly:

- *"When you try to speak affirming words, what holds you back?"*
- *"What messages did you receive growing up about giving praise or affection?"*

Many clients are surprised to find that they *do* have the ability to speak affirming words, but they've just never been invited to speak them with intentionality.

As they begin practicing, remind them that specificity beats sentimentality. Help them find language that sounds like them, not like a Hallmark card. Encourage short, sincere statements tied to real moments:

- *"You did such a good job with that meeting. I'm proud of how you handled it."*
- *"Thanks for making dinner tonight. I needed that."*
- *"You've been really patient with me lately. I see it, and I appreciate it."*

You might even create a personal affirmation "bank" together: a short list of real compliments or appreciations the client can draw from and build on. This gives them a scaffold for growth, rather than expecting fluency from the start.

Finally, help clients manage their expectations for how their affirmations are received. If their partner seems skeptical or dismissive, it's not necessarily a failure—it may be a sign that trust is still forming. Encourage consistency over grandiosity. As research in behavioral psychology shows, small, repeated acts of emotional support create stronger bonds over time than rare, elaborate gestures (Skinner, 1953; Gottman & Silver, 1999).

With coaching, even the most hesitant clients can learn to speak this language—not as performance, but as practice. And for the partner at the receiving end, those few, genuine words may bring more healing than the client could imagine.

Coaching Clients Who Crave Words of Affirmation

For clients whose primary Love Language is Words of Affirmation, love is heard and felt verbally. They may not need extravagant praise or constant encouragement, but when meaningful words are absent, they often feel emotionally disconnected, even if everything else in the relationship seems fine.

What they're longing for isn't just compliments. It's confirmation: *I matter to you. I'm seen. I'm safe here.*

But here's the challenge: Even clients who crave Words of Affirmation often struggle to admit it. Asking for affirmation can feel like asking for attention, validation, or ego-stroking. Some clients fear they'll come across as needy, high-maintenance, or insecure. Others carry shame around this desire—especially if they've been criticized, mocked, or emotionally neglected in the past. The result is a deep longing that goes underground, surfacing instead as resentment, withdrawal, over-functioning, or quiet disappointment.

Clients in this position might say things like:

- *"I know it's silly, but it would just mean so much to hear that he's proud of me."*
- *"I do so much in this relationship. It would be nice to feel appreciated—not just assumed."*
- *"She says she loves me, but I can't remember the last time I really felt it in her words."*

From a coaching perspective, these are not surface complaints. They are signals of emotional depletion. Research shows that perceived verbal affirmation in romantic relationships significantly correlates with higher relationship satisfaction and personal wellbeing (Keely & Malouff, 2022). The absence of affirming words—especially when a partner speaks a different Love Language—can slowly erode trust and attachment security over time (Mikulincer & Shaver, 2007; Jensen-Campbell & Graziano, 2001).

Your role as a coach is to help the client:

1. Understand and own the legitimacy of this need
2. Clarify what kind of affirmation resonates (dialect)
3. Find language to express that need without pressure or apology

That starts by normalizing the importance of verbal connection. Clients often soften when they hear that longing for affirmation is not about vanity—it's about emotional resonance. You might say, *"It sounds like words help you feel emotionally anchored in the relationship. That's not shallow—that's your signal for connection."*

Next, help them define what actually fills their tank. Is it compliments? Encouragement? Appreciation? Public praise or private reassurance? Vague requests like *"I just want them to be more affirming"* rarely lead to meaningful change. But when a client can say, *"What really lands for me is when they notice what I've done and name it specifically,"* they're setting their partner—and themselves—up for success.

Once clarity is in place, expression becomes the next challenge. Here, coaching can focus on tone, timing, and delivery. Help clients distinguish between assertiveness and demand. Instead of saying, *"You never say nice things to me,"* they might say,

> *"When you told me last month that you were proud of how I handled that meeting—I carried that with me. That kind of thing means a lot."*

Or:

> *"One thing that really makes me feel close to you is when you notice something I've done and tell me what it meant to you."*

This kind of vulnerability requires safety. It also requires some inner work. Clients who crave affirmation may have to wrestle with the part of themselves that believes they shouldn't need it—or that they're not worthy of it. That internal script often comes from early experiences of conditional love or withheld praise, and it's worth unpacking gently in session (Siegel, 2012; Rogers, 1951).

Finally, don't forget to coach emotional regulation when this need isn't met. Clients with this primary language often experience a "low love tank" more quickly than others (more on love tanks in a later chapter). When words are missing—or delivered poorly—they may spiral into assumptions about the relationship's health. Helping them slow the story down, check the facts, and practice self-affirmation in the meantime can be grounding. You might offer: *"It's okay to need words. And it's also okay to take care of yourself while you're waiting to be heard."*

Summary

Words shape worlds. For clients whose Love Language is Words of Affirmation—whether they're trying to give it or longing to receive it—language becomes the link between emotion and connection. It's not about poetic delivery or over-the-top praise. It's about being specific, sincere, and emotionally present in what is spoken.

As a coach, your role is to help clients clarify their relationship to this language—especially if it doesn't come naturally. You're guiding them to identify what kind of words resonate, to notice what stands in the way of speaking or receiving them, and to practice with intentionality.

Whether clients light up from encouragement, appreciation, or compliments, Words of Affirmation remains one of the most precise and personal Love Languages—and one of the easiest to get wrong. But with awareness, empathy, and repetition, clients can build fluency. And as they do, they unlock the kind of emotional clarity that builds trust, repairs distance, and reminds someone, *"I see you. I choose you. And I want you to know it."*

QUESTIONS TO PONDER

1. What's your personal comfort level with Words of Affirmation (both giving and receiving)?
2. How do you distinguish between affirmations that are emotionally present versus those that are performative?
3. How would you help a client express this Love Language if they associate it with discomfort, shame, or inauthenticity?
4. When a client says they feel "unappreciated," what deeper emotional themes might be underneath?
5. How do you coach someone to express their need for affirmation without sounding demanding or dependent?

Chapter 8

Coaching Quality Time

Marcus shifted in his chair and stared out the window.

"She says we never spend time together," he muttered, his tone somewhere between confusion and fatigue. "But we're in the same house every night. We eat dinner. We talk. I don't know what more she wants."

His coach nodded gently, giving him space.

"It's like nothing counts unless it's candles and eye contact," Marcus added, half-joking, half-defensive. "Honestly, I feel like I can't win."

What Marcus didn't realize yet—and what his coach would help him see—is that proximity isn't the same as presence. While Marcus thought they were connecting through routine and logistics, his wife experienced those same moments as hollow, distracted, or rushed.

She didn't want him to do more. She wanted him to be more—more emotionally present, more tuned in, more intentional. Her Love Language was Quality Time, and while Marcus wasn't ignoring her, he also wasn't meeting her in the way she most deeply felt loved.

This is one of the most common misfires coaches encounter with couples: a disconnect not in effort, but in interpretation. In this chapter, we'll explore the heart of Quality Time, unpack its dialects, and show how coaches can help clients bridge the space between being physically together and being emotionally connected.

Understanding the Heart of Quality Time

At the core of Quality Time is a desire for undivided attention. Clients who speak this Love Language don't just want to be near their partner—they want to feel *with* them. They want shared space that feels emotionally rich, distraction-free, and relationally prioritized. Quality Time says, "When you give me your time, I feel like I matter. When you don't, I feel like I'm competing with everything else."

Unlike some of the other Love Languages, Quality Time isn't tied to a specific behavior or gesture—it's defined by intentional presence. What counts isn't the activity itself but the emotional engagement within it. A walk around the block. A dinner without phones. A deep conversation in the car. These simple moments become profoundly affirming when a client experiences their partner's full attention.

Psychologically, this Love Language reflects the human need for attunement and joint attention, especially in emotionally significant relationships. From early development, the experience of being noticed, mirrored, and shared in a moment creates emotional security and belonging (Schore, 2001; Siegel, 2012). In adulthood, these same patterns show up as a longing to feel chosen—not just in words, but in the *allocation of time and focus*.

What makes Quality Time emotionally rich is also what makes it easy to miss. In today's culture of distraction, multitasking, and digital saturation, uninterrupted presence can feel rare (Turkle, 2015). For clients whose Love Language is Quality Time, the relational cost of constant interruptions or shallow interactions is high. Research on emotional presence and relationship satisfaction shows that perceived attentiveness—especially in emotionally significant conversations—is a strong predictor of relational closeness and trust (Reis & Shaver, 1988; Gordon & Chen, 2016).

From a coaching perspective, this Love Language also opens a window into how clients interpret attention as love—or absence as rejection. It's not unusual to hear clients say things like:

- *"We're always doing something, but I don't feel like we're together."*
- *"They're physically there, but mentally somewhere else."*
- *"I'd rather have one meaningful hour than a full weekend of surface-level interaction."*

These aren't time complaints—they're presence complaints. And they're coaching gold. When a client expresses dissatisfaction with time, it's rarely about the calendar. It's about connection. They're not asking for more hours, they're asking for more access.

For some clients, Quality Time is tied to identity. *When you carve out space for me, I feel like I matter to you.* For others, it's about rhythm: *Our connection feels solid when we check in regularly, even for a few minutes.* And for some, it's a bid for safety: *When we don't spend time together, I start to spiral.*

Helping clients name what Quality Time looks like for them—and how its absence registers emotionally—is a key first step in coaching. Because what's often dismissed as a scheduling conflict is, at its core, a signal of relational need.

The Dialects of Quality Time

Quality Time about how that time is experienced together. For clients who crave this Love Language, the key to connection lies in the type of shared time that makes them feel most emotionally nourished. That's where dialects come in.

The 5 Love Languages Premium Assessment identifies four distinct dialects of Quality Time. Each one reflects a unique preference around structure, spontaneity, and the emotional flavor of time spent together. Helping clients name their preferred dialect—and recognize when it's not being spoken—can shift vague frustration into clear, actionable insight.

Here's a coaching guide to the four Quality Time dialects:

1. **Improvising**

   Present-oriented, unscheduled, easygoing, and fully present

   Clients who favor this dialect feel most loved when time together is unhurried, spontaneous, and emotionally attuned. They value freedom from agendas, a relaxed pace, and being *with* someone in the moment—without needing a plan. It's less about what happens and more about the emotional flow of the time together.

   Examples:

   - A slow coffee on a Saturday morning—no phones, no rush.
   - An impromptu walk after dinner that turns into a deep conversation.
   - Laughing on the couch watching a show—without multitasking.

   These clients often say things like:

   "I don't care what we do—I just want to be together without distractions."

When misunderstood, Improvising clients may be labeled as passive or noncommittal, but what they're actually craving is attuned presence without pressure.

2. **Managing**

   Present-focused and scheduled, punctual and paced

   Clients with the Managing dialect feel loved when time together is reliable, consistent, and paced with intention. They thrive on shared routines, regular check-ins, and structured moments that create relational rhythm. It's not rigid—it's dependable.

   Examples:

   - A nightly 20-minute debrief with no phones.
   - A shared lunch break every Tuesday.
   - Starting the day together over coffee before the chaos begins.

   These clients may say:

   "When we build time for each other into our lives, I feel secure."

   What they're longing for is connection through consistency. Missed time slots or canceling routines can feel like emotional disconnection not just logistical inconvenience.

3. **Planning**

   Future-oriented and scheduled, efficient and prepared

   Clients who speak this dialect feel most loved when someone invests advanced thought and care into shared time. They love making plans, researching options, and knowing their partner's thoughts ahead. Quality Time, for them, means intentional design—not just physical presence.

   Examples:

   - Booking a weekend getaway two months in advance.
   - Planning a surprise dinner with a favorite meal and playlist.
   - Setting goals together for an upcoming project or season.

   These clients might say:

   "It means so much when you plan something just for us. I feel chosen."

   The risk for clients with the Planning dialect is that if things feel too casual or last-minute, they may interpret it as a lack of care—even if the other person is physically present.

4. **Dreaming**

   Future-focused and unscheduled, spontaneous and visionary

   Dreaming clients feel loved when they're invited to imagine the future together (for the distant future or five minutes from now)—through long talks, loose plans, or shared hopes. These clients are energized by *possibility*, and time spent visioning with a partner is deeply bonding.

   Examples:

   - Talking for hours about "what if" goals over wine.
   - Dreaming aloud about a shared future or new venture.
   - Watching the sunset and imagining where life might take you next.

   They often say things like:

   "I love it when we just talk about the future—it makes me feel like we're on the same team."

   When this dialect is neglected, these clients may feel the relationship is stagnant or uninspired—even if there's time being spent together. What they want is shared emotional momentum.

Helping clients (and their partners) identify these four dialects of Quality Time gives clarity to a Love Language that is often described too vaguely, even by the person who identifies with it. Naming the dialect moves the conversation from *We never spend time together* to *What kind of time helps me feel most connected?*

And that shift—from general complaint to specific insight—is where coaching creates the most lasting change.

Coaching Clients Who Want to Learn to Give Quality Time

Some clients come into coaching knowing that their partner's Love Language is Quality Time, but they're stuck. Not because they don't care, but because being emotionally present on purpose feels confusing or time-consuming. For these clients, love isn't the problem—*access* is.

They often say things like:

- "I'm just not wired for long conversations."
- "We're around each other all the time—how is that not enough?"
- "I don't get the big deal. I'm busy, but I'm here."

What they're bumping into isn't resistance—it's a different relational operating system. For clients who don't naturally prioritize Quality Time, love is often expressed through doing, not being. Coaching helps them learn how to pause their productivity reflex and become more comfortable offering presence as a gift—not just completing tasks or showing up physically.

Start by validating the challenge. Learning to give this language is less about scheduling more time and more about changing the emotional texture of the time already being spent. It's about quality, not quantity. That shift may feel subtle to the client, but for their partner, it's everything.

Many clients who struggle with this language fall into one of these common patterns:

- They associate attention with obligation ("Do I have to stop everything just to connect?").
- They fear they'll have nothing to say or that it'll feel awkward.
- They're chronically distracted or pulled toward multitasking.
- They assume presence equals proximity ("If we're both in the room, that counts, right?").

The coach's job is to make this Love Language feel doable rather than daunting. For example, you might help the client identify windows of time they already share with their partner—like evenings, car rides, or meals—and find simple ways to increase presence and minimize distraction during those times.

You can also use the dialects to help the client find a style that feels natural. A client who resists structured time may thrive in an Improvising rhythm—suggesting a spontaneous walk after work. A goal-oriented client might love Planning a weekend outing. Matching the *giving style* to the giver—while still honoring the receiver—creates a bridge between difference and connection.

Coaching questions to explore include:

- *"When have you felt most emotionally close to your partner? What were you doing?"*
- *"What kind of time together has worked well in the past?"*
- *"What distractions tend to get in the way when you're trying to connect?"*
- *"If you had 30 minutes with your partner today, what would be the most meaningful way to spend it?"*

You might also help clients frame their presence verbally. Some people need coaching around *what to say* to make Quality Time feel connected. Sentence starters like these can help the conversation deepen without becoming emotionally overwhelming:

- *"How's your heart today?"*
- *"What was something that made you laugh this week?"*
- *"What are you most looking forward to right now?"*

It's also important to address performance anxiety. Some clients worry that if they attempt to create Quality Time and it falls flat, they'll feel embarrassed or rejected. Not every effort will be perfect, but consistent, sincere effort builds trust over time. According to Reis and Shaver's (1988) *interpersonal process model of intimacy*, emotional closeness increases when a partner expresses understanding, validation, and care—even in small ways.

For many clients, learning to give Quality Time requires slowing down long enough to notice their partner's emotional world—and believing that their focused presence is enough. With coaching, they can begin to see that love isn't always a grand gesture. Sometimes, it's just ten minutes of undivided attention that says, *"Right now, you're what matters most."*

Coaching Clients Who Crave Quality Time

Because clients who crave Quality Time are all about presence, they often don't need constant attention or elaborate plans. What they long for is attuned, intentional time that makes them feel emotionally prioritized. When that's missing, even in an otherwise functional relationship, they often feel disconnected, unseen, or emotionally alone.

These clients may say things like:

- *"I feel like we're roommates, not partners."*
- *"Even when we're together, their mind is somewhere else."*
- *"I'd trade a hundred errands for one real conversation."*

Craving this Love Language can be deeply vulnerable. Many clients hesitate to admit it very often, fearing they'll be perceived as too needy, too dependent, or overly idealistic. Some internalize guilt for wanting more than what their partner seems able—or willing—to give. Others have been subtly shamed by their partner for wanting to "talk about the relationship" or "schedule quality time," and now approach their need with hesitation or resentment.

As a coach, your task is to help the client reclaim the legitimacy of their emotional longing. Craving Quality Time isn't immaturity—it's attachment in motion. Secure bonds are built and maintained through shared attention, responsiveness, and co-regulated presence (Mikulincer & Shaver, 2007). For some clients, the lack of Quality Time doesn't just feel disappointing—it activates old wounds of emotional neglect or abandonment.

Clients who need Quality Time often don't just want their partner to be there physically. They want them to be there fully present, engaged, and emotionally available. That's why simply "doing things together" may fall short for some people with this Love Language. The client may experience shallow time as more painful than no time at all. This distinction is essential in coaching, as it helps the client name the difference between proximity and presence, and invites them to speak that distinction clearly.

Coach your client to move from frustration to specificity. Instead of "*We never spend time together,*" help them try:

- *"I love when we talk without distractions—even if it's just for 15 minutes."*
- *"It means a lot to me when we carve out time where we're really with each other."*
- *"When you're fully present with me, it helps me feel grounded in the relationship."*

You can also help clients explore what kind of time fills them up. Use the dialects from the Premium Assessment to deepen the discovery:

- Do they long for unscheduled spontaneity (Improvising)?
- Do they crave a consistent rhythm of connection (Managing)?
- Do they feel most seen when their partner plans ahead (Planning)?
- Or do they light up when dreaming about shared goals and future plans (Dreaming)?

Clients who crave Quality Time may also need coaching around emotional regulation when their need isn't consistently met. Because this language is time-based, it's often the most impacted by life stress, parenting demands, or mismatched priorities. Help clients manage the story they tell themselves during disconnection:

- *"When they don't make time for me, what does that mean to me?"*
- *"Is there another possible explanation that doesn't involve rejection?"*

While validating their need, you can also equip them with coping strategies—ways to stay grounded in their worth and relational security even in the absence of ideal connection. For example:

- Practicing self-initiated bids for time (without passive waiting or blame).
- Using transitional rituals (like a weekly check-in) to create rhythm.
- Learning to voice longings in a way that is clear, vulnerable, and non-accusatory.

Ultimately, craving Quality Time is not about being emotionally high maintenance. It's about wanting to be chosen in the currency of attention, which is one of the most meaningful forms of love we have to offer in a distraction-heavy world. When someone gives you their full attention, even briefly, it tells you: "*You matter right now. There's nothing more important than this moment we're sharing.*"

Helping clients honor and express that longing without apology may be one of the most powerful outcomes of your coaching.

Summary

At its core, Quality Time is about emotional presence that communicates, "*I choose you, right now.*" For clients who speak this Love Language, love isn't measured by how much time is spent together but by how fully seen and emotionally engaged they feel during that time.

As a coach, your work is to help clients understand this need, name their preferred dialect, and develop the skills to either offer or request presence with courage and clarity. Whether you're guiding someone who's learning to be more present or someone who's longing to feel chosen, your role is to make space for what time alone can't do: connection with intention.

In an age of constant distraction, coaching around Quality Time is more important than ever. Because when clients learn to show up fully (or to ask someone else to), they're not just spending Quality Time. They're strengthening the emotional infrastructure of the relationship itself.

QUESTIONS TO PONDER

1. How do I personally relate to the idea of emotional presence versus physical proximity?
2. In what ways might I be tempted to coach this Love Language as a scheduling issue rather than an emotional one?
3. How can I help clients clarify what kind of time actually nourishes them—beyond vague requests?
4. What blind spots might a client have if they assume "being together" always equals connection?
5. How do I help clients who feel rejected or resentful when their bids for time go unanswered?

Chapter 9

Coaching Receiving Gifts

Tina looked down, twisting the ring on her finger.

"It's not about the stuff," she said. "I don't need fancy things. But when there's nothing—no note, no little gesture—it feels like I don't cross his mind."

She paused, then added more quietly, "It's not that he doesn't love me—I know he does. But sometimes I wonder if he actually sees me . . . or remembers me."

Tina's husband, Evan, was practical and deeply loyal. He fixed things around the house before she even noticed they were broken. He rarely missed a family dinner. He said "I love you" every night. And on her birthday, he did remember—but it was a generic card from the drugstore with a little gift certificate tucked inside. Thoughtful, maybe. But impersonal. When their anniversary came and went with little more, something inside Tina withdrew.

"He says gifts feel materialistic," Tina explained. *"But to me, they're reminders. Like bookmarks in the story of our relationship. Something that says, 'I thought of you. You matter.'"*

This is the emotional landscape of Receiving Gifts—a Love Language that is often misunderstood as shallow or indulgent, when in reality it is one of the most symbolically rich and emotionally precise forms of connection.

In this chapter, we'll explore why Receiving Gifts matters deeply to some clients, what it looks like in different dialects, and how coaches can guide individuals and couples to understand, express, and receive this language without judgment or misfire.

Understanding the Heart of Receiving Gifts

Of all the Love Languages, Receiving Gifts is the most likely to be misunderstood. On the surface, it may look like materialism—but at its core, this language is about symbolic meaning and emotional memory. For clients who speak this Love Language, a gift is not about the item—it's about what the item represents. It's a tangible reminder that says, *"I see you. I remembered. You matter to me."*

A well-chosen gift can serve as a relational anchor—a way of marking a moment, affirming connection, or carrying love across distance or time. This reflects what Belk (1979) describes as the symbolic nature of gift-giving—an extension of the self that communicates identity, affection, and intention beyond what words alone can express.

The object itself is rarely the point. It's the thought behind it, the intentionality in it, and the emotion woven through it that makes it matter.

Research in emotional communication supports this idea: symbolic acts, including gift-giving, are powerful tools for expressing affection and building relational intimacy—especially when they reflect the recipient's values or personal story (Floyd & Morman, 2001; Grote & Clark, 2001). In many cases, the size or cost of a gift is irrelevant. What resonates is whether the giver truly knows and honors the recipient's inner world.

Clients who crave this language are often especially attuned to nonverbal demonstrations of care. While other Love Languages are experienced in real time—like touch, time, or words—gifts have staying power. They can be held, revisited, and remembered. A meaningful token can become a kind of emotional artifact: a seashell from a beach walk, a book with a note in the margin, a ring handed down from a grandparent. These objects hold emotionally encoded meaning, especially when given with awareness and care.

On the flip side, when this language is dismissed or neglected, it can feel deeply wounding. A forgotten birthday. A last-minute purchase. A partner who says, *"You know I love you—I don't need to buy you something."* For clients whose primary language is Receiving Gifts, these moments can register as indifference, forgetfulness, or emotional distance. They're not asking for extravagance. They're asking for significance.

Coaches may notice that clients who resonate with this language often light up when recalling moments when someone *got it right*—not because of the cost, but because of the meaning. Conversely, they may carry quiet disappointment or shame for "caring too much" about something others see as superficial.

Part of your role as a coach is to help reclaim the dignity of this language. You might say, *"It sounds like gifts help you feel remembered and emotionally anchored. That's not materialism—that's how you connect."* Helping clients articulate that need without apology can shift the conversation from defense to clarity.

You can also help clients unpack why this language matters to them. Sometimes, it's tied to early memories—parents who showed love through care packages or cultural traditions where gift-giving was central. Other times, it may have developed in response to emotional scarcity—where small, symbolic gestures carried enormous relational weight.

Understanding this Love Language is about understanding the psychology of symbolic communication. It's not about acquiring—it's about meaning-making. And when a client begins to speak, receive, or ask for this language with clarity and confidence, it often leads to a new level of relational richness.

The Dialects of Receiving Gifts

Not all gifts are created equal—at least not emotionally. For clients whose primary Love Language is Receiving Gifts, the form, function, and feeling behind a gift matter deeply. What makes one client feel cherished might feel excessive to another. That's why the 5 Love Languages Premium Assessment breaks this Love Language into four dialects: Fanciful, Functional, Sensible, and Sentimental.

Each dialect reflects a unique emotional pattern of what kind of gifts land—and why. Helping clients name their dialect allows coaches to guide both givers and receivers with far more accuracy. Instead of the vague complaint, *"They never get me anything meaningful,"* a client can learn to say, *"I'm sentimental—I treasure small, heartfelt tokens. It doesn't have to be big—it has to be thoughtful."*

Here's how each dialect works:

1. **Fanciful: Heartfelt and Extravagant**

   Clients who speak this dialect feel loved through grand, meaningful gestures. They often associate love with being *swept off their feet*, and when someone invests significant thought, time, or money into a gift, it registers as, *"I'm worth the effort."* These gifts may be rare, but when they appear, they leave a lasting emotional imprint.

Examples:

- A surprise anniversary trip to a dream location
- A piece of jewelry with a personalized inscription
- A luxury item paired with a heartfelt note

For Fanciful clients, the extravagance isn't about materialism—it's about feeling deeply pursued.

2. **Functional: Practical and Extravagant**

These clients feel most loved when they receive useful gifts with a high impact—items that improve their life, reflect their needs, or demonstrate deep attentiveness. A high-end kitchen appliance, new tech device, or ergonomic chair might not sound romantic, but for a Functional client, it communicates love through enhanced wellbeing.

Examples:

- A thoughtfully researched smartwatch
- A subscription to something that solves a recurring issue
- Paying for a service that lifts their mental load

Functional clients are deeply moved by gifts that say, *"I see what you need—and I invested in your flourishing."*

3. **Sensible: Practical and Simple**

This dialect values low-cost, useful items that reflect everyday attentiveness. Sensible gifts are often humble—small, timely, and rooted in daily life. Their power comes from emotional precision: the giver noticed a need, remembered a preference, or anticipated something helpful.

Examples:

- Picking up their favorite snack on the way home
- A new phone charger because theirs was fraying
- A practical item wrapped with intentionality

Sensible clients may say, *"It's not about how much—it's about whether they thought of me."*

4. **Sentimental: Heartfelt and Simple**

   Sentimental clients are moved by emotionally meaningful tokens, often inexpensive or even handmade. They're drawn to gifts that carry story, symbolism, or memory—a book with a note in the margins, a photo in a handmade frame, a playlist of shared songs. These clients value emotional resonance over functionality or cost.

   Examples:
   - A pressed flower from a shared walk
   - A handwritten letter tucked into a lunch bag
   - A framed map of where they first met
   - For Sentimental clients, these gifts serve as emotional bookmarks—holding space for shared meaning, long after the moment has passed.

When clients discover their dialect in this Love Language—or learn their partner's—it can instantly reframe years of missed connections. A client who loves Sentimental gestures might feel disappointed by a Functional gift that felt impersonal. Or a Fanciful partner might feel their Sensible spouse's gifts are underwhelming. Dialect mismatch doesn't mean failure; it means there's room for better translation.

Helping clients articulate their dialect gives them the language to say:
- *"It doesn't have to be big—it just has to be thoughtful."*
- *"When you plan something extravagant, it makes me feel truly seen."*
- *"I love it when you give me something I'll actually use—it shows me you're paying attention."*

And for the giver? Understanding dialects makes the task feel less confusing and more purposeful. It's not about guessing right—it's about learning to speak love in a way that lands.

Coaching Clients Who Want to Learn How to Give Gifts

Many clients arrive knowing their partner treasures Receiving Gifts—but they're at a loss for how to give gifts that land. Their natural expression may center on service or words, so gift-giving feels like unfamiliar territory. In coaching these clients, your goal is to help them shift from random acts of shopping to intentional, emotionally resonant gift-giving—tailored to their partner's dialect.

Normalize the Learning Curve

Start by validating the challenge. Gift-giving can feel high-stakes: "*What if I get it wrong?*" Clients often worry about cost, timing, or missing the subtle signal. Remind them that meaningful gift-giving is a skill—one that can be developed with curiosity and practice (Solomon, 1983). Learning any new skill involves trial and feedback. Encourage them to treat early efforts as experiments rather than finals.

Match Gift to Dialect

Use the four dialects—Fanciful, Functional, Sensible, Sentimental—to guide brainstorming:

- **Fanciful** givers: Coach them to create one grand gesture (e.g., a surprise getaway or tickets to a concert) tied to a shared dream.
- **Functional** givers: Help them research a tool or service that eases a daily pain point (e.g., a premium coffee grinder or organizing app subscription).
- **Sensible** givers: Brainstorm small, everyday tokens (favorite snack, a cozy pair of socks) wrapped with thoughtful notes.
- **Sentimental** givers: Encourage crafting or choosing an item rich in shared memories (photo collage, handwritten letter, playlist).

This mapping transforms a client's vague intention into a clear prompt: "*I'll plan a functional gift because they light up when things get easier.*"

Plan for Emotional Impact

Gift-giving isn't a one-step process. Coaches can guide clients through a simple three-phase model:

1. **Discovery:** Observe partner's hints, preferences, and everyday routines. What do they mention wanting? What do they carry with them?
2. **Design:** Sketch a gift concept that aligns with the dialect. Invite clients to jot down why this gift matters—this builds emotional intentionality (Grote & Clark, 2001).
3. **Delivery:** Coach them on presentation—when, where, and how to give the gift so it feels special. As Sherry (1983) notes, the ritual of gift-giving—the wrapping, the timing, the reveal—is often as emotionally important as the object itself, heightening its perceived value and symbolic impact. Context

amplifies meaning: a late-night note vs. a hurried morning encounter can change the reception dramatically.

Cultivate Resourcefulness

Not every client has a big budget—or time. Emphasize that thoughtfulness outshines price (Floyd & Morman, 2001). A Sensible or Sentimental gift can cost under ten dollars but carry immense weight. Help clients brainstorm small but personalized tokens: a handwritten letter, a book from a favorite author, or a coupon for a shared walk.

But what if the partner's dialect is Fanciful or Functional—and they light up at big gestures or high-impact gifts? This is where creative pacing and intentional timing come in. Clients can plan toward occasional, well-timed gifts that feel extravagant without being frequent or impulsive. Help them think seasonally or symbolically:

- "What's one big surprise I could save for on our anniversary?"
- "How might I space out gifts so they feel rare and meaningful—rather than rushed or routine?"

Coaches can also help clients frame the gift as a sacrifice or celebration: *"This took planning, but it was worth it to show you how much I care."* That context adds weight, especially for a Fanciful partner, where emotional effort often matters as much as the item itself.

Finally, invite clients to pair a modest gift with a meaningful message. A lower-cost item—like a watchband, candle, or scarf—can feel elevated when paired with a card that explains its significance or how it made them think of their partner.

Address Underlying Fears and Beliefs

Many clients believe *"I shouldn't need to buy love."* Explore these internal scripts:

- Where did this belief originate?
- How does it limit their willingness to give?
- What new narrative could empower them to express affection through gifts?

Reframing gift-giving as emotional communication—not transactional—helps clients release guilt and own their intention to connect.

Set Realistic Expectations and Feedback Loops

Guide clients to set small goals: one thoughtful gift per quarter, for example. After giving, encourage them to debrief:

- How did their partner respond?
- What words, gestures, or emotional cues revealed the gift's impact?
- What might they adjust next time?

This feedback loop transforms each gift into a learning opportunity, reducing anxiety and building confidence.

Practice Generosity Without Obligation

Finally, coach clients to give with generosity, not obligation. Gifts given purely out of duty can feel hollow. Encourage them to find genuine reasons—celebrations, moments of gratitude, or simple surprises *just because.* When the gift stems from authentic care, its emotional resonance naturally increases. Through intentional discovery, thoughtful design, and reflective practice, even the most reluctant gift-giver can learn to speak this language fluently—bringing warmth, memory, and emotional depth into their relationships.

Coaching Clients Who Crave Gifts

For clients whose primary Love Language is Receiving Gifts, a simple token can feel like a relational lifeline. A small, well-timed gift says, "*You thought of me. I matter enough to mark this moment.*" But when those gestures are absent—or missed entirely—clients may feel forgotten, unimportant, or emotionally disconnected, even in otherwise loving relationships.

The pain isn't about "wanting stuff." It's about longing for emotional symbolism made tangible.

Still, many clients who crave this Love Language carry shame or defensiveness about it. They've been told they're materialistic. They've internalized the belief that "if I need gifts to feel loved, something must be wrong with me." As a coach, one of your first roles is to help them reframe the desire for gifts as a legitimate emotional need—not a character flaw.

You might say:

"It sounds like gifts help you feel remembered, valued, and emotionally anchored. That's not shallow—it's your way of receiving love."

Clients who crave this language often report repeated relational hurts, such as:

- A partner who says, *"You know I love you—I don't need to prove it with things."*
- Missed birthdays, anniversaries, or milestones.
- Last-minute or thoughtless gifts that felt obligatory rather than meaningful.
- A pattern of being told their needs are "too much."

These experiences can compound into emotional narratives like:

"I shouldn't need anything."
"If I have to ask for it, it doesn't count."
"It's easier to pretend I'm fine than to be disappointed again."

Coaches can gently surface and challenge these scripts by exploring:

- Where did you learn that needing something tangible is wrong?
- When was a time when a small gift made a big impact on you?
- How does receiving a thoughtful gift affect your sense of connection?

From there, you can help clients name their dialect—Sentimental, Sensible, Functional, or Fanciful—and articulate that preference clearly and calmly to their partner. The goal is not to demand, but to express. Instead of *"You never buy me anything,"* a client might learn to say:

- *"One of the ways I feel really loved is through small, meaningful gifts—especially when there's some thought behind them."*
- *"I know it's not your default, but when you surprise me with something that shows you were thinking of me, I carry that with me for days."*

Crucially, coaches must also help clients regulate disappointment. Because this Love Language is rooted in anticipation and surprise, unmet expectations can feel especially disorienting. You can help clients:

- Develop resilience around missed gestures without self-blame.
- Practice self-soothing and self-affirmation in moments of emotional absence.
- Explore proactive communication rather than quiet hoping.

Encourage clients to anchor gifts in shared meaning, not in price or performance. A Fanciful dialect might love an elaborate gesture—but can also cherish one well-planned event each year. A Sentimental dialect may find more joy in a $5 memento from a meaningful location than in a designer item with no story.

Help clients create rituals of request, like sharing a "wish list," expressing what certain dates mean to them, or reflecting on meaningful gifts from the past. These touchpoints can give their partner clear direction without pressure—and offer the client a sense of empowerment rather than helplessness.

Above all, affirm this: Receiving Gifts is not about greed—it's about memory, mindfulness, and being emotionally chosen. Helping clients own this truth without apology can open up new conversations, deeper vulnerability, and the kind of connection that lasts long after the gift is given.

Summary

Receiving Gifts is not about materialism—it's about meaning made tangible. For clients who speak this Love Language, a gift is never just an object. It's a symbol, a signal, a memory. Whether simple or elaborate, functional or sentimental, the right gift communicates, *"I see you. I thought of you. You're worth the effort."*

As a coach, your job is to help clients move past misconceptions and into clarity. You'll support those who struggle to speak this language—helping them understand that thoughtful gifts aren't about cost, but about emotional resonance. You'll also guide clients who crave to receive this language—helping them voice their need with vulnerability, not shame.

When spoken fluently, Receiving Gifts becomes one of the most enduring and emotionally rich forms of connection. Because gifts don't just express love in the moment—they hold it, carry it, and remind us of it long after the words have faded.

QUESTIONS TO PONDER

1. What are my own assumptions about gift-giving? Have I ever unintentionally minimized this Love Language in my relationships or coaching?
2. How comfortable am I guiding a client to give or request something tangible as an expression of love?
3. How can I help clients distinguish between materialism and meaningful symbolism?
4. What strategies can I use when a client feels shame or defensiveness about craving this Love Language?
5. How might I support clients in recognizing their dialect and guiding their partner without creating pressure or guilt?

Chapter 10

Coaching Acts of Service

Jason exhaled hard and ran a hand through his hair.

"I just wish she'd notice."

His voice was quiet but tight. *"I've been doing everything—laundry, the dishes, getting the kids to school. And when I told her I was exhausted, she said, 'But we haven't really connected in days.'"*

He looked up at his coach, confused and frustrated. *"I thought all of that was connection. I've been trying so hard to hold things together. Doesn't that count for something?"*

Jason's experience is common. He's expressing love through Acts of Service—doing, providing, relieving stress—but his efforts are going unseen or unrecognized. His partner, meanwhile, is speaking a different language, looking for emotional engagement rather than completed tasks.

This disconnect—between *doing* and *feeling loved*—is at the heart of Acts of Service. When it's a client's primary Love Language, love looks like help. It sounds like initiative. It feels like being supported without having to ask.

In this chapter, we'll unpack the emotional engine behind Acts of Service, explore its dialects, and equip coaches to help clients give and receive this language with clarity, empathy, and mutual understanding.

Understanding the Heart of Acts of Service

For clients who speak Acts of Service as their primary Love Language, love is expressed not in what is said, but in what is *done*. It's action-oriented affection—a kind of embodied empathy. When someone steps in to help, lightens a load, or anticipates a need, the message lands as: *"I care about your wellbeing—and I'm proving it."*

This Love Language is often rooted in the belief that commitment shows up in reliability. For these clients, feeling emotionally supported is closely tied to feeling practically supported. The partner who picks up groceries without being asked, who folds laundry during a hard week, or who fixes the leaky sink before it becomes an issue isn't just being helpful—they're expressing love in its most meaningful form.

Acts of Service also taps into the psychology of prosocial behavior, which plays a critical role in relationship satisfaction and longevity. Studies show that when one partner engages in helpful, intentional actions—especially those that reduce the other's stress or increase their capacity—the result is often increased trust, gratitude, and emotional security (Algoe et al., 2010; Feeney & Collins, 2015).

This Love Language can also reflect early relational modeling. Clients who grew up in families where love was shown through "doing" may naturally associate care with acts of responsibility. Others may crave this language because they didn't receive practical help as children—and now associate it with safety and stability in adulthood. In either case, the emotional thread remains the same: *"If you love me, show up for me—not just emotionally, but tangibly."*

Yet this language can be easily misunderstood. For someone outside this Love Language, the act may feel transactional or invisible. A client who puts in hours of effort—cleaning, organizing, serving—may feel deeply rejected when their partner says, *"I still don't feel close to you."* That's because the emotional meaning behind the service wasn't registered.

This is where coaching becomes essential. You're not just helping clients "do more"—you're helping them identify what kind of actions actually feel loving to their partner. And when a client craves this language, your job is to help them express the need clearly and without apology, so it's not buried beneath resentment or disguised as competence.

It's also important to recognize how gender norms and cultural expectations can affect this language. Research shows that women are often socialized to perform Acts of Service as a duty, while men may associate it more with roles of provision or protection—and these patterns persist across generations and even into dual-earning households (Offer, 2012; Pepin & Cotter, 2018; Ruppanner et al., 2021). In either case, the emotional meaning of the act can be distorted or assumed—unless it's made explicit.

When understood and spoken fluently, Acts of Service becomes a powerful relational force. It fosters shared agency, mutual support, and proactive care—not just helping out, but showing up in ways that say, *"You're not alone. I've got your back."*

The Dialects of Acts of Service

Acts of Service may look straightforward—doing something helpful—but the emotional *why* behind each act varies dramatically. That's why the 5 Love Languages Premium Assessment breaks this Love Language into four dialects, each reflecting a distinct emotional payoff the client is hoping to receive: Saves Time, Alleviates Stress, Instills Security, and Conveys Care.

Helping clients name their dialect gives precision to an otherwise vague request like *"I just want more help."* With insight, that becomes *"When you do something that eases my stress, I feel deeply loved."*

Here's a breakdown of each dialect and how it functions emotionally:

1. **Saves Time: The act lightens a time burden and creates margin**
   For these clients, love is felt when a partner helps reclaim their most limited resource: time. And time-related support is strongly linked to relational satisfaction and perceived responsiveness (Cutrona, 1996; Feeney & Collins, 2015). Whether it's running errands, prepping meals, or knocking out tasks that free them up for rest or meaningful connection, the emotional message is: *"You value my time enough to give some of yours."*

   Example acts:

   - Picking up the kids so your partner can finish work early
   - Prepping a week of lunches to reduce morning chaos
   - Handling email follow-ups or calendar logistics

   Coaching tip: Help clients articulate not just the task, but the timing: "It means a lot to me when you do something that gives me back my evening."

2. **Alleviates Stress: The act reduces mental, emotional, or physical strain.** This dialect is about relief. When a partner steps in to shoulder a stressful load—or simply anticipates a pressure point before it escalates—it creates space for the client to breathe, rest, and regulate. Alleviating stress through tangible support plays a vital role in emotional co-regulation and couple wellbeing (Shrout, 2017; Feeney & Collins, 2015). The act says: *"I'm paying attention to what's hard, and I want to make it easier."*

   Example acts:
   - Taking over dinner plans after a long day
   - Calling the insurance company so your partner doesn't have to
   - Stepping in with the kids during a moment of emotional overload

   Coaching tip: Invite clients to identify recurring stressors and guide their partners toward actions that target those areas, not just generic "help."

3. **Instills Security: The act reinforces safety, trust, and stability.** Clients who resonate with this dialect often connect service with emotional safety and relational reliability. Partners who feel supported through consistent, dependable actions are more likely to report secure attachment and relationship satisfaction (Mikulincer & Shaver, 2007; Reis et al., 2004). When their partner consistently follows through, manages responsibilities, or supports in high-stakes moments, it communicates: *"You can count on me."*

   Example acts:
   - Creating financial spreadsheets or managing bills
   - Driving during long trips so their partner can relax
   - Being physically present during a doctor's appointment or difficult moment

   Coaching tip: Help clients and their partners view these acts not just as logistical—but as attachment-oriented behaviors that build trust over time.

4. **Conveys Care: The act expresses emotional attentiveness in a physical form.**

   This is the most emotionally expressive dialect. Even minor acts of relational mindfulness can enhance emotional bonding and perception of partner responsiveness (Gordon & Chen, 2016). The act may be small or mundane, but the message is deeply personal: *"I noticed, I remembered, I care."* For these clients, the act is a love letter in motion—less about solving a problem and more about showing up intentionally.

Example acts:

- Bringing your partner coffee just the way they like it
- Warming up their car on a cold morning
- Folding their laundry "the way they like it"

Coaching tip: Help clients name what types of acts feel the most relational—not just helpful. These gestures often matter most during low-stakes moments, where they reinforce emotional connection.

When couples speak the same Love Language but different dialects, they often miss each other entirely. One partner may be trying to alleviate stress, while the other is hoping for something that instills security or conveys emotional closeness. Helping clients distinguish the underlying emotional need helps reduce resentment, clarify expectations, and invite generosity—not just effort. As a coach, your role isn't to assign tasks. It's to translate effort into emotional meaning.

Coaching Clients Who Want to Learn to Give Acts of Service

Many clients enter coaching knowing their partner's primary Love Language is Acts of Service, but they feel unsure, uncomfortable, or even resistant when it comes to expressing love through action. For some, service feels like obligation. For others, it simply doesn't occur to them—they've never been taught to look for needs or to anticipate how practical help might carry emotional weight.

This is especially true for clients whose natural Love Language is words, time, or affection. They might say things like, "I tell them I love them every day," or "We're together all the time—doesn't that count?" They're expressing care, just not in a form that feels impactful to their partner. Coaching in this area isn't about chore distribution—it's about reframing practical help as emotional investment. The task is to help clients move from a mindset of compliance to one of connection.

The first coaching move is to normalize the learning curve. Acts of Service often requires relational interruption, stepping away from one's own plans or preferences to meet someone else's need. It requires attentiveness and emotional flexibility. These are coachable skills, not moral traits. As Feeney and Collins (2015) note, thriving relationships are built in part on responsive support—acts that are attuned to a partner's inner world and offered without keeping score.

Much of the work involves helping clients understand what kind of service actually matters to their partner. Using the dialects from the Premium Assessment can be especially clarifying here. A partner whose dialect is "Saves Time" may need a task taken off their plate during a busy week. Another who feels most loved when service "Instills Security" may crave consistency or follow-through with long-term logistics. The client who doesn't know what to do often isn't unwilling—they're simply misfiring. Coaching helps them connect effort with emotional meaning.

It's also important to address an assumption many clients bring: that love should be enough on its own, and anything that looks like obligation cheapens it. They may say things like, "I don't want to have to prove it all the time," or, "If I do it because I have to, does it even count?" But here, coaching opens space for nuance. Giving service doesn't negate love—it delivers it in a form the other person can fully receive. The meaning behind the act is what makes it loving, not the act itself. As Gordon and Chen (2016) show, even small gestures, when motivated by awareness and care, can dramatically increase perceived emotional responsiveness.

Some clients also struggle with the simple reality that they don't notice what their partner needs. The mental load involved in home life, parenting, and emotional labor often runs quietly in the background—and unless a client has been taught to see it, they may move through the relationship unaware of the burdens their partner is carrying. Helping these clients develop observational skills and curiosity is part of the coaching process. You might ask, "What kinds of things does your partner do that no one acknowledges?" or "Where do you see stress building up for them during the week?" Clients often begin to recognize not just tasks, but relational opportunities.

It can also help to work with clients to create a few recurring practices—small, repeatable Acts of Service that match their partner's dialect and can be offered with consistency. Making the bed each morning. Taking over dinner one night a week. Filling the gas tank before their partner heads out. When the act is given not from obligation but from intention, it creates a relational rhythm of reassurance. Over time, these simple patterns build emotional trust and help clients become fluent in a language they once avoided.

Lastly, some clients will need to unpack emotional resistance to serving. This often comes from fear . . . fear of being taken for granted, of reinforcing gendered expectations, or of losing autonomy in the relationship. Rather than arguing against these concerns, it's more effective to explore them. Service without boundaries leads to resentment. But service offered with agency and clarity can strengthen intimacy. As Brown (2012) points out, many of us are more comfortable performing than connecting—because vulnerability is required in giving what someone else needs, not just what we're good at offering.

When coached with empathy and precision, even the most reluctant giver can learn to see Acts of Service not as a list of duties—but as an invitation to love in action.

Coaching Clients Who Crave Acts of Service

Clients whose primary Love Language is Acts of Service often find themselves caught between two difficult positions: doing everything and feeling emotionally empty. They may not even realize their primary language is service until they begin to notice how deeply discouraged they feel when they're constantly helping others, yet no one steps in to help them.

They'll often say things like, *"I just want someone to take something off my plate,"* or, *"It would mean the world if I didn't have to ask."* But underneath those statements is a deeper emotional desire: *to be noticed, supported, and valued—not for what they do, but through what is done for them.*

For these clients, service is not about productivity—it's about presence. A partner folding laundry, picking up groceries, or prepping coffee in the morning might seem like small gestures to others, but to a client who speaks this language, those acts carry disproportionate emotional weight. They register as attentiveness. They say, *"I thought about you. I care enough to act."*

And yet, asking for this Love Language can feel deeply vulnerable. Many clients have been conditioned to believe that needing help is a weakness—or worse, an imposition. Some carry internal scripts that say: *If I have to ask, it doesn't count,* or *I'm the one who's supposed to be holding it all together.* Especially for high-functioning, caregiving-oriented individuals, this need can feel like something to be hidden, not honored.

Coaching becomes a space to unearth and validate that longing. It may begin by simply reflecting what you observe: "It sounds like you feel most loved when someone steps in without being asked—when they notice what's hard and do something about it." That alone can bring relief. You're naming what they've often struggled to articulate.

It's also helpful to explore which dialect of service they most resonate with. Some clients crave time-saving gestures—a partner who does the dishes or handles the bedtime routine. Others feel most loved when stress is alleviated—someone stepping in during overwhelming moments. Still others long for acts that create structure and dependability—behaviors that instill a sense of security. And for many, the most powerful moments are when someone offers a service that, while small, clearly conveys care. A warm cup of tea left beside them. A note that says, *I took care of it.*

Helping clients name this dialect not only clarifies what they're craving—it helps their partner know how to love them more effectively. You can also guide clients to express these needs with grace rather than guilt. Instead of saying, "You never help," say, "I feel most supported when you take initiative—especially when I've had a long day." Or, "Even small things like taking out the trash without being asked make me feel like I'm not alone in this."

The coach's task is to normalize the need without minimizing the nuance. That may include working through past disappointments or resentment that's been building over time. It may also involve coaching clients to differentiate between wanting help and needing everything done "their way." Sometimes, the barrier to receiving love through service isn't that no one is trying—it's that the expression isn't landing because perfection is being prioritized over connection.

It's equally important to help clients regulate their expectations. Because this Love Language is tangible, it's highly sensitive to inconsistency. A partner who forgets to follow through may trigger old wounds of feeling unseen or unimportant. In these moments, coaching helps the client process their emotional reaction without spiraling into all-or-nothing thinking. You might ask, "What else do you know to be true about your partner's intentions?" or "How can you express the impact without framing it as failure?"

At its best, Acts of Service becomes a channel for mutual care. When a client receives a small act of help and interprets it as love, they unlock a new level of relational security. And when they can voice their longing without shame, they give their partner the opportunity to succeed—not through grand gestures, but through ordinary, intentional acts of connection.

Summary

Acts of Service is a Love Language built on action—but its power lies in emotional meaning. To the client who speaks this language, love is most clearly expressed when someone steps in to help, lightens a burden, or anticipates a need. But without clarity, this language is easily misread—as obligation, as performance, or as mere task management.

As a coach, your role is to bring awareness and intention into these interactions. You help clients identify their own dialect—whether they feel loved when time is saved, stress is reduced, security is created, or care is conveyed. And you help those who struggle to give this language discover how simple, thoughtful acts can express volumes—if done with sincerity and presence.

At its heart, Acts of Service is not about checking boxes. It's about showing up for someone in tangible ways that communicate: *You matter enough for me to act.*

QUESTIONS TO PONDER

1. How do I personally relate to the idea of love being expressed through action?
2. Have I ever dismissed or minimized a client's desire for practical help in favor of more verbal or emotional expressions?
3. How can I help clients distinguish between acts that are "helpful" and those that are emotionally resonant?
4. What signs of burnout or overfunctioning might I watch for in clients who constantly give but struggle to receive this language?
5. How do I ensure my coaching encourages mutuality in service rather than reinforcing unhealthy role expectations?

Chapter 11

Coaching Physical Touch

Lauren crossed her arms and gave a soft, nervous laugh.

"It's not that I don't love him—I do," she said. *"But every time he reaches for me, I flinch. I don't even know why. I feel bad, like I'm rejecting him, but sometimes I just want space."*

Across from her, Mark sat quietly, eyes low.

"It's confusing," he said finally. *"I know she cares, but I miss feeling close. It's like we're fine, but the spark—the warmth—it's just . . . gone."*

Lauren and Mark aren't fighting. They're not angry. But they're disconnected in a way that's hard to name. He experiences love most deeply through physical closeness—touching feet under the covers, resting his hand on hers at dinner, the quiet comfort of a hug at the end of a long day. She, on the other hand, has begun to associate Physical Touch with pressure, even guilt. Somewhere between parenting, stress, and emotional fatigue, it stopped feeling like connection and started feeling like demand.

This is the delicate terrain of Physical Touch. When it's a client's primary language, love is felt through proximity, presence, and physical connection—but when misread or resisted, it can become a source of tension, rejection, or emotional erosion. In this chapter, we'll explore the psychology behind this language, its many dialects, and how to coach clients to give and receive touch with empathy, safety, and intention.

Understanding the Heart of Physical Touch

For clients whose primary Love Language is Physical Touch, love is not just something they hear or observe—it's something they experience somatically (Uvnäs-Moberg, 2009). It's expressed through proximity, comfort, and physical reassurance: the gentle squeeze of their hand, a warm embrace, an arm around their shoulder. Touch, for these clients, is not optional. It is the primary channel through which love is affirmed and internalized.

And yet, Physical Touch is frequently misunderstood. It's often conflated with sexuality, especially with couples where one partner feels emotionally disconnected from their partner's desire for sex. But the language of touch is far broader—and far deeper. For those who truly have this as their primary Love Language, it includes nonsexual touch, casual affection, nurturing gestures, and even simple rituals of physical presence that communicate emotional safety and support.

Touch is, in fact, one of the earliest and most enduring forms of emotional communication. Long before language develops, infants rely on physical contact to regulate stress, form secure attachments, and build trust (Hertenstein et al., 2006). These early neurological patterns continue into adulthood. Research has shown that affectionate touch in romantic relationships contributes to lower cortisol levels, higher relationship satisfaction, and increased feelings of relational security (Jakubiak & Feeney, 2017; Debrot et al., 2013).

Clients whose primary Love Language is Physical Touch often struggle to explain why its absence hurts so deeply. They may say, *"I know my partner loves me, but I don't feel it,"* or *"It's not about sex—I just miss being close."* When touch disappears, so does their sense of closeness. Without physical connection, even verbal affection can feel hollow. Conversely, when touch is warm, consistent, and attuned, it serves as a nonverbal anchor of emotional presence (Field, 2010).

But this language isn't without its risks. Because touch is so intimate, it requires trust (Trotter & Leach, 2017). For clients who've experienced trauma, coercion, or violations of physical boundaries, touch may come with ambivalence—or even fear. They may crave closeness but flinch at contact. Others may carry cultural or familial conditioning that made affection rare or emotionally confusing. Coaching in these moments invites clients to explore not only their present needs, but the early emotional associations they developed around physical connection.

Coaches must also be mindful of relational mismatches. It's not uncommon for one partner to crave physical reassurance while the other is more verbally or practically expressive. Coaching helps translate this dynamic—not by demanding sameness, but by cultivating empathy. When clients understand that touch is not a "bonus" but a core emotional need for their partner, the conversation shifts. It becomes less about preference and more about presence.

Physical Touch, at its healthiest, grounds love in the body. It says, without words: *"I'm here. I see you. You're not alone."* And when spoken consistently, it has the power to regulate anxiety, deepen attachment, and create a rhythm of relational safety that words alone cannot sustain.

The Dialects of Physical Touch

Not all touch communicates the same thing. *The Love Language That Matters Most* and the 5 Love Languages Premium Assessment identify seven distinct dialects of Physical Touch, each shaped by its emotional purpose and relational context. Helping clients name the kind of touch they need—or the kind they naturally give—can dramatically reduce misunderstanding and strengthen emotional connection.

These dialects provide clients and couples with the vocabulary to move from vague frustration ("We're just not connecting") to specific clarity ("I need comforting touch right now, not playful touch"). Here's a brief overview of each:

Comforting: Touch that soothes or calms during stress or sadness.
This touch is grounded, slow, and stabilizing. A hand on the back during grief. A long hug after a hard day. Clients who resonate with this dialect often say, "When I'm upset, I don't need advice—I need to feel held." *Coaching tip: Encourage partners to offer presence over solutions, using physical connection as a way to co-regulate emotional distress.*

Affectionate: Casual, frequent touch that expresses warmth and connection.
These are the everyday gestures that say, "I'm here, I like you, I see you." Holding hands, an arm around the shoulder, a kiss on the cheek in passing. It's less about timing and more about rhythm. *Coaching tip: Help clients recognize how these "small" touches maintain a relational baseline of closeness, especially outside of high-emotion moments.*

Playful: Light, fun, teasing touch that creates shared joy.
This dialect includes tickling, light wrestling, back-and-forth physical games, or quick loving taps. It brings levity and lightness into the relationship, and is often tied to shared laughter and spontaneity. *Coaching tip: Remind clients that playfulness fosters bonding and emotional safety, especially in long-term relationships that feel weighed down by stress or routine.*

Romantic: Touch that signals desire, anticipation, or flirtation.
This is about emotional spark and attraction. A slow caress, a brush of the hair, the kind of touch that invites connection and signals romantic interest. For some clients, this is the glue of their intimacy. *Coaching tip: Encourage clients to offer this kind of touch without it always leading to sex—allowing space for affection and desire to build relational trust.*

Protective: Touch that offers safety, steadiness, or shielding in public or private.
Clients who resonate with this dialect feel secure when their partner physically "has them"—holding their hand while walking through a crowd, wrapping them in a jacket, or staying close in vulnerable spaces. *Coaching tip: Explore how this touch reinforces trust, especially in clients with anxious attachment or histories of feeling unsafe.*

Expressive: Touch that conveys emotion (joy, sadness, tenderness, etc.) without words.
This dialect is more about emotional tone than context. A reassuring pat on the shoulder after a hard conversation. A tight squeeze after good news. It's touch that mirrors emotional presence. *Coaching tip: Invite clients to reflect on how expressive touch has played a role in significant moments—and how to make room for it more intentionally.*

Restorative: Touch that calms the body and helps recharge emotionally or physically.
Clients who speak this dialect often describe cuddling or lying together in silence as essential. It's not about stimulation—it's about emotional rest. *Coaching tip: Help clients distinguish this need from laziness or withdrawal. Restorative touch can be one of the most healing practices in a relationship under strain.*

When clients can identify which kinds of touch matter most—and when—they move from generalized craving to actionable communication. And when couples can name and honor each other's touch dialects, they don't just reconnect physically. They reconnect emotionally, with precision and empathy.

Coaching Clients Who Want to Learn to Give Physical Touch

For clients who didn't grow up in physically affectionate homes, or for whom touch feels unfamiliar, learning to express love through physical connection can feel awkward at best—and, at worst, threatening to their sense of identity or comfort. They may enter coaching with a sincere desire to love their partner well, but the *how* of Physical Touch feels foreign or forced.

Some clients simply aren't "touchy." They describe themselves as more verbal or practical, and they may see physical affection as optional or uncomfortable. Others have internalized cultural or familial messages that equate Physical Touch with sexuality, vulnerability, or obligation. In either case, the coaching work is not to push physicality but to gently expand the client's emotional fluency into the physical realm—honoring both their boundaries and their partner's needs.

It's important to begin with permission, not pressure. Learning to give this Love Language must never come at the cost of a client's consent or emotional safety. But it does require openness. Coaching can help clients explore the emotional meaning of touch for their partner, reframing it not as a demand but as a relational dialect. What feels unnecessary to one person may be the very thing that signals love, security, or significance to another (Jakubiak & Feeney, 2017).

It's also helpful to connect intent with impact. Clients often say, "I'm showing up. I help. I say I love them. Why isn't that enough?" But when a partner's primary language is touch, those efforts may not register. Unmet needs in relationships aren't always about neglect. Sometimes they're about misalignment in how love is expressed and received (Chapman, 2024). Coaching helps translate effort into emotional resonance.

The seven dialects of Physical Touch can be especially valuable here. A client may never feel entirely comfortable initiating romantic touch at first—but may find ease in affectionate or protective gestures. Starting with simple, low-pressure expressions of physical presence (sitting close during a movie, a reassuring hand on the shoulder, or a goodbye hug) allows the client to grow their comfort gradually. According to Hertenstein et al. (2006), even brief physical contact can effectively communicate distinct emotional messages, including sympathy, gratitude, and love.

Clients who fear "getting it wrong" often benefit from a shift in mindset—from performance to presence. Coaching toward emotional attunement helps relieve pressure. The goal is not perfect technique, it's relational mindfulness: noticing their partner's emotional state and responding with intentional touch. A small, well-timed gesture can speak volumes.

For some, it may help to build a short list of "go-to" touch gestures that feel both authentic and repeatable. A daily goodbye kiss. A light hand on the back during hard conversations. These acts become rituals of reassurance—not obligations, but anchors.

When a partner has trauma history or touch sensitivity, the coaching becomes even more delicate. Rather than avoiding touch altogether, help the client engage in collaborative curiosity: "What kind of touch feels safe for you?" or "Are there times when you're most open to physical closeness?" These conversations don't just set the stage for physical connection—they build emotional trust.

Lastly, many clients need to reframe their internal narrative around what touch means. For those who experienced touch as a form of control or duty, it may be healing to rediscover it as an expression of empathy. With coaching, clients can begin to reframe physical contact as something they're free to offer, not merely obligated to give. When rooted in safety and sincerity, Physical Touch becomes less about compliance and more about care.

Even for those who don't naturally speak this language, fluency is possible. And when they begin to express it with warmth and intention, their partner doesn't just feel loved. They feel *chosen.*

Coaching Clients Who Crave This Love Language

For clients whose primary Love Language is Physical Touch, the absence of contact can feel like the absence of love itself. These clients may have difficulty putting their longing into words—but they feel it in their bodies: the loneliness of sleeping back-to-back, the subtle ache of walking side by side without holding hands, the quiet erosion of intimacy when days pass without a hug or kiss.

Some will say it directly: *"I just miss being touched."* Others will express it indirectly, describing emotional disconnection without naming the underlying physical gap. Still others won't voice it at all—especially if they've learned that their need is perceived as needy, inconvenient, or too sexual.

Craving touch comes with vulnerability. It opens the client to potential misunderstanding: *"Is that all you care about?"* or *"I don't like being pawed at,"* or worse, silence and withdrawal. Over time, many clients stop asking. They internalize a story that says: *"My need is too much,"* or *"If I have to ask, it doesn't count."*

Coaching offers a safe space to unearth that craving, validate it, and reclaim it without shame. The research is clear: touch isn't optional. It's an essential human need. Studies show that affectionate touch promotes emotional bonding, reduces stress, and strengthens attachment security across the lifespan (Coan, Schaefer, & Davidson, 2006). Even completely nonverbal touch can activate neural pathways associated with safety, social belonging, and calm (Morrison, 2016).

But relationally, what matters most is not just that touch happens—it's how it lands. For clients who crave this language, the touch must be intentional, attuned, and consistent. Sporadic affection feels confusing. Absent affection feels wounding. Consistent, meaningful contact builds trust.

It's also helpful to explore *which kind of touch* matters most. The seven dialects offer a path forward. One client may long for comforting touch after emotional strain, physical reassurance that says, *"You're not alone."* Another may feel connected through playful touch, craving lightness in the weight of routine. Others find safety in restorative touch, quiet closeness without conversation. Helping clients identify the form of touch that speaks to their heart sharpens their ability to express that need clearly.

Yet, clarity alone isn't always enough. Many clients face relational resistance. Their partner may be physically reserved, emotionally withdrawn, or even avoidant. In these cases, coaching should help the client navigate their longing without bitterness. That includes learning how to ask for touch vulnerably, without accusation. Instead of saying, *"You never touch me,"* they might say, *"When you reach for me, I feel safe and close to you."*

Sometimes, coaching also includes grieving what isn't happening. For clients in relationships where touch is limited due to trauma, illness, conflict, or personal preference, there's often a quiet grief that must be honored. Coaching helps clients name that sadness without turning it into blame, while also exploring new ways to experience closeness that may include (but aren't limited to) physical contact.

You may also encounter clients whose need for touch stems from emotional depletion in other areas. In this case, physical contact becomes a proxy for unspoken connection. Here, coaching becomes an exercise in curiosity. What are they really longing for? Is it reassurance? Attention? Intimacy? By helping clients differentiate between contact and connection, you equip them to speak their need more precisely.

Clients who crave Physical Touch often live with a feeling they struggle to explain: *"I'm close to someone, but I still feel distant."* The coaching gift is to name that gap—and guide them toward the kind of connection that closes it.

Summary

Physical Touch is often the most visible of the 5 Love Languages—but also one of the most emotionally layered. It can offer profound reassurance, spark joy, or cultivate intimacy, yet it also requires trust, attunement, and mutual willingness. When clients crave it, they're not asking for surface-level gestures—they're seeking embodied presence, emotional grounding, and a tangible expression of connection.

Coaching around this language involves far more than encouraging more contact. It calls for careful attention to comfort levels, boundaries, histories, and meaning. For clients learning to give this language, the work is often about reclaiming touch as a relational gift. For those who crave it, the journey is learning how to voice that desire without shame.

When spoken with clarity and care, Physical Touch becomes more than a habit. It becomes a way of saying, *"I'm here, I'm with you, and I want you to feel that—not just hear it."*

QUESTIONS TO PONDER

1. How do I personally experience or avoid Physical Touch in relationships, and how might that shape my coaching?
2. What assumptions do I bring into the conversation about touch—especially around gender, sexuality, or cultural expression?
3. How can I help clients name the kind of touch they long for, instead of assuming all physical contact serves the same purpose?
4. What safety considerations do I need to remain aware of, especially when coaching around past trauma or current boundaries?
5. How do I coach partners toward emotional consent and relational curiosity, not just increased contact?

PART 3

THE 5 LOVE LANGUAGES PREMIUM ASSESSMENT

"What gets measured gets managed."

—ATTRIBUTED TO PETER DRUCKER

Insight is powerful . . . but insight with data? That's next level. In this section, you'll learn how to integrate the 5 Love Languages Premium Assessment into your coaching process, turning intuitive conversations into targeted transformation. You'll discover how to interpret results, unpack emotional nuance, and design a personalized coaching plan that meets your clients right where they are. This isn't just about scoring or sorting—it's about using the assessment as a mirror that reflects patterns, reveals blind spots, and accelerates growth. With the right tools, your sessions won't just feel meaningful, they'll become measurably effective.

Chapter 12

The Value of Assessments in Coaching Relationships

"I feel like I'm guessing," Melissa admitted, glancing at her notes between sessions.

She had been coaching David and Brianna for weeks. They were kind, motivated, and surprisingly self-aware. They showed up ready to talk, made space for one another, even used "I" statements. But something was missing. Conversations circled. Insights stalled.

Melissa couldn't put her finger on it. Until she introduced an assessment.

It was simple, really. A short tool designed to reveal patterns in how each partner expressed and received love. And suddenly, the sessions changed.

David, who had insisted he was "doing everything right," realized his steady stream of compliments wasn't landing with Brianna—because her emotional currency was Quality Time.

Brianna, who thought she didn't have a Love Language, saw how often she pulled away from touch because it had become associated with obligation rather than comfort.

In one session, the emotional air shifted. They weren't guessing anymore. They were translating.

Coaching relies on intuition. It draws on empathy, observation, and a thousand subtle signals between people. But even the most attuned coaches can unknowingly operate in emotional fog. That's where assessments come in. Not to replace intuition, but to refine it. To sharpen the focus. To give coaches and clients alike a shared framework and a place to begin.

In this chapter, we'll explore why well-designed assessments are one of the most valuable tools in a coach's toolkit. We'll look at when to use them, how to choose the right one, and how they help unlock insights that might otherwise stay buried beneath good intentions and habitual misfires.

We'll also walk through a few trusted assessments that relationship coaches often rely on—from comprehensive tools like Prepare/Enrich and SYMBIS to the HeartChart and Better Love. And, of course, we'll lay the foundation for why the 5 Love Languages Premium Assessment is of prime importance to your coaching—not because it's the only lens, but because it consistently opens one of the most important relational doors: *how love is expressed, missed, and received.*

Why Assessments Matter in Coaching

Coaching, at its best, is a conversation. But not just any conversation—it's one marked by reflection, insight, movement. And often, what stands in the way of that movement is not resistance or unwillingness. It's a lack of clarity.

Assessments give clients something that intuition alone rarely delivers: language for what they've felt but couldn't name. They don't diagnose or prescribe. They illuminate. They offer a mirror that helps both individuals and couples see their patterns more clearly and speak about them more constructively.

That clarity is especially helpful when coaching couples. In relational work, conversations can easily slide into patterns: the same frustrations, the same missed cues, the same defensiveness. Assessments introduce new data points—not just about the problem, but about each person's way of thinking, processing, and expressing themselves. This often shifts the dynamic from blame to curiosity.

It's not uncommon for a coach to hear:

"That's exactly what I've been trying to say—but I didn't have the words for it."

Or:

"Reading this helped me understand that my partner isn't ignoring me. They're showing love in a way I haven't recognized."

When that happens, the assessment becomes transformational, not merely informative. It becomes a bridge between intention and impact.

Assessments also increase engagement. Clients are often more open when looking at results on paper than when confronted with direct feedback. The tool becomes the neutral third party. It helps shift the dynamic from *you vs. me* to *us vs. the problem*. As Ting and Scisco (2006) note in their work on coaching, structured feedback through assessments can enhance openness, reduce defensiveness, and accelerate goal-setting.

This is supported by more recent findings in relational coaching and psychology. Research by Jarvis, Lane, and Fillery-Travis (2021) emphasizes that assessments help create a reflective container—particularly when couples face emotionally charged or patterned interactions. And studies on insight-oriented interventions suggest that when clients can view their relationship through structured feedback, they are more likely to adopt constructive coping strategies and measurable behavior changes (Peterson & Seligman, 2020).

In short, assessments support what coaching already values: self-awareness, growth, and actionable insight. They don't override the relationship between coach and client. They enhance it. And when used wisely, they allow the coach to move beyond surface-level listening and into targeted, meaningful exploration.

That's the difference between conversation and transformation. And for many clients, it begins with a well-chosen tool.

When and How to Use Assessments in Coaching

Knowing that assessments are helpful is one thing. Knowing *when* and *how* to use them is where coaching wisdom comes in. Assessments aren't one-size-fits-all, nor are they always best introduced in the first session. Their impact often depends on timing, pacing, and emotional readiness.

Some coaches find value in offering an assessment before the first session. It gives structure to the intake process, provides a starting point for deeper questions, and gives the client something concrete to reflect on, not to mention giving the coach a preview into what they're about to encounter. This works well when the couple is eager for insight and open to structured feedback. However, if you know that a new client is skeptical, defensive, or unsure of what coaching is meant to offer, you may want to meet with them first to build trust and rapport before introducing any tools. It's simply a judgment call, and you generally can't go wrong either way.

In general, assessments are most useful at three strategic moments:

- **At the beginning**, to establish shared language and surface core dynamics.
- **At a midpoint**, when sessions feel repetitive or when new insight is needed to break a logjam.
- **As a maintenance or reevaluation tool**, helping clients reflect on growth, identify blind spots, or prepare for transitions.

Regardless of timing, how an assessment is introduced matters. Coaches should avoid presenting tools as tests or diagnoses. Instead, you should frame it as a mirror—ways of seeing oneself more clearly, not being judged more closely. Clients respond best when assessments are described as conversation starters, not scorecards. You can say something like: *"This isn't about labeling you—it's about unlocking language that helps you move forward."*

The tool becomes a third voice in the room, one that can name what clients may feel but struggle to articulate. This allows partners to say, "The assessment showed that . . ." rather than, "You always . . ." It softens defensiveness and invites reflection.

It also helps when coaches model openness to interpretation. No assessment is perfect. Encourage clients to sit with what resonates and leave behind what doesn't. The goal is to spark insight, not impose categories. In fact, research on adult learning and self-awareness suggests that tools are most impactful when they generate a sense of agency, not compliance (Kolb & Kolb, 2018).

And finally, while assessments provide valuable structure, the coach's presence still does the deeper work. No "score" can replace curiosity. No chart can match empathy. Assessments help illuminate what's been hidden—but the real transformation comes when a skilled coach helps clients see themselves, and each other, with new understanding.

A Snapshot of Trusted Relationship Tools

While no single assessment can capture the full picture of a relationship, certain tools have become trusted staples in the coach's toolkit—each offering a different lens. Some provide diagnostic breadth. Others go deep into emotional patterns or communication habits. The key is knowing what each tool offers, when it's best used, and how to layer them wisely across the arc of a coaching relationship.

HeartChart

As a general rule, we recommend starting with the HeartChart. For starters, it's very brief and it's free. More importantly, it's highly effective for getting you and your client a clear sense of the overall state of the relationship—especially around connection and commitment. In less than four minutes, the HeartChart surfaces relational vitality and investment, placing the respondent within a simple framework.

The HeartChart differs from personality or compatibility tools in one key way: it doesn't measure *traits—it reveals* the current *state* of the relationship (one of thirteen different states). It captures how each person is experiencing the connection in real time (they could be "steady," "hopeful," "frayed," "stuck," "thriving," etc.).

When coaching an individual whose partner isn't in the room, it helps the client reflect honestly on where things stand—without over-explaining. When coaching a couple, it gives both partners a shared visual language to discuss where they feel aligned, where they feel distant, and what might help them move forward.

In addition to being a powerful starting point, the HeartChart is also well-suited for use as a pre- and post-coaching measure. It's easy for clients to see their movement over time—even if their language hasn't caught up with their growth. Many coaches find that revisiting the HeartChart at the end of a coaching cycle allows for a reflective, hope-filled conversation about how far the couple has come—and what's still ahead.

It doesn't replace deeper assessments. It prepares the ground for them. It invites the kind of self-awareness that allows clients to engage more meaningfully with tools like the 5 Love Languages Premium Assessment. In this way, the HeartChart functions like a relational thermometer—quickly identifying whether you're coaching a thriving, strained, or disconnected bond.

Before we take a deep dive into the 5 Love Languages Premium Assessment, here is a brief look at a few other widely used assessments that relationship coaches may integrate:

Prepare/Enrich

This tool has been around for nearly fifty years and is widely used with premarital and married couples looking for a comprehensive relationship inventory. It's research-based, detailed, and highly structured. Excellent for surfacing strengths and growth areas across key domains (communication, conflict, family systems, etc.). It requires the coach or counselor to be trained online or in person (about three hours) in using it.

SYMBIS Assessment (Saving Your Marriage Before It Starts)

Like Prepare/Enrich, SYMBIS works exceptionally well with couples at any stage (it becomes SYMBIS+ when using it with couples who are married). It's a positive, strengths-based entry into relationship coaching. It's 15-page infographic report is delivered in approachable language and maps out personality, expectations, and relational dynamics.

Better Love Assessment

As a coach you may sometimes be called upon to do a group, class, event, or retreat with couples, and Better Love is ideal for these kinds of settings. The couples receive their report directly, and you lead the group through it together. It's relatively brief (10 pages), visually appealing, and has a low barrier to entry. Helpful for couples looking to reflect and reconnect without deep diagnostics.

Together, these tools help coaches see what's happening in a relationship—not just through observation, but through structured reflection. Some open the door. Others help clients walk through it. What matters most is using the right tool at the right time—with clarity, context, and care.

In the next section, we'll explore why the 5 Love Languages Premium Assessment offers something unique within this landscape: a precise, emotionally attuned window into how people express, receive, and misinterpret love—and how coaches can use that insight to guide breakthrough moments.

The 5 Love Languages Premium Assessment

Among the many assessments available to relationship coaches, no tool has more intuitive simplicity and relational depth of the 5 Love Languages Premium Assessment. Its widespread appeal is undeniable, but its coaching potential goes well beyond popularity. It gives individuals and couples language for something deeply emotional, often misunderstood, and frequently mishandled: *how we express and interpret love.*

While tools like Prepare/Enrich or SYMBIS provide comprehensive insight across domains like communication, finances, family systems, or personality dynamics, the 5 Love Languages Premium Assessment focuses squarely on emotional expression. It surfaces the everyday actions that either reinforce connection or quietly erode it. And unlike many assessments that measure personality traits or compatibility factors, the Premium Assessment report centers on felt experience—how love is given, received, missed, and misread.

This is your go-to assessment as a Love Language Coach. Think of the Premium Assessment as a stethoscope for a relationship coach. You wouldn't try to diagnose a heartbeat by guesswork, and you shouldn't try to coach love and connection without first listening in.

The emotional precision of this tool makes it ideal for coaching sessions where one partner feels "unseen" or "unappreciated," even when both are "doing their best." The report doesn't just identify a primary Love Language, it also breaks down specific dialects within each language, allowing for deeper exploration. A client may already know they value Quality Time, for example, but the Premium Assessment helps them see that what they most long for is *dreaming together about the future* or *being fully present without distraction*. That level of specificity changes conversations. It moves coaching from broad categories to targeted empathy.

What makes the Premium version especially rich is that it doesn't just stop with Love Languages; it integrates personality patterns into the results, offering a more nuanced and dynamic portrait of how each person expresses and interprets love. This customization helps clients feel seen not only in what they value, but *why they value it—making the feedback more resonant, and the coaching conversation more personalized.*

Another benefit of the Premium Assessment is that it is actionable immediately for your client. The language is accessible, the insights are intuitive, and the emotional weight is real. It invites the client to say: *"This is how I feel most loved. How about you?"* That simple exchange can open emotional doors that years of miscommunication had kept closed.

Finally, it pairs beautifully with other tools. The HeartChart gives clients a snapshot of where they are. The Premium Assessment helps them understand why they might be there—and what to do next. Where one measures the state of the relationship, the other uncovers the relational habits and emotional languages that sustain or strain it.

Of course, the Premium Assessment is fully integrated into the latest edition of *The 5 Love Languages* as well as *The Love Language That Matters Most*, offering readers a seamless bridge from reading and reflection to real-world application with you in your sessions. It's not just a companion, it's a catalyst for the deeper value you bring as a Love Language coach.

In short, the 5 Love Languages Premium Assessment doesn't attempt to solve everything. It zeroes in on one of the most foundational dynamics in any relationship: how people seek connection, and how that connection is either nurtured or missed.

For the coach, that's not just useful; it's indispensable.

That's why in the remaining chapters of Part 3, we'll take a deeper dive into exactly how to use the 5 Love Languages Premium Assessment in your practice. You'll learn how to walk clients through their results, interpret both individual and couple dynamics, and guide coaching conversations that move from static insight to real emotional change. We'll explore how to customize your coaching approach based on each client's dialect, how to use the tool to build a personalized growth plan, and how to reintroduce the assessment over time to track progress and deepen connection.

The goal is to help your clients experience lasting transformation through the language of love.

Summary

Assessments aren't shortcuts. They're structure. In the hands of a skilled coach, they offer clarity, spark curiosity, and create a shared language that accelerates growth. Whether it's the high-level insight of Prepare/Enrich, the strengths-based tone of SYMBIS, the emotional clarity of the HeartChart, or the actionable depth of the 5 Love Languages Premium Assessment, each tool plays a role in helping people name what's working, uncover what's missing, and move toward deeper connection.

The best assessments don't replace coaching, they fuel it. They invite clients to reflect more honestly and engage more openly. That's why every Love Language Coach should have a core toolkit of assessments at the ready, using them not just to inform, but to transform.

QUESTIONS TO PONDER

1. Which assessments have I used most often—and what have they revealed about how I guide client insight?
2. How do I decide *when* to introduce a tool, and do I give clients a meaningful "why" behind it?
3. In what ways might I be underutilizing assessment data during follow-up sessions?
4. Do I default to one assessment, or do I have a flexible toolkit based on client needs and stages?
5. How comfortable am I interpreting assessments that focus on emotional needs versus personality traits?
6. What's one new assessment I could begin using—or one I could revisit with fresh intentionality?

Chapter 13

Exploring the 5 Love Languages Premium Assessment

Tori and Caleb both scored highest in Quality Time. On paper, it looked like a win: a perfect match. But as they sat side by side in their session, the silence said otherwise.

Tori had tears in her eyes. *"It's like we live in different worlds,"* she whispered.

Caleb blinked. *"But we do everything together. We even carpool to work."*

Same language, different dialect.

Tori's results revealed a craving for uninterrupted, present-moment connection—"Improvising" and "Dreaming" were her highest dialects. What she wanted was slow mornings with no agenda, playful conversations about their future, the kind of connection that made her feel emotionally seen.

Caleb's dialects leaned hard into "Managing" and "Planning." He was a schedule guy—Quality Time meant efficiency, shared goals, taking care of errands together. To him, the fact that they were constantly in motion side by side *was* connection.

The love was real. The effort was there. But they were missing each other—every day.

This is what the 5 Love Languages Premium Assessment helps surface: not just a preferred category of love, but the emotional shape it takes. The way it's offered, missed, and misunderstood.

Clients often arrive in coaching frustrated or confused. They're giving love, but it's not landing. They're craving love, but unsure how to name it. The Premium Assessment gives them a shared framework, a richer vocabulary, and a mirror they didn't know they needed.

But a report alone doesn't create change. It's the interpretation and guidance from a coach that unlocks transformation. In this chapter, you'll learn how to walk through the assessment with clients in a way that feels less like reading results and more like reading between the lines of their relationship.

We'll explore how to unpack primary and secondary languages, understand dialects in context, and make sense of surprises, resistance, and gaps. We'll also look at the personality overlays and emotional skill ratings that bring nuance and clarity to what might otherwise seem straightforward.

Used with care, this tool becomes more than an assessment. It becomes a bridge—from *what clients mean to give to what their partner needs to receive.*

Inside the Report: What It Measures—And Why It Matters

The 5 Love Languages Premium Assessment is more than a personality snapshot. It's a layered map of how love is experienced, expressed, and often misunderstood—complete with emotional indicators, behavioral patterns, and relational blind spots. Understanding the order and design of the report not only helps you guide clients through it more confidently, it ensures you're listening for the emotional signal behind the data.

Here's how the report is structured—and how each section opens up specific coaching opportunities.

Page 3: Your Love Languages

This page is where it all begins. The report offers an ordered ranking of the 5 Love Languages, accompanied by personalized narrative descriptions for the client's primary, secondary, and lowest-scoring (foreign) language. Each is expressed as a percentile, which gives

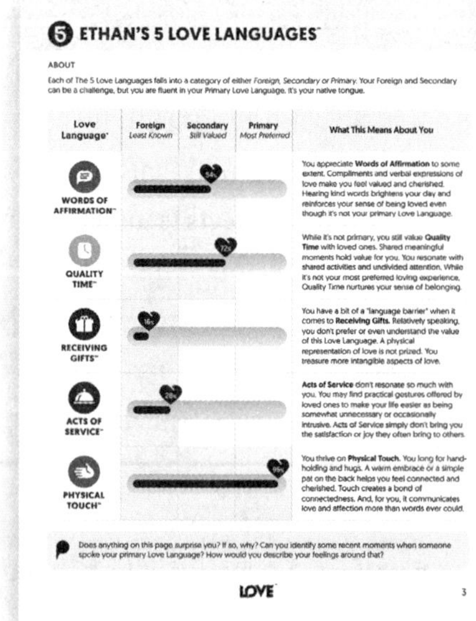

5 ETHAN'S 5 LOVE LANGUAGES™

ABOUT

Each of The 5 Love Languages falls into a category of either *Foreign, Secondary or Primary.* Your Foreign and Secondary can be a challenge, but you are fluent in your Primary Love Language. It's your native tongue.

Love Language™	Foreign *Least Known* / Secondary *Still Valued* / Primary *Most Preferred*	What This Means About You
WORDS OF AFFIRMATION™	54%	You appreciate **Words of Affirmation** to some extent. Compliments and verbal expressions of love make you feel valued and cherished. Hearing kind words brightens your day and reinforces your sense of being loved even though it's not your primary Love Language.
QUALITY TIME™	72%	While it's not primary, you still value **Quality Time** with loved ones. Shared meaningful moments hold value for you. You resonate with shared activities and undivided attention. While it's not your most preferred loving experience, Quality Time nurtures your sense of belonging.
RECEIVING GIFTS™	16%	You have a bit of a "language barrier" when it comes to **Receiving Gifts.** Relatively speaking, you don't prefer or even understand the value of this Love Language. A physical representation of love is not prized. You treasure more intangible aspects of love.
ACTS OF SERVICE™	28%	**Acts of Service** don't resonate so much with you. You may find practical gestures offered by loved ones to make your life easier as being somewhat unnecessary or occasionally intrusive. Acts of Service simply don't bring you the satisfaction or joy they often bring to others.
PHYSICAL TOUCH™	99%	You thrive on **Physical Touch.** You long for hand-holding and hugs. A warm embrace or a simple pat on the back helps you feel connected and cherished. Touch creates a bond of connectedness. And, for you, it communicates love and affection more than words ever could.

Does anything on this page surprise you? If so, why? Can you identify some recent moments when someone spoke your primary Love Language? How would you describe your feelings around that?

LOVE™ 3

you more than a label—it gives you insight into *intensity*.

For example, a client scoring 92% in Words of Affirmation will likely feel a much stronger emotional impact (or absence) than someone at 65%. A client with a foreign language at 5% may not just be indifferent to that form of love, they may actively misinterpret it.

This section doesn't provide answers—it offers a launch point for questions. What resonates? What surprises them? What behaviors have they mistaken for love—or overlooked entirely?

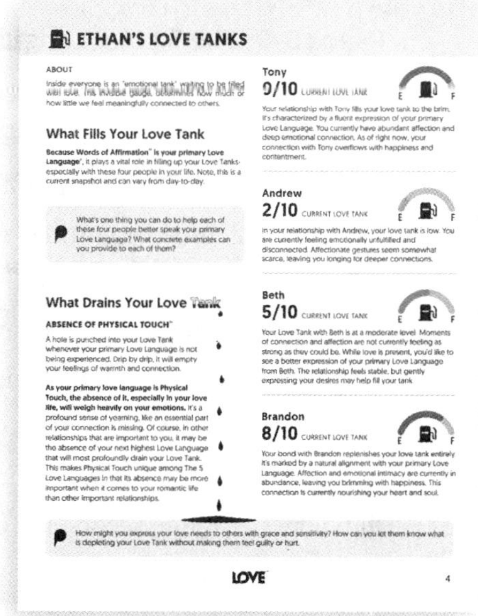

ETHAN'S LOVE TANKS

ABOUT

Inside everyone is an "emotional tank" waiting to be filled with love. This invisible gauge determines how much or how little we feel meaningfully connected to others.

What Fills Your Love Tank

Because Words of Affirmation™ is your primary Love Language®, it plays a vital role in filling up your Love Tanks-especially with these four people in your life. Note, this is a current snapshot and can vary from day-to-day.

What's one thing you can do to help each of these four people better speak your primary Love Language? What concrete examples can you provide to each of them?

What Drains Your Love Tank

ABSENCE OF PHYSICAL TOUCH™

A hole is punched into your Love Tank whenever your primary Love Language is not being experienced. Drip by drip, it will empty your feelings of warmth and connection.

As your primary love language is Physical Touch, the absence of it, especially in your love life, will weigh heavily on your emotions. It's a profound sense of yearning, like an essential part of your connection is missing. Of course, in other relationships that are important to you, it may be the absence of your next highest Love Language that will most profoundly drain your Love Tank. This makes Physical Touch unique among The 5 Love Languages in that its absence may be more important when it comes to your romantic life than other important relationships.

Tony
9/10 CURRENT LOVE TANK

Your relationship with Tony fills your love tank to the brim. It's characterized by a fluent expression of your primary Love Language. You currently have abundant affection and deep emotional connection. As of right now, your connection with Tony overflows with happiness and contentment.

Andrew
2/10 CURRENT LOVE TANK

In your relationship with Andrew, your love tank is low. You are currently feeling emotionally unfulfilled and disconnected. Affectionate gestures seem somewhat scarce, leaving you longing for deeper connections.

Beth
5/10 CURRENT LOVE TANK

Your Love Tank with Beth is at a moderate level. Moments of connection and affection are not currently feeling as strong as they could be. While love is present, you'd like to see a better expression of your primary Love Language from Beth. The relationship feels stable, but gently expressing your desires may help fill your tank.

Brandon
8/10 CURRENT LOVE TANK

Your bond with Brandon replenishes your love tank entirely. It's marked by a natural alignment with your primary Love Language. Affection and emotional intimacy are currently in abundance, leaving you brimming with happiness. This connection is currently nourishing your heart and soul.

How might you express your love needs to others with grace and sensitivity? How can you let them know what is depleting your Love Tank without making them feel guilty or hurt.

LOVE 4

Page 4: Your Love Tank

This page is simple but emotionally rich. At a glance, it offers a visual snapshot of how love is currently being experienced in the client's key relationships, as well as how their own love tank is functioning internally.

The top of the page identifies what fills the client's love tank and what drains it. These aren't generic stressors or guesses—they're *self-reported emotional indicators* that give immediate access to what energizes the client relationally and what depletes them. For example, a client might list "being truly listened to" as filling their tank, while "constant criticism" drains it. These statements are brief, but they speak volumes and often become interpretive keys to other sections of the report.

On this same page, the client has identified up to four key people in their life—typically a spouse or partner, but also children, friends, siblings, in-laws, or other significant figures. For each one, the client sees how full that person's love tank *feels* to them. In other words, it captures the client's perception of how well they feel loved by that person.

This creates a layered view of relational connection. The top half speaks to the client's personal sense of emotional nourishment. The bottom half captures how they believe others are showing up in their lives. For some clients, this alignment is affirming. For others, it may reveal a painful disconnect.

While brief, this page often surfaces key questions that drive meaningful coaching: Where is love being given but not felt? Where is the client exhausted, despite their best intentions? And where might their perception of how others' loving expressions toward them be missing the mark, or hitting it?

It's not a diagnostic—it's a check-in on the current status. But for many clients, it's the first time they've paused to ask: *What actually fills me? What quietly drains me? And how am I experiencing expressions of love in the relationships that matter most?*

Pages 5–9: The 5 Love Languages (Dialects Breakdown)

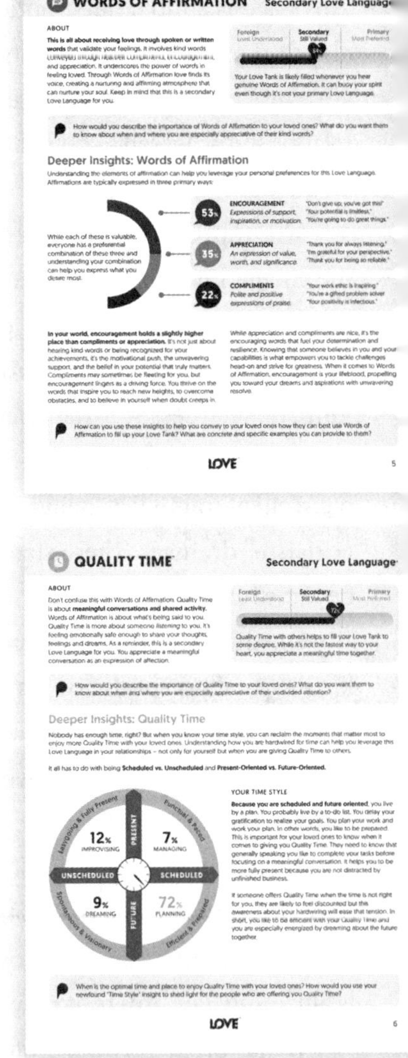

This five-page section is the emotional core of the report and the reason the Premium Assessment goes far beyond the free online quiz. While most clients come in familiar with the concept of a "primary Love Language," what they often haven't encountered is the emotional precision the pages in this section deliver.

Each of the five pages in this section is devoted to one Love Language, regardless of whether it's the client's primary, secondary, or lowest ranked. That's one of the most important features: the *upper-right corner* of every page clearly states where that language falls in the client's personal ranking, giving coaches an immediate sense of both relevance and emotional weight.

At the top of each page, the report provides a fuller description of that specific Love Language—grounding the client in its broader meaning before zooming in. This is particularly helpful for clients who may dismiss a language that doesn't "feel like them" or who are struggling to articulate how they express love outside their top preference.

But the most valuable content on each page

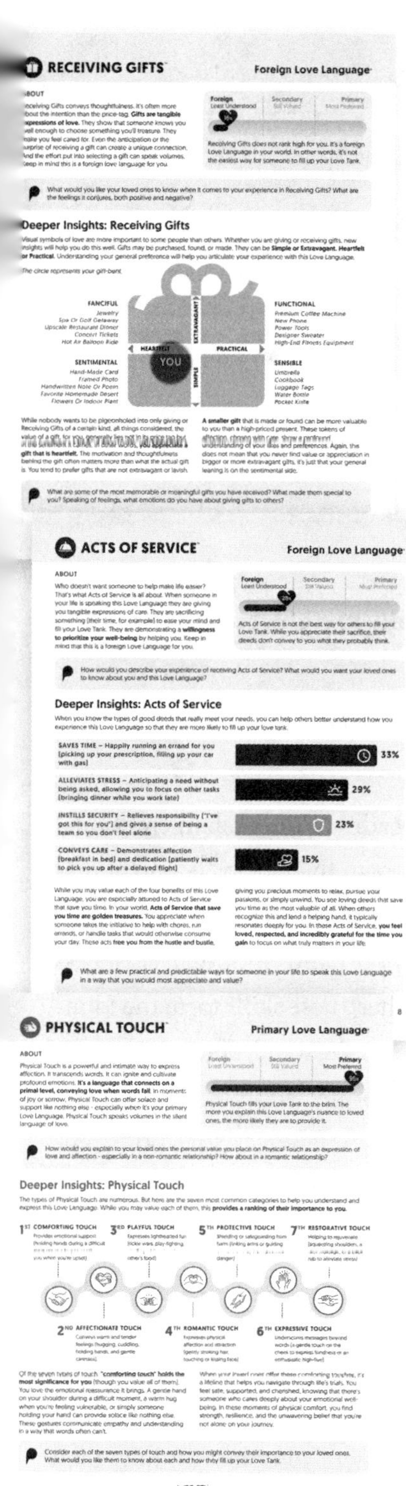

RECEIVING GIFTS

Foreign Love Language

ABOUT

Receiving Gifts conveys thoughtfulness. It's often more about the intention than the price-tag. **Gifts are tangible expressions of love.** They show that someone knows you well enough to choose something you'll treasure. They make you feel cared for. Even the anticipation or the surprise of receiving a gift can create a unique connection. And the effort put into selecting a gift can speak volumes. Keep in mind this is a foreign love language for you.

Foreign Least Understood | Secondary Still Valued | Primary Most Preferred

Receiving Gifts does not rank high for you. It's a foreign Love Language in your world. In other words, it's not the easiest way for someone to fill up your Love Tank.

What would you like your loved ones to know when it comes to your experience in Receiving Gifts? What are the feelings it conjures, both positive and negative?

Deeper Insights: Receiving Gifts

Visual symbols of love are more important to some people than others. Whether you are giving or receiving gifts, new insights will help you do this well. Gifts may be purchased, found, or made. They can be **Simple or Extravagant, Heartfelt or Practical.** Understanding your general preference will help you articulate your experience with this Love Language.

The circle represents your gift-bent.

While nobody wants to be pigeonholed into only giving or Receiving Gifts of a certain kind, all things considered, the value of a gift, for you, generally lies not in its price tag but in the sentiment it carries. In other words, **you appreciate a gift that is heartfelt.** The motivation and thoughtfulness behind the gift often matters more than what the actual gift is. You tend to prefer gifts that are not extravagant or lavish.

A smaller gift that is made or found can be more valuable to you than a high-priced present. These tokens of affection, chosen with care, show a profound understanding of your likes and preferences. Again, this does not mean that you never find value or appreciation in bigger or more extravagant gifts, it's just that your general leaning is on the sentimental side.

What are some of the most memorable or meaningful gifts you have received? What made them special to you? Speaking of feelings, what emotions do you have about giving gifts to others?

ACTS OF SERVICE

Foreign Love Language

ABOUT

Who doesn't want someone to help make life easier? That's what Acts of Service is all about. When someone in your life is speaking this Love Language they are giving you tangible expressions of care. They are sacrificing something (their time, for example) to ease your mind and fill your Love Tank. They are demonstrating a **willingness to prioritize your well-being** by helping you. Keep in mind that this is a foreign Love Language for you.

Foreign Least Understood | Secondary Still Valued | Primary Most Preferred

Acts of Service is not the best way for others to fill your Love Tank. While you appreciate their sacrifice, their deeds don't convey to you what they probably think.

How would you describe your experience of receiving Acts of Service? What would you want your loved ones to know about you and this Love Language?

Deeper Insights: Acts of Service

When you know the types of good deeds that really meet your needs, you can help others better understand how you experience this Love Language so that they are more likely to fill up your love tank.

SAVES TIME – Happily running an errand for you (picking up your prescription, filling up your car with gas)	33%
ALLEVIATES STRESS – Anticipating a need without being asked, allowing you to focus on other tasks (bringing dinner while you work late)	29%
INSTILLS SECURITY – Relieves responsibility ("I've got this for you") and gives a sense of being a team so you don't feel alone	23%
CONVEYS CARE – Demonstrates affection (breakfast in bed) and dedication (patiently waits to pick you up after a delayed flight)	15%

While you may value each of the four benefits of this Love Language, you are especially attuned to Acts of Service that save you time. In your world, **Acts of Service that save you time are golden treasures.** You appreciate when someone takes the initiative to help with chores, run errands, or handle tasks that would otherwise consume your day. These acts **free you from the hustle and bustle,** giving you precious moments to relax, pursue your passions, or simply unwind. You see loving deeds that save you time as the most valuable of all. When others recognize this and lend a helping hand, it typically resonates deeply for you. In these Acts of Service, **you feel loved, respected, and incredibly grateful for the time you gain** to focus on what truly matters in your life.

What are a few practical and predictable ways for someone in your life to speak this Love Language in a way that you would most appreciate and value?

8

PHYSICAL TOUCH

Primary Love Language

ABOUT

Physical Touch is a powerful and intimate way to express affection. It transcends words. It can ignite and cultivate profound emotions. **It's a language that connects on a primal level, conveying love when words fail.** In moments of joy or sorrow, Physical Touch can offer solace and support like nothing else - especially when it's your primary Love Language. Physical Touch speaks volumes in the silent language of love.

Foreign Least Understood | Secondary Still Valued | Primary Most Preferred

Physical Touch fills your Love Tank to the brim. The more you explain this Love Language's nuance to loved ones, the more likely they are to provide it.

How would you explain to your loved ones the personal value you place on Physical Touch as an expression of love and affection - especially in a non-romantic relationship? How about in a romantic relationship?

Deeper Insights: Physical Touch

The types of Physical Touch are numerous. But here are the seven most common categories to help you understand and express this Love Language. While you may value each of them, this **provides a ranking of their importance to you.**

Of the seven types of touch, **"comforting touch" holds the most significance for you** (though you value all of them). You love the emotional reassurance it brings. A gentle hand on your shoulder during a difficult moment, a warm hug when you're feeling vulnerable, or simply someone holding your hand can provide solace like nothing else. These gestures communicate empathy and understanding in a way that words often can't.

When your loved ones offer these comforting touches, it's a lifeline that helps you navigate through life's trials. You feel safe, supported, and cherished, knowing that there's someone who cares deeply about your emotional well-being. In these moments of physical comfort, you find strength, resilience, and the unwavering belief that you're not alone on your journey.

Consider each of the seven types of touch and how you might convey their importance to your loved ones. What would you like them to know about each and how they fill up your Love Tank.

LOVE

9

is found in the "Deeper Insights" section, where the language is broken down into dialects—emotionally specific variations that reveal how the client most naturally gives or receives that type of love.

These dialects are not arbitrary—they are research-informed and psychologically grounded, crafted to capture how emotional needs express themselves through behavior. For coaching, this is gold.

Two people may both speak the same primary language and still feel disconnected—not because they don't love each other, but because they're speaking different dialects. One may think they're offering what the other craves, but it's landing flat or even causing frustration. These dialects bring that misalignment into focus and offer a tangible way to course-correct.

In short, this section is where the report moves from identification to interpretive depth. It doesn't just tell clients *what* they value. It shows them *how* that value expresses itself—so they can recognize it, request it, and offer it with greater precision. For coaches, that precision turns guesswork into clarity—and intention into impact.

Page 10: Your Love Skills

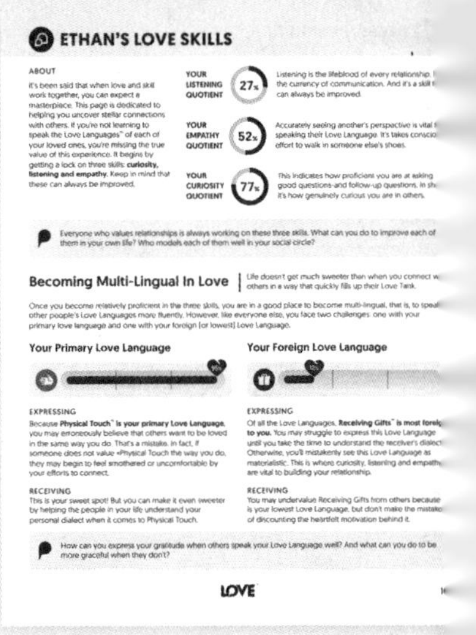

ETHAN'S LOVE SKILLS

ABOUT

It's been said that when love and skill work together, you can expect a masterpiece. This page is dedicated to helping you uncover stellar connections with others. If you're not learning to speak the Love Languages™ of each of your loved ones, you're missing the true value of this experience. It begins by getting a lock on three skills: **curiosity, listening and empathy.** Keep in mind that these can always be improved.

YOUR LISTENING QUOTIENT 27%
Listening is the lifeblood of every relationship. the currency of communication. And it's a skill can always be improved.

YOUR EMPATHY QUOTIENT 52%
Accurately seeing another's perspective is vital speaking their Love Language. It's takes conscio effort to walk in someone else's shoes.

YOUR CURIOSITY QUOTIENT 77%
This indicates how proficient you are at asking good questions and follow-up questions. In sh it's how genuinely curious you are in others.

Everyone who values relationships is always working on these three skills. What can you do to improve each of them in your own life? Who models each of them well in your social circle?

Becoming Multi-Lingual In Love | Life doesn't get much sweeter than when you connect w others in a way that quickly fills up their Love Tank.

Once you become relatively proficient in the three skills, you are in a good place to become multi-lingual, that is, to speak other people's Love Languages more fluently. However, like everyone else, you face two challenges: one with your primary love language and one with your foreign (or lowest) Love Language.

Your Primary Love Language

EXPRESSING
Because **Physical Touch™ is your primary Love Language,** you may erroneously believe that others want to be loved in the same way you do. That's a mistake. In fact, if someone does not value Physical Touch the way you do, they may begin to feel smothered or uncomfortable by your efforts to connect.

RECEIVING
This is your sweet spot! But you can make it even sweeter by helping the people in your life understand your personal dialect when it comes to Physical Touch.

Your Foreign Love Language

EXPRESSING
Of all the Love Languages, **Receiving Gifts™ is most forei to you.** You may struggle to express this Love Language until you take the time to understand the receiver's dialect Otherwise, you'll mistakenly see this Love Language as materialistic. This is where curiosity, listening and empathy are vital to building your relationship.

RECEIVING
You may undervalue Receiving Gifts from others because is your lowest Love Language, but don't make the mistake of discounting the heartfelt motivation behind it.

How can you express your gratitude when others speak your Love Language well? And what can you do to be more graceful when they don't?

LOVE

This page shifts the report from emotional preference to emotional capacity. While the previous pages reveal how someone feels most loved, this Love Skills page reveals how likely the client is to offer love *effectively.* This page is divided into two parts: core skill scores and a framework called "Becoming Multilingual in Love."

At the top of the page, clients receive percentile scores in three core relational skills:

- **Curiosity: The willingness to lean in, ask questions, and seek to understand.**
- **Listening: The ability to remain emotionally present, receptive, and responsive.**
- **Empathy: The capacity to feel with another person and attune to their emotional reality.**

These three competencies are supported by decades of research in emotional intelligence and attachment theory. Studies have shown that curiosity and empathy are linked to increased relationship satisfaction (Kashdan et al., 2011), while listening quality significantly predicts perceived support and emotional closeness in couples (Bodie, 2011; Reis & Shaver, 1988). Together, these skills form the foundation of relational attunement: the ability to notice, understand, and respond to a partner's emotional needs in ways that feel safe and connected.

Unlike Love Languages, which reflect emotional preferences, love skills represent relational development areas. They are not fixed traits but *learnable* capacities. The scores don't diagnose—they illuminate. A client may have a strong preference for Words of Affirmation, for example, but low empathy or listening scores—which may explain why their partner still feels emotionally distant despite frequent verbal praise.

The lower half of the page introduces a practical framework titled "Becoming Multilingual in Love." This section encourages the client to reflect on how they currently express and receive their primary Love Language and their lowest foreign

Love Language. By identifying this, clients begin to see love not as a fixed style but as a dynamic skill set.

This section bridges preference and growth. It reminds the client—and the coach—that emotional connection isn't just about knowing your language and dialect. It's about being willing to learn fundamental relationship skills as well as someone else's Love Language, even when it's unfamiliar. The Love Skills page plants that vision: not just to love instinctively, but to love wisely.

Pages 11–12: You and the 5 Love Languages

This two-page section brings together two essential dimensions: the client's core personality traits and how those traits may influence their experience of the 5 Love Languages. It's one of the most nuanced sections of the Premium Assessment—because it helps clients see not just *what they prefer, but why that preference may look or feel the way it does.*

Rather than assigning a type or locking someone into a static category, this section uses an adapted version of the Big Five personality framework to offer a dynamic, relational lens. It explores how emotional temperament shapes both the expression and reception of love (McCrae & Costa, 2008).

The first page of this section invites the client to explore their personality continuum across three paired dimensions. Unlike traditional trait labels, these dimensions are presented as relational tendencies, offering clients a psychologically accessible way to reflect on their behavior:

ETHAN AND THE 5 LOVE LANGUAGES Part One

ABOUT

Who you are, your personality, plays a featured role in all of your relationships. **Your personal hardwiring shapes your Love Language.** Relationships are more complex than the simple model of The 5 Love Languages. This page is dedicated to understanding how your personality traits and dispositions interact with your primary Love Language.

Introversion ⟷ Extroversion

Your tendency to seek social interaction

INTROVERSION — EXTROVERSION

As an extrovert, you are uniquely geared toward a world of social interaction and vibrant energy. **You thrive in the company of others,** finding joy and energy in bustling gatherings, lively conversations and exciting social events. You appreciate Acts of Service™ that enable you to enjoy these kinds of experiences. Because you relish the spontaneity and dynamism of social interactions, you especially value Acts of Service from someone who directs their actions toward this for you (particularly if they are not an extrovert). You flourish with **Acts of Service that bring about exciting and collaborative experiences** that feed your outgoing spirit.

Cautious ⟷ Curious

Your tendency to be open and creative

CAUTIOUS — CURIOUS

Relative to others, you are pragmatic and probably data-driven. Some may even perceive you as a bit dogmatic or closed-minded. **You can come across as skeptical and you're likely averse to change.** This means that you may have a precise or particular way an Act of Service is provided to you. Are you finicky? Maybe. And, if your loved ones are motivated but still struggling to speak your Love Language, perhaps that's something you need to own. Acknowledging your lack of openness, and being a bit self-deprecating about it, can go a long way in building better connections.

Carefree ⟷ Dependable

Tendency to be organized and diligent

CAREFREE — DEPENDABLE

Some people are hardwired to be driven. Some are more lackadaisical. You are somewhere in the middle. You appreciate goal setting and you value diligence. But these qualities don't always come easy for you - especially if your loved ones are not feeding your soul through Acts of Service. **But when they help your life to be a little easier, you get in gear.** Motivation often kicks in and you become more responsible and goal-directed. In short, Acts of Service not only fills your Love Tank, **it can ignite your drive and self-discipline.** It energizes the conscientious part of your personality.

LOVE 11

ETHAN AND THE 5 LOVE LANGUAGES Part Two

Cool ⟷ Warm

Tendency to trust and agree with others

COOL — WARM

When it comes to social sensitivity, people tend to fall along a continuum of being highly sensitive, polite, and cheerful on one end, and opinionated, disagreeable and harsh on the other end. **You are in the middle. But when your Love Tank begins to fill with Acts of Service™, you lean into your better self.** You become more cooperative and less competitive. You become more trusting and less skeptical. More empathic, less manipulative. In short, you become more inclined to put others needs before your own.

Now that you have information about yourself on these four dimensions of personality, review each of them and identify what you agree with most. What resonates most for you? What do you disagree with? Feel free to scratch off any content that is not helpful, however, ask a loved one you trust to weigh in before you do.

Your Emotional Wellbeing

How you think and feel about yourself

[illegible] name of the game when it comes to thriving relationships. When you grow, your relationships grow.

We all have work to do when it comes to being the best version of ourselves. Nobody can do this internal work for you. Nobody in your life is a shortcut to personal wholeness. They can help you, as iron sharpens iron, but ultimately, **you are responsible for your own emotional wellbeing.** This work may be the most important thing you ever do for your relationships. This section will heighten your self-awareness when it comes to your overall emotional wellbeing.

EVEN-TEMPERED
CALM
RESILIENT
CONFIDENT

IRRITABLE
WORRIED
REACTIVE
SELF-CONSCIOUS

While you likely contend with your share of negative thinking (and perhaps stress and anxiety), you are likely benefiting from emotional self-care. Room for improvement? Sure. But you're not likely to suffer extreme sensitivity or emotional drama. This means that Acts of Service can be incredibly uplifting for you. You recognize the heart-felt motive and sacrifice behind them. In fact, these kind acts likely motivate you to learn how to better speak the Love Languages of your loved ones.

What are you currently doing to improve your own emotional wellbeing? What is one practical step you can take this week toward achieving this? How might that improve your relationships?

LOVE 12

1. Introversion ⟷ Extroversion

This scale reflects a client's preferred social energy. The narrative on the report connects their tendencies (e.g., outgoing or reserved) with how they may receive and interpret specific Love Languages.

2. Cautious ←→ Curious

This dimension relates to openness, risk tolerance, and creative flexibility. Clients who score more cautiously may resist relational spontaneity or interpret certain expressions of love through a more pragmatic lens.

3. Carefree ←→ Dependable

A reflection of conscientiousness, this scale highlights a client's level of structure, discipline, and personal responsibility. The narrative helps the client consider how this orientation may influence how they offer love—and how they expect to receive it.

The second page continues the personality exploration with a fourth dimension:

4. Cool ←→ Warm

This spectrum explores social sensitivity and emotional accessibility. Clients who lean warm may be naturally empathetic and affirming, while cooler-leaning individuals may be more skeptical or reserved—something that can influence how emotional connection is initiated and maintained.

Each of these dimensions is anchored with examples of how the client's personality traits influence and shape their experience with their primary Love Language.

The lower portion of this page is dedicated to the Emotional Wellbeing section, and it gently acknowledges that emotional health is the foundation of strong relationships. Regardless of one's Love Language, a person who is highly reactive, anxious, irritable, or self-protective will likely struggle to give and receive love—even if their partner is speaking the right language fluently.

That's the point of this section. It introduces a powerful but subtle shift: *Love is not just about how others show up for you. It's about how well you're able to show up in your own emotional skin.*

For coaches, this page is essential—not as a detour from the Love Languages, but as a reminder that no language of love can flourish in soil that's chronically stressed, guarded, or emotionally depleted. This is the part of the report that shifts the conversation from preference to readiness. And in some coaching journeys, that's where real change begins.

Page 13: Your Dialect

This page is one of the most interactive and empowering features of the Premium Assessment. It marks the moment when insight becomes articulation and the client doesn't just understand their Love Language *in theory* but how it looks *in practice*.

Titled "Your Dialect," this page offers a curated menu of behavior-specific options tied to the client's primary Love Language, and it guides them through a personal selection process:

ETHAN'S DIALECT — PHYSICAL TOUCH™

ABOUT

The better a person understands the nuances of your Love Language®, the more they will speak the language of your heart. Helping others know your Love Language is helpful. But helping them to speak it with **your particular dialect can be transforming.** Your dialect has to do with personal and nuanced behaviors that fill up your Love Tank. Below is a list of concrete and specific expressions for Physical Touch. Some will resonate with you more than others.

Identify a handful of behaviors from this list that are especially likely to fill up your Love Tank. Choose as many as you like.

COMFORTING TOUCH
- Comforting arm around the shoulder during tough times
- Rest their head on your shoulder
- Offer a supportive touch during moments of vulnerability
- A quick shoulder squeeze as a sign of solidarity
- Brush away a tear to offer comfort
- Write your own

AFFECTIONATE TOUCH
- Cuddle on the couch during a movie night
- Give and receive frequent kisses
- Sit close and lean on each other
- Walking with arm over your shoulder
- Share a gentle touch while watching a sunset
- Write your own

PLAYFUL TOUCH
- Engage in physical games or sports together
- Spin and dance with each other during a favorite song
- Playfully tickle or caress each other
- Lightly tapping your nose with a playful gesture
- Playfully wrestle or have a pillow fight
- Write your own

PROTECTIVE TOUCH
- Hold hands during a thunderstorm
- Shield each other from the rain under a shared umbrella
- A soft touch on the lower back to guide through a crowd
- Offer a hand to hold during a suspenseful movie
- Walk arm-in-arm, providing stability on uneven paths
- Write your own

ROMANTIC TOUCH
- Share a passionate and romantic kiss
- Trace circles on each other's palms while holding hands
- Slowly dance together
- Share a lingering and affectionate embrace
- Nestle into each other's arms by a fireside
- Write your own

EXPRESSIVE TOUCH
- A soft pat on the back to acknowledge a job well done
- An energetic fist bump to celebrate a shared victory
- Interlocking pinky fingers as a promise or pledge of mutual trust
- A secret handshake to greet a long-time friend
- A high five to signal excitement about the start of a new project
- Write your own

RESTORATIVE TOUCH
- Brushing or playing with hair to relax and unwind before sleep
- Offer soothing back scratches for relaxation
- Gently massaging temples to ease a headache
- Write your own

Now that you've selected the items that are part of your dialect, circle your top three - the ones that make you feel most loved when you experience them with others. How might you convey to specific loved ones the importance of these to you?

LOVE 13

- First, clients identify the specific actions or expressions that are most likely to fill their love tank—real-life behaviors that reflect their preferred dialects.
- Then, they're invited to circle their top three, prioritizing the gestures that make the biggest emotional impact.
- Finally, the page prompts them to consider how they might share these preferences with loved ones, encouraging relational clarity and vulnerability.

Each list is tailored to the client's highest-scoring language and broken into refined subcategories. Clients can also add their own options, reinforcing that love is personal, and language becomes fluent only when tailored to individual experience.

This page functions like a mirror and a map: a *mirror* that helps the client see what deeply resonates in the details of love, and a *map* for others, making it easier to love the client well with emotional precision.

For coaches, this is a turning point. The selections made here often illuminate why previous attempts to love someone fell short. They also provide a starting point for helping clients communicate clearly and ask for what they need.

The next page (Section 7) extends this work by helping clients translate these insights into the specific relationships they care about most.

Page 14: Your Love Language in Action

After identifying their personal dialect on the previous page, the client is now guided to consider how their Love Language plays out differently across relationships. This page marks the transition from self-reflection to interpersonal clarity—from *"this is what I need"* to *"this is how that looks in real life, with real people."*

The page invites the client to list up to four key relationships—typically a

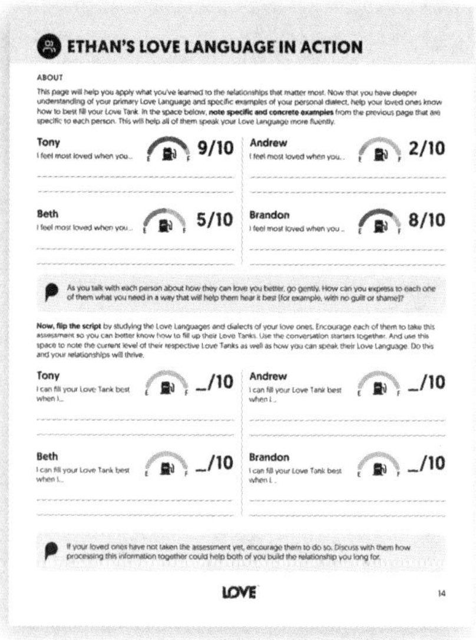

ETHAN'S LOVE LANGUAGE IN ACTION

ABOUT

This page will help you apply what you've learned to the relationships that matter most. Now that you have deeper understanding of your primary Love Language and specific examples of your personal dialect, help your loved ones know how to best fill your Love Tank. In the space below, **note specific and concrete examples** from the previous page that are specific to each person. This will help all of them speak your Love Language more fluently.

Tony 9/10
I feel most loved when you...

Andrew 2/10
I feel most loved when you...

Beth 5/10
I feel most loved when you...

Brandon 8/10
I feel most loved when you...

As you talk with each person about how they can love you better, go gently. How can you express to each one of them what you need in a way that will help them hear it best (for example, with no guilt or shame)?

Now, flip the script by studying the Love Languages and dialects of your love ones. Encourage each of them to take this assessment so you can better know how to fill up their Love Tanks. Use the conversation starters together. And use this space to note the current level of their respective Love Tanks as well as how you can speak their Love Language. Do this and your relationships will thrive.

Tony _/10
I can fill your Love Tank best when I...

Andrew _/10
I can fill your Love Tank best when I...

Beth _/10
I can fill your Love Tank best when I...

Brandon _/10
I can fill your Love Tank best when I...

If your loved ones have not taken the assessment yet, encourage them to do so. Discuss with them how processing this information together could help both of you build the relationship you long for.

LOVE 14

partner, child, parent, or close friend (the same ones they noted on the love tank page of the report)—and write down how they most want to receive love from each person, specifically within the frame of their primary Love Language and dialect.

This page reinforces a crucial coaching truth: Love is not one-size-fits-all—even from one relationship to the next.

Bonus Page: How to Love [Client's Name]

At the very end of the report, the client receives a personalized summary titled *"How to Love [Client's Name]."* It's intentionally designed to be shared, posted, or handed off—a visual snapshot of the client's emotional blueprint that others can easily reference.

Unlike the previous pages, which focus on self-discovery and reflection, this page is outward-facing. It's written for others in clear, direct language, offering practical and emotionally specific suggestions for how to love the client well.

The tone is encouraging, not prescriptive. It reads like a relational invitation: "Here's what matters most to me. If you want to love me well, start here."

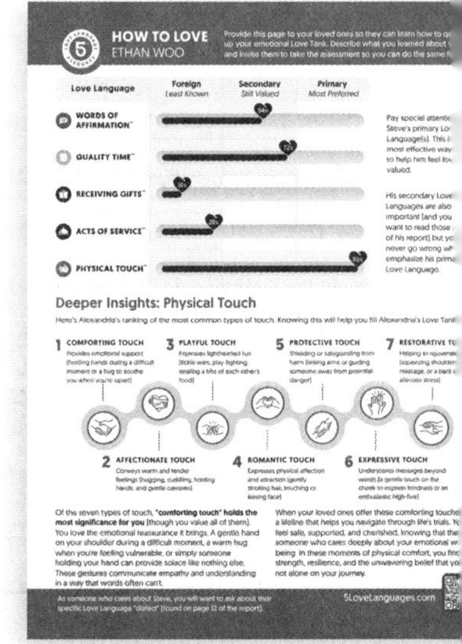

HOW TO LOVE
ETHAN WOO

Love Language	Foreign *Least Known*	Secondary *Still Valued*	Primary *Most Preferred*
WORDS OF AFFIRMATION™			
QUALITY TIME™			
RECEIVING GIFTS™			
ACTS OF SERVICE™			
PHYSICAL TOUCH™			

Deeper Insights: Physical Touch

1 COMFORTING TOUCH

2 AFFECTIONATE TOUCH

3 PLAYFUL TOUCH

4 ROMANTIC TOUCH

5 PROTECTIVE TOUCH

6 EXPRESSIVE TOUCH

Of the seven types of touch, **"comforting touch" holds the most significance for you** (though you value all of them). You love the emotional reassurance it brings. A gentle hand on your shoulder during a difficult moment, a warm hug when you're feeling vulnerable, or simply someone holding your hand can provide solace like nothing else. These gestures communicate empathy and understanding in a way that words often can't.

As someone who cares about Steve, you will want to ask about their specific Love Language "dialect" (found on page 12 of the report).

5LoveLanguages.com

It's the kind of page that can be posted on a fridge, taped inside a journal, or sent to a partner as a gentle but honest road map. It doesn't demand, it guides. And in many relationships, it can serve as a bridge-builder during emotionally dry or confusing seasons.

At its core, this bonus page reinforces one of the deepest hopes in any relationship: to be known, understood, and loved—not merely in general, but specifically.

COACHING
INTRO

ETHAN WOO

A Note to the Coach

This version of the report is designed specifically for you—the coach. On each page, you'll see a scaled-down view of what your client is seeing, surrounded by tools and insights created to help you coach with excellence. This guide will help you bring your client's Love Language results to life with confidence and clarity—turning awareness into real relationship growth.

Warmup

Each page begins with a brief section designed to ground you before your session. These notes connect relevant chapters from your primary resources: The 5 Love Languages, The Love Language That Matters Most and The 5 Love Language Coaching Handbook. They give you context, key terms, and research that deepens your understanding for a better session.

Tailored Tips

This section is the heart of your coaching guide. It will help you interpret what each page means for your client and offer practical direction for your dialogue. It's designed to help you create "aha" moments that move your client from awareness to action.

- Listen for themes, not just answers. Notice patterns in what your client values or avoids —it often reveals where love is felt or missed.
- Reflect before you redirect. Mirror what your client says before offering insight; this helps them feel understood and ready for growth.
- Aim for clarity, not complexity. Help your client leave each session with one clear takeaway or next step they can immediately apply.

Review these notes before each session, but let the conversation stay fluid each point is meant to spark curiosity, not provide a script.

Prompts

invite your client to think aloud, deepen awareness, and apply insight in real time.

Coaching Assignment

At the end of each section, you'll find a short coaching assignment. This helps your client carry the insight beyond the session- translating discovery into practice. Keep it light and doable; even a small step reinforces lasting growth.

LOVE Coaching 1

The Coach's Version of the Premium Assessment

As a certified Love Language coach, you'll notice that the 5 Love Languages Premium Assessment includes a **Coach's Version**, a companion report designed exclusively for you. This version is typically not shared with the client, but there's nothing secretive here. It's built to support *your* preparation, *your* discernment, and *your* confidence as you guide the conversation.

The Coach's Version goes beyond results and summaries. It offers curated insights tailored to the specific pages and profiles you are walking through in a given session, along with discussion starters, coaching prompts, and interpretive guidance that help you know not just *what* the results say but *how* to work with them. Think of it as a behind-the-scenes view that helps you anticipate key moments, name patterns with clarity, and ask questions that open the conversation.

COACHING
WORDS OF AFFIRMATION

ETHAN WOO

Warmup

Chapter 5 takes a deep dive into love tanks and will give you terms to help you describe nuances.

Chapter 4 provides research supporting the concept and several pragmatic coaching tips.

Revising the opening section of Chapter 1 to see how Dr. Chapman introduced the concept.

Tailored Tips

As Ethan's secondary Love Language, Words of Affirmation serves as an emotional enhancer—it doesn't define connection but powerfully fills his love tank when expressed in the right dialect.

- Note Ethan's dialect spread: Encouragement (53%), Appreciation (35%), and Compliments (22%). His strongest response to Encouragement suggests he feels most loved when others express belief in his growth or perseverance—not just when they notice achievements.
- Explore how Appreciation validates effort and reliability, while Compliments meet the need to be

How do you tend to affirm others—and how does that compare to what you most long to hear yourself?"

es, or verbal remarks—and write briefly about affirmation this week that mirrors what he most language refines how he receives it

6

COACHING
LOVE LANGUAGES OVERVIEW

ETHAN WOO

Warmup

Chapter 5 takes a deep dive into love tanks and will give you terms to help you describe nuances.

Chapter 4 provides research supporting the concept and several pragmatic coaching tips.

Revising the opening section of Chapter 1 to see how Dr. Chapman introduced the concept.

Tailored Tips

This page reveals more than Ethan's preferences—it's a map of how he regulates connection. Invite him to view these five scores not as labels, but as his personal rhythm of giving and receiving love.

- Notice the spread between his top and bottom scores. A narrow gap suggests relational adaptability; a wide gap signals possible blind spots in empathy.
- Explore whether his primary language compensates for unmet needs in childhood or current relationships—it often does.
- Discuss his lowest language as a growth edge, not a deficit. Mastery there expands his emotional range and resilience.
- Identify relational asymmetry: where Ethan offers one language but desires another in return. Highlight how this mismatch can quietly fuel unmet expectations.

personality chart, will help clients see how they're wired to love and how they're wired to miss it.

Prompts

1 "When you look at your five Love Languages as a whole, what story do they tell about how you've learned to give and receive love over time?"

2 "Where do you notice a disconnect between the love you most express and the love you most crave—and what might that reveal about your current relationship

Next Steps

Invite Ethan to trace one meaningful relationship through the lens of his five Love Languages. Have him note which languages shaped connection and which went unspoken. The goal is to see how he instinctively gives love versus how he feels it most—because insight begins where those two diverge.

LOVE Coaching 4

Used well, this report allows you to stay fully present with your client while still drawing on a deep well of support. It's there to sharpen your instincts, expand your options, and help you pace the session wisely. The client experiences insight and discovery; you experience confidence and clarity. That's the value of the Coach's Version of the report, supporting your work without ever stepping into the spotlight.

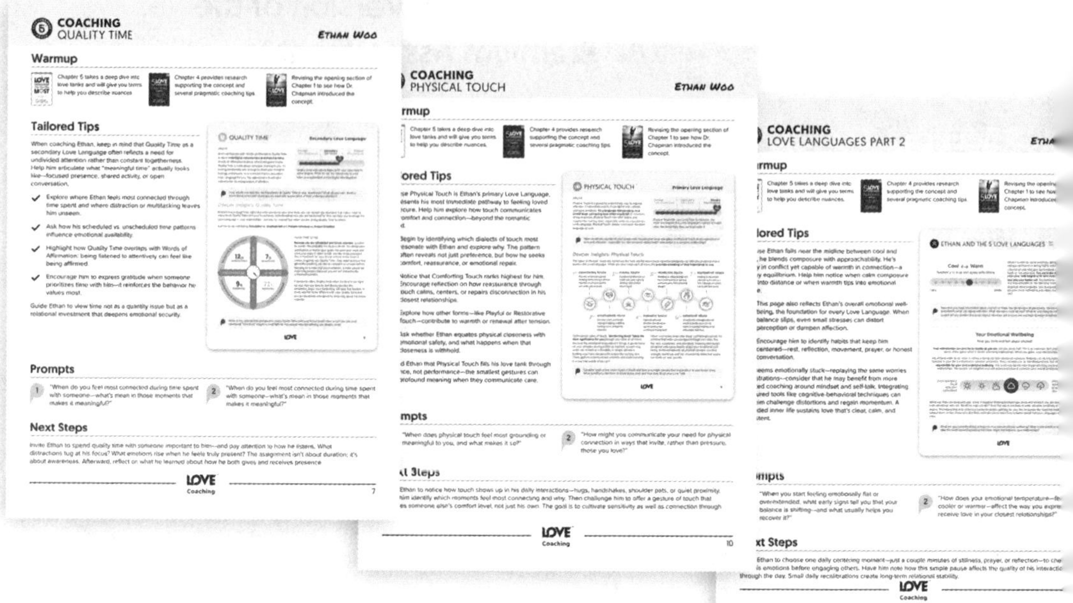

Summary

The 5 Love Languages Premium Assessment offers far more than a label. It provides clients with a personalized, emotionally intelligent road map for understanding how they give and receive love—layered with dialects, personality patterns, skill indicators, and relational insights.

Each section of the report is designed with coaching in mind:

- It begins with clarity (Love Language rankings)
- It deepens with nuance (dialects and behavioral specifics)
- And it broadens into self-awareness (emotional wellbeing and relational skills)

This tool is not meant to categorize people. It's designed to humanize them, to bring emotional needs into language, behavior, and reflection. For coaches, this chapter serves as an orientation, not on how to fix or advise but on how to see clients more fully.

The next step is to turn this insight into movement, which begins in the next chapter as we explore how to translate assessment results into a personalized coaching plan.

QUESTIONS TO PONDER

1. At this stage, which part of the report do I personally find most insightful?
2. Are there sections I tend to skim over? What might I be missing in those areas?
3. How comfortable am I discussing topics like emotional wellbeing, personality traits, or low skill scores with clients?
4. When I walk through the report with a client, do I give space for reflection or rush to interpretation?
5. How might I better introduce the assessment in a way that sets the tone for safety, curiosity, and growth?

Chapter 14

Walking Through the Assessment Results with Clients

Rachel stared at the page for a long time before speaking. Then, barely above a whisper, she said, "I've never had something describe me so clearly."

Her Love Language wasn't new. She'd taken the free online quiz before and gotten the same result: Words of Affirmation. But this time was different. Seeing her dialect laid out—specifically "Encouragement" and "Appreciation"—felt like someone had finally connected the dots she hadn't been able to name. It wasn't just *what* she needed, it was *why* it mattered.

Then came the moment of impact. She looked up at her coach and said, "I think this explains why I've been angry for so long. I kept trying to tell him what I needed, but I didn't have the words until now."

That's the power of a well-paced walk-through. It's not just about reviewing results—it's about holding space for clients to recognize themselves, maybe for the first time, in the language of love and emotional need. The assessment gives you the material. But it's the coaching presence that allows it to land.

This chapter is designed to help you facilitate those moments with skill and care. It's not about delivering a perfect interpretation or rushing toward action. It's about walking beside your client as they begin to hear the deeper story their report is telling—one page at a time. And if you are using the online video certification to become a Certified Love Language Coach, you'll discover that the video training walks through each of these pages in more detail.

You'll learn how to guide clients through each section of the Premium Assessment with emotional safety, clarity, and permission. And you'll practice framing your role not as an expert reading a report but as a companion helping someone decode the language of their own heart.

Inviting the Client to Take the Assessment

It begins with you inviting your client to take the assessment. Your online coaching dashboard makes this easy. Here's a simple way to frame the invite to your client that helps them understand why it matters:

"I'd love for you to take the 5 Love Languages Premium Assessment before our next session. It goes beyond just identifying your top language—it gives us insight into how you personally receive love best, and what specific behaviors tend to fill (or drain) your emotional tank. It helps us coach with more clarity and less guesswork."

Be sure to:

- Invite them to take the assessment through your coaching dashboard
- Let them know approximately how long it takes (typically 15 minutes)
- Encourage them to take it when they can be focused, not rushed

If you're coaching a couple, encourage both partners to take it separately (they'll each receive a separate invite from you to take the assessment) without talking about it together until after they've completed it.

Keep in mind that you will have access to your Coach's Version of their reports in your dashboard once they complete the questions. In fact, you will be notified as soon as it's ready to review. This makes it easy to review it on your own in preparation for the coaching session.

Creating the Right Environment

Whether clients arrive eager, uncertain, or quietly skeptical, your job is to set the tone before you even open the first page. This isn't a reading. It's a conversation, and the way you begin determines how open, reflective, and emotionally honest the client is likely to be (Rogers, 1959).

That's why your first role as a coach is not to interpret the report—it's to create a safe, reflective space where they can process what the report stirs up. This approach accomplishes three things:

1. It centers the client's voice before yours.
2. It shifts the goal from analyzing to reflecting.
3. It creates emotional permission for nuance, surprise, or disagreement.

Frame the session as a discovery—not a diagnosis. You're not trying to confirm the "correctness" of their results but to explore the emotional meaning behind them. Think of it as a discussion starter as much as diagnostic. This also softens defensiveness, especially in areas like low love skill scores or personality descriptors that may touch a nerve.

It can be helpful to remind the client: "This isn't a test. There's no pass/fail. This is a snapshot of what might be most meaningful to you when it comes to giving and receiving love."

That reminder positions the entire session as an invitation—one that encourages curiosity over certainty, grace over judgment, and presence over performance.

Walking Through the Report, Page by Page

Once the session begins and the client has their report in hand, the temptation might be to dive straight into interpretation. But a more fruitful approach is to move through the report slowly and relationally—treating each page not as something to explain, but as something to explore *together*.

What follows isn't a script, but a suggested flow. You can spread this over several sessions. There's no pressure. The goal is not to rush through insight but to listen deeply—to what surprises the client, what validates their experience, and what catches them emotionally off guard.

Page 3: Your Love Languages

Begin with the most familiar territory: the client's top, secondary, and lowest Love Languages. Invite curiosity, not confirmation.

Try questions like:

- "What did you expect to see here, and what caught you off guard?"
- "When do you feel this language most clearly in your current relationships?"
- "What's a moment when this Love Language was missing or misunderstood?"

Pay attention to the percentile scores—they can help uncover emotional intensity. A 93% in Physical Touch speaks differently than a 65%.

Page 4: Your Love Tank

This page offers a snapshot of how the client is currently experiencing love across key relationships. Invite reflection:

- "What fills your tank most consistently?"
- "What kinds of things drain it—subtly or significantly?"
- "When you look at the four relationships you listed, which one surprises you most?"

This isn't a page for blame—it's a gentle check-in. Treat the love tank as emotional data. Sometimes even *naming* what's empty is the first step to refilling it. There's more to come on the love tank metaphor in an upcoming chapter.

Pages 5–9: The 5 Love Languages (Dialect Breakdowns)

Spend time here. Each page unpacks *how* a Love Language is most meaningfully experienced. Ask:

- "Which of these dialects feels most like you?"
- "Do any of them surprise or confuse you?"
- "Have you ever tried to express this, only to feel misunderstood?"

If the client has a partner who shares the same primary language, this is where subtle mismatches become visible. "We both like Quality Time, but I need it to be spontaneous. He wants it scheduled and purposeful." That's not failure, it's dialect divergence.

Page 10: Your Love Skills

Approach this page with sensitivity. The scores in Curiosity, Listening, and Empathy often illuminate *why* love might not be landing, even if effort is high.

You might say: "These aren't right or wrong scores—they're relational muscles. Some might be stronger than others right now. What do you notice?"

Be cautious not to assume low skill scores indicate disinterest. More often, they point to emotional fatigue, unawareness, or habits formed in early relationships.

Pages 11–12: You and The 5 Love Languages (Personality & Wellbeing)

These pages provide temperament and wellbeing context. You might ask:

- "Does this description of your personality feel accurate?"
- "How do you think your emotional state affects how you receive love—or how open you are to it?"

Pay attention to the emotional wellbeing spectrum—this can be a key indicator of whether the client is currently resourced enough to receive love, even if it's being expressed well. More to come on this in a moment.

Page 13: Your Dialect

These are two of the most actionable and emotionally clarifying pages. Use them to validate what the client already knows intuitively:

- "Are these behaviors ones that you've already asked for? If so, how?"
- "Which of the relationships listed here feels most out of sync—and why?"
- "Is there a conversation you've been wanting to have but haven't had language for until now?"

These pages help the client personalize the results. They are the bridge between awareness and action.

Page 14: Your Love Language in Action

If the client feels safe and open, end here. This is their invitation to others. It's also a mirror of how well they understand themselves.

You might say: "How does it feel to read this page—as if someone else were reading it to love you better?"

Some clients will light up. Others may tear up. This is where the coaching posture matters most. You're not asking them to evaluate the page—you're giving them space to feel seen.

Once again, this isn't a diagnosis as much as it is a dialogue. Let the client lead. Let emotion surface. And let the silence be part of the story.

Reading Between the Lines

Not everything that matters in the report is printed in bold. Some of the most important coaching insights aren't in the scores or categories—they emerge in the pauses, the emotional reactions, the sideways comments, or the body language when a client lands on a page they weren't expecting.

This section is about cultivating the art of *interpretive listening*—the ability to read emotional subtext, notice internal tension, and gently reflect what may be going unsaid.

Emotional Dissonance: When the Report and the Client Don't Match

Sometimes a client will say something like, *"I know my top language is Physical Touch, but I still don't feel connected,"* or *"I scored high in affirmation, but compliments just make me uncomfortable."*

That's not a contradiction. That's where coaching begins.

These are signs of emotional friction, where desire and receptivity are out of sync (Neff & Germer, 2018). Instead of correcting or reinterpreting, try opening the conversation:

- "It sounds like that result doesn't quite line up with your experience—tell me more."
- "Have you had times where someone tried to love you in that way and it missed the mark?"
- "Is there any part of this that feels vulnerable, awkward, or unfamiliar?"

Your role isn't to resolve the contradiction. It's to hold space for it—because in that tension, clients often discover the story beneath the score.

Language Gaps Between Partners

If you're walking through the report with a couple—or reviewing both partners' assessments separately—watch for assumed alignment. A couple may both score highest in Quality Time but be *living out entirely different dialects.*

One partner may light up at long, meandering conversations ("Dreaming"), while the other finds deep meaning in doing chores side by side ("Planning").

The deeper work is not in saying, "You both need Quality Time." It's in helping them name what it *actually looks like* for each person.

The Emotional Wellbeing Spectrum: Readiness to Receive

Nowhere is the "between the lines" work more critical than in the Emotional Wellbeing section of the report. This part doesn't just reflect how a client feels—it offers insight into whether they are resourced enough to receive (and give) love.

A client who is consistently anxious, irritable, reactive, or withdrawn may intellectually recognize their Love Language, but still feel emotionally blocked when it's expressed. It's not about stubbornness or resistance—it's about emotional safety and internal capacity.

You might say: "Sometimes when we're depleted or emotionally stretched thin, even love that's offered well can be hard to absorb. Does any part of that feel true for you right now?"

This isn't a detour from Love Language work; it's foundational to it.

If a client is emotionally offline—caught in survival mode, grief, or chronic relational stress—your coaching focus may need to shift toward restoring regulation and trust before jumping into behavioral change (Kashdan et al., 2011).

Clients often feel ashamed when they "should" feel loved but don't. Your attuned presence here allows them to be honest without shame—and honesty is always the beginning of healing.

Of course, as a coach, you are not expected to carry everything. If a client's emotional wellbeing appears severely compromised—marked by persistent anxiety, emotional numbness, depression, or trauma responses—it's important to recognize when you may be out of your depth. There is no shame in referring a client to a psychologist, counselor, or medical professional who can provide the specialized care they need. In fact, it's one of the most loving, responsible moves you can make. Once more: Don't try to help where you're not qualified.

Tone, Timing, and Tenderness

Remember, clients aren't just processing information, they're engaging emotional history. Some pages will validate. Others may sting. Your ability to slow down, attune to their response, and *not rush to insight* is what builds trust.

What matters most is not what you notice—it's how gently you process it.

Try: "Can I reflect something I'm noticing?" or "There's no pressure to respond now—I just want to name that this part seemed to land differently."

This posture lets you coach in real time without crossing into interpretation that feels invasive or premature.

In the quiet spaces between scores, clients often hear themselves most clearly. As a coach, reading between the lines is not about decoding—it's about creating room for resonance. It's listening not only to what the report says, but to how the client responds to what it says.

And when you do that with care, what starts as a report becomes something far more powerful: a relational mirror, framed in compassion.

When the Client Doesn't Identify with Their Top Love Language

Every now and then, a client will read their results, look up, and say something like, *"I don't know . . . this doesn't really feel like me."*

This can be a disorienting moment for them—and a revealing one for you. It's not a flaw in the assessment. It's a signal that the client may be bumping into a blind spot, a defense, or even a gap between their *idealized self* and their *actual experience of emotional need.*

As a coach, your task isn't to convince the client that the report is right. It's to stay curious with them:

- "What part of it feels off?"
- "Does this language feel unfamiliar, or maybe even uncomfortable to receive?"
- "Have you had experiences where someone tried to love you this way, and it missed the mark?"

Sometimes, the disconnect is about emotional readiness (Siegel, 2010). A client may have long dismissed a particular Love Language because it feels too vulnerable. A low-touch client might be surprised to score high in Physical Touch—until they realize they've gone years without safe, comforting affection.

Other times, it's about seasonality. Love Languages can shift in intensity depending on stress levels, life transitions, or relational roles. A highly verbal client might suddenly crave Acts of Service during a new season of parenthood—not because their core self changed but because their capacity did.

And occasionally, it's because the client may have misunderstood some of the directions. That's okay. Invite them to make meaning of the report they have—not to accept it as gospel, but to use it as a mirror that might show one angle of the truth. And, of course, you can suggest they take it again after some time has passed.

When you help clients feel safe to disagree, you empower them to stay engaged with the process. You're not asking for agreement. You're cultivating self-reflective ownership—which, in the end, is what coaching is all about.

Summary

As a coach, your role in walking through the report isn't to deliver answers but to hold space for discovery. Page by page, you invite your client to explore emotional preferences, name longings, and reflect on patterns that may have gone unspoken for years.

The walk-through is not a test review. It's a conversation. It's where insight meets presence, and where a client's emotional world starts to come into focus—not just through what they say, but through what they feel, hesitate over, or finally name.

Ultimately, the walk-through isn't about the data. It's about connection. And when done well, it can be the *first time a client feels fully seen—not as a personality type, but as a person who longs to love and be loved well.*

QUESTIONS TO PONDER

1. When I walk through a report with a client, do I tend to explain or invite?
2. Which section of the report do I feel most confident guiding clients through? Which feels more uncertain or underdeveloped?
3. Have I ever dismissed or moved too quickly through a moment when a client disagreed with their results? What could I have done differently?
4. How do I handle emotionally charged discoveries during a walk-through, especially when they're unexpected?
5. What's one thing I can do in my next session to make the report walk-through more emotionally safe, spacious, or client-led?

Chapter 15

Using the Premium Assessment to Support Growth Over Time

By the time a client has walked through their 5 Love Languages Premium Assessment results with you, they've likely had a few "aha" moments. They've seen themselves in the language of love, recognized the behaviors that resonate, and maybe even felt the sting of how long those needs have gone unmet. That's a powerful moment. But it's not the finish line. It's the trailhead.

As a coach, your task now shifts. You're no longer walking through the report—you're helping the client walk forward with it. Once you have completed your experience together of unpacking the pages of the report (as outlined in the previous chapter), you can pass along their report to them for future use and growth. Why? Because a map is only useful if you take the journey. Insight without action tends to fade. Even the most emotionally accurate report can sit in a drawer while the old patterns quietly return.

This chapter is about coaching for sustainable change. You'll learn how to:

- Translate a client's dialect into daily relational habits
- Help clients set realistic, emotionally anchored goals
- Revisit the report over time as a checkpoint for growth
- Recognize when it's time to shift direction—or deepen a practice
- Equip clients to use the assessment as a tool for emotional fluency in all areas of life

The Premium Assessment is not a one-and-done resource. It's a relational framework that can evolve with your client's growth, season, and self-awareness. Your role is to keep that framework alive, dynamic, and practical—so that love becomes not just a language, but a lifestyle.

Translating Report Results Into Actionable Goals

Insight is valuable. But insight alone doesn't change relationships. Coaches know this well: Clients often nod in recognition, feel genuinely moved by a discovery, and still fall back into the same old relational routines. Why? Because *knowing* something is not the same as *doing* something consistently, especially when emotions, habits, or past hurts are in play.

This section equips you, the coach, to bridge that gap. The goal is to help clients take what they've discovered in their assessment and translate it into small, concrete, emotionally meaningful actions they can begin practicing right away.

1. Start With One Relationship

Begin by asking your client to choose one relationship they want to focus on. Often this is a romantic partner—but it could also be a child, parent, or close friend. Narrowing the focus helps the client avoid overwhelm and gives the coaching process a relational anchor point.

Ask:

- "Which relationship feels most in need of attention or intentionality right now?"
- "Where do you feel the biggest gap is between what you give and what's received—or what you crave and what's actually happening?"

Starting small increases follow-through. Research on behavior change consistently shows that focusing on one domain at a time leads to greater success and sustainability than trying to apply insight everywhere at once (Fogg, 2020; Duhigg, 2012).

Whichever one they choose, that other person in the relationship might want to take the Premium Assessment as well.

2. Use the Dialect and Key Relationships Pages as Action Templates

The most practical pages for goal-setting are:

- **"Your Dialect" (p. 13)**: where clients selected specific behaviors that resonate
- **"Key Relationships" (p. 14)**: where they named how they'd like to receive love from specific people

These two pages offer a ready-made map for what to *do*. But your role is to slow it down and coach toward precision. Ask things like: "You mentioned wanting more 'protective touch'—how might that show up in a normal week?"

The more emotionally vivid the action, the more likely it is to feel meaningful and stick. This aligns with research from self-determination theory, which suggests that goals tied to emotional needs and internal values are more likely to lead to lasting change (Ryan & Deci, 2000).

3. Set the Scale to "Small but Consistent"

The goal isn't to overhaul a relationship overnight. It's to build a rhythm of intentionality. That's where coaching becomes a powerful accountability structure. Invite the client to choose:

- **One micro-habit** to practice regularly (e.g., "Send one note of appreciation each week")
- **One moment of intentionality** to initiate (e.g., "Plan a 15-minute check-in each Sunday")

The smaller the action, the greater the likelihood it will be done (Fogg, 2020). Behavior change is not about dramatic declarations; it's about emotional deposits that, over time, create a new pattern of connection.

4. Name Emotional Barriers Before They Become Obstacles

Finally, help your client anticipate what might get in the way:

- "What's the hardest part about actually doing this?"
- "What's a pattern you've seen in yourself when you want to change something in a relationship?"

Encourage honesty, not performance. Some clients will say, "I just forget." Others will say, "I'm scared it won't be received." Naming the resistance makes space for compassion and for planning around it.

Helping clients normalize resistance and keep the focus on practice over perfection increases engagement and reduces self-judgment (Neff & Germer, 2018).

Insight without follow-through fades quickly. But when you help a client connect their emotional discoveries to concrete, doable actions—especially in the context of one important relationship—you build a bridge between awareness and change. That's where coaching becomes not just helpful, but transformational.

Dialect-Specific Coaching Strategies

Understanding a client's primary Love Language is helpful. But where meaningful coaching really begins is in helping clients understand and act on their dialect—the emotionally specific way they prefer to receive love within that broader category. Dialects give you coaching precision. They translate "I need more Quality Time" into "I crave unhurried conversation without distraction."

This section will help you coach clients toward practical, emotionally resonant behavior changes—rooted in their dialect and aligned with their real-life context.

Words of Affirmation: Speak the Right Words, the Right Way
Dialect coaching themes:

- *Encouragement*: Coach clients to express belief in their partner's potential, especially in times of doubt.
- *Appreciation*: Coach around noticing effort and naming it (e.g., "I see how hard you're working for our family").
- *Compliments*: Help clients articulate what they admire with specificity—not just "You look nice," but "That color brings out your eyes."

Coaching caution: Some clients feel awkward using expressive language. Normalize that. Start with small phrases or written notes if verbal feels unnatural.

Quality Time: Match the Rhythm, Not Just the Minutes
Dialect coaching themes:

- *Improvising* (spontaneous presence): Brainstorm flexible, screen-free ways to be present.
- *Managing* (structured connection): Help clients block protected time for shared focus.

- *Planning* (future-oriented): Lean into shared routines or goal-setting as connection rituals.
- *Dreaming* (visionary, hopeful): Coach around building in time for "what if" conversations or shared imagination.

Coaching caution: Time isn't always about quantity. It's about attunement—showing up mentally, not just physically. Research emphasizes that turning toward bids for connection (even small ones) builds long-term intimacy (Gottman & Silver, 1999).

Acts of Service: Know the Meaning Behind the Motion
Dialect coaching themes:

- *Saves Time*: Look for tasks that free the partner from mental or logistical load.
- *Alleviates Stress*: Ask what tasks consistently weigh them down—and how to help.
- *Instills Security*: Focus on follow-through, reliability, and anticipation.
- *Conveys Care*: Emphasize unexpected gestures that communicate, "I'm thinking of you."

Coaching caution: Especially with women, be mindful of over-functioning or invisible labor dynamics. Normalize asking, *"What would feel helpful—not just done, but appreciated?"*

Receiving Gifts: Make the Gesture Match the Emotion
Dialect coaching themes:

- *Sensible*: Keep it practical, but emotionally meaningful (e.g., a favorite snack or candle).
- *Functional*: Provide tools that empower or support their day-to-day life.
- *Fanciful*: Coach clients to save up for larger, symbolic gestures that reflect emotional investment.
- *Sentimental*: Encourage personalized items, photos, or memory-based mementos.

Coaching caution: It's not about money—it's about *symbolism*. Research shows that gift-giving strengthens bonds when the giver demonstrates personal understanding of the recipient (Ward & Broniarczyk, 2016).

Physical Touch: Choose the Emotion Before the Action

Dialect coaching themes:

- *Comforting* and *Restorative*: Grounding touch—e.g., hand-holding, an arm around the shoulder during stress.
- *Playful* or *Romantic*: Help clients initiate fun or passion without pressure.
- *Expressive* and *Protective*: Talk about how safe, warm touch builds trust and security—not just desire.

Coaching caution: Touch requires emotional safety. Past trauma, relational history, or cultural context may affect a client's experience of physical contact. Be mindful and always ask about comfort and consent.

Emotional Fluency Is Learned

Your job isn't to get clients to master every dialect—but to help them practice emotional attunement in the one that matters most right now. You're teaching them how to *notice, reflect, and respond*—not from guesswork, but from emotionally anchored clarity.

Over time, many clients become more confident speaking their partner's dialect—even if it doesn't come naturally. That's emotional fluency. And like any language, it's learned through repetition, reflection, and relational practice (Weger Jr. et al., 2014).

Adapting Over Time—Life Stages, Stress, and Change

Love is not static—and neither are Love Languages. While a client's primary emotional preference often remains relatively stable, the way they *receive, express, and prioritize love* can shift over time. Stress, relationship dynamics, major life transitions, and even subtle emotional changes can influence how a Love Language shows up—or goes quiet.

As a coach, it's important to normalize this: "Your Love Language doesn't disappear—but how you access or express it might shift depending on the season you're in." Helping clients recognize this can reduce shame and increase adaptability. Below are several common patterns and coaching opportunities.

Life Transitions Alter Emotional Capacity

Major transitions—like becoming a parent, changing careers, caregiving for a loved one, or grieving a loss—can alter a client's emotional bandwidth. During these times, what once felt emotionally energizing may now feel irrelevant or inaccessible.

- A previously touch-oriented client may feel emotionally numb during postpartum recovery.
- A client who thrived on affirmation may be too depleted to believe praise, even when offered sincerely.

Rather than asking *"What's your language?"* during these seasons, it's often more helpful to ask:

- "What kind of love feels most nourishing right now?"
- "What's something that would feel emotionally manageable but still meaningful?"

This aligns with findings in relational psychology that emotional availability fluctuates with perceived support and psychological resilience (Reis & Gable, 2003).

Stress and Emotional Overload Can Skew Preferences

Under prolonged stress, many clients regress into relational survival mode. They may pull back from what they usually crave or overly focus on one form of love as a coping mechanism.

For example:

- A client may reject Quality Time not because they don't want connection, but because they feel emotionally taxed and can't "perform" presence.
- Another might double down on Acts of Service to compensate for emotional distance—"I can't say I love you, but I'll mow the lawn and pay the bills."

As a coach, help clients distinguish between their authentic Love Language and their *adaptive strategies*. You might ask:

"Are you still drawn to this language or is it just what feels safest right now?"

Love Languages in Different Relationships

Some clients experience subtle variation in their preferences depending on the relationship. They may crave Physical Touch from a partner but prioritize Words of Affirmation in friendships. They may express one language fluently at work (e.g., Acts of Service as a leader) but struggle with it at home.

The Premium Assessment acknowledges this nuance through the "Key Relationships" page—and as a coach, you can deepen the insight:

- "What does this language look like between you and your spouse . . . your kids . . . your aging parent?"
- "Is there a relationship where this dialect used to thrive but now feels distant?"

Understanding these shifts over time and across relationships can reduce frustration and strengthen intentionality.

Growth May Lead to New Dialect Access

As clients grow emotionally—especially through coaching, therapy, or spiritual transformation—they often develop the capacity to receive or express love in new ways.

A client who previously dismissed Receiving Gifts as superficial may come to embrace the symbolism of a thoughtful, personal gesture. A client who feared touch may learn to associate it with safety, not threat.

Change here is not disloyalty to one's past—it's a sign of healing. Coaches can mark these shifts as emotional progress: "It sounds like you're becoming more fluent in this dialect. How does that feel?"

Love Languages Are a Framework, Not a Formula

Your job is not to help a client "lock in" their type—it's to help them reflect, adapt, and grow. The best use of the assessment is to revisit it over time—not to see if someone's language changed, but to explore how it's evolving in their story. Love Languages are not rigid categories but "ways of keeping emotional love alive" (Chapman, 2024). And staying alive means staying responsive to change.

Using the Assessment as a Growth Tracker

The 5 Love Languages Premium Assessment isn't just a tool for discovery—it can also become a relational dashboard over time. When used strategically, it helps clients (and coaches) observe emotional movement, relational growth, and evolving patterns of connection. In other words, it doesn't just show *where the client is*—it helps track how far they've come.

This kind of longitudinal insight is especially valuable in coaching, where the goal isn't just clarity—it's transformation over time.

Schedule a Follow-Up Assessment

Encourage clients to retake the Premium Assessment every twelve months or so, particularly:

- After a season of intentional relational growth
- Following a major life transition (new job, new child, loss, relocation)
- At the end of a formal coaching journey

The comparison isn't about "getting a different result." It's about noticing how dialect preferences, emotional capacity, or love skill scores may have shifted. Even subtle differences can signal growth, strain, or new relational needs.

Coaching prompt: "Looking at your results from last year and today, what's shifted—and what might that mean?"

Research on self-monitoring in behavioral change consistently shows that structured reflection increases accountability, resilience, and follow-through (Michie et al., 2009).

Pair It With the HeartChart for Context

When possible, pair the 5 Love Languages Premium Assessment with a HeartChart assessment (it's free and you'll find it at MyHeartChart.com)—especially in couple coaching or when focusing on relationship recovery.

- The **HeartChart** gives you a state-based snapshot of the overall relationship: How connected are they? How committed?
- The **5 Love Languages Premium Assessment** gives you specific emotional data: Which behaviors matter most? Which dialects are being missed?

Together, they offer a full picture. One tells you where the couple stands, the other tells you how they want to be loved. Used together over time, they help coaches track both emotional climate and communication fluency—vital indicators of sustainable change.

Use the Love Skills Page as a Coaching Baseline

The "Your Love Skills" page (Curiosity, Listening, Empathy) functions as an emotional performance snapshot—and should be revisited with care. Improvements may reflect greater awareness, increased regulation, or strengthened habits. Declines may indicate new relational strain, emotional fatigue, or reduced relational capacity.

Rather than framing these as scores to "improve," coach clients to observe and interpret them relationally:

- "What have you been doing differently over the past few months?"
- "Where are you finding it hardest to stay emotionally present lately?"

This positions the skills not as personal report cards, but as relational barometers.

Encourage Clients to Update Their "How to Love Me" Page

Perhaps the simplest—but most powerful—way to track growth is through the "How to Love [Client's Name]" summary page. Invite clients to revisit this page periodically and share it with loved ones.

This page becomes a living document—an evolving articulation of emotional needs and values. Coaching prompt: "If someone you care about read your current page, what would you most want them to understand?"

Over time, this page often becomes more specific, more vulnerable, and more confident. That's growth—measured not in numbers but in language and ownership.

Growth Is Often Subtle

Many clients expect to see major changes right away. But relational growth tends to unfold in quiet increments: a partner who begins to check in more, a child who seems more relaxed, a client who no longer hesitates to name what they need.

Using the assessment as a growth tracker helps clients notice what's working, stay grounded in the process, and celebrate movement—even if it's slow. Because when love is offered more clearly, and received more openly, change isn't just possible—it's already happening.

Equipping the Client to Lead Their Own Growth

The most meaningful coaching equips clients to own their growth and communicate their needs in everyday life. The 5 Love Languages Premium Assessment provides an elegant starting point, but it's your job as a coach to help clients keep growing from it—not just in coaching sessions, but in conversations, conflicts, celebrations, and changes.

This section outlines how to help clients step into relational leadership—with love, not control—as they use what they've learned to build healthier connections and deepen emotional safety.

Normalize Asking for What They Need

Many clients hesitate to articulate their emotional needs. They fear sounding needy, selfish, or too much. Your role is to reframe clarity as a gift, not a demand:

- "When you say this, you're not asking for perfection—you're giving your partner the best possible road map."
- "This isn't about what you're missing. It's about what helps you feel emotionally full."

Asking with clarity increases the likelihood of getting needs met. Research on relational assertiveness shows that clear, non-defensive communication improves relationship satisfaction and reduces resentment over time (Schrodt et al., 2007).

Encourage Ongoing Curiosity About Others' Dialects

Love Languages aren't just for receiving—they're also about recognizing the emotional reality of others. As clients grow, help them ask questions like:

- "What seems to matter most to the people I love?"
- "What do they do when they're trying to connect?"
- "Have I been loving them in the way *I* prefer, or in the way *they* receive?"

The goal is emotional fluency—not mastering every dialect but becoming curious enough to learn another person's emotional grammar. That kind of relational empathy is deeply connected to long-term emotional intimacy (Clark & Lemay, 2010).

Build Rituals Around What Works

Sporadic gestures are easy to forget. Rituals are what build emotional rhythm. Help clients think about how to incorporate their dialect into regular habits:

- A weekly "Affirmation Friday" message
- A monthly "Sensible Gift Day" (practical but personalized)
- A nightly check-in using Quality Time that matches their preferred pacing

Small rituals, when repeated consistently, create emotional safety and predictability—hallmarks of secure, satisfying relationships (Fiese et al., 2002).

Celebrate Emotional Growth, Not Perfection

Clients often expect quick results, especially in relationships that have been dry or disconnected for some time. Part of your work is helping them track **emotional courage**, not just outcomes.

Try asking:

- "What's something you did this week that stretched your comfort zone emotionally?"
- "Where did you love more clearly, even if it wasn't received the way you hoped?"

Helping clients focus on what's within their control (effort, clarity, vulnerability, etc.) keeps them grounded in growth rather than frustrated by what isn't changing yet.

Release the Coach, Retain the Practice

Eventually, the coaching relationship ends. Your goal is not to create dependence on you—it's to create confidence in them. When your client can say, "I know what helps me feel loved. I can ask for it with grace. And I'm learning how to love others better, even when it doesn't come naturally," that's coaching success.

The 5 Love Languages Premium Assessment is a powerful companion on that journey. But it's your coaching presence that helps turn that companion into a guide for lifelong connection.

Summary

True change happens when insight leads to intentional practice—when a client begins to live out their dialect with clarity, courage, and care. As a coach, your role is to help clients not just identify what fills their tank but build relational habits around it. To support them in communicating their needs without shame. And to encourage curiosity about how others receive love best.

You've learned how to:

- Translate dialects into clear, doable actions
- Set relational goals that are specific, small, and sustainable
- Adapt coaching to different seasons of life, stress levels, or emotional capacity
- Use the Premium Assessment as an ongoing growth tracker
- Equip clients to lead their own growth, even after coaching ends

When coaching is done well, clients leave not only feeling understood but also empowered. They carry with them a clearer emotional vocabulary, a stronger relational posture, and a personalized road map they can keep returning to as they grow.

QUESTIONS TO PONDER

1. When working with a client's Love Language results, do I stay in interpretation or help them move into intentional action?
2. Which dialects am I most confident coaching around? Which ones do I need to explore more deeply?
3. How can I better help clients anticipate emotional resistance or stress-related shifts in their preferences?
4. Am I using the assessment as a one-time tool or am I leveraging it for long-term growth check-ins?
5. What's one way I can help a client take ownership of their emotional needs without fear of seeming demanding?

PART 4

COACHING COUPLES TOGETHER

"Between what is said and not meant, and what is meant and not said, most of love is lost."

—ATTRIBUTED TO KHALIL GIBRAN

There's nothing quite like being in the room with both partners. When you're coaching a couple together, the stakes are higher—and so is the opportunity for breakthrough. In this section, you'll learn how to navigate dual dynamics, track emotional cues in real time, and create a space where both people feel seen, safe, and stretched. You'll explore what makes coaching a couple different from working with individuals, how to interrupt toxic patterns with care, and how to guide conversations that are charged with both history and hope. This is where your presence matters most—because what you model in the room often becomes the pattern they take home.

Chapter 16

Helping Couples Understand Each Other's Love Language

"I tell him I love him all the time. I text him during the day. I compliment him. But he still says he feels alone."

"I do stuff for her constantly. I keep our house running. I fix everything before she even notices. And it's like none of it counts."

You've probably heard some version of this in a session. Two people are trying, giving, even sacrificing, yet somehow missing each other completely. Not because they don't care. But because they're speaking different emotional dialects.

This is where Love Language coaching with couples gets real.

While the first step is helping each partner understand their own Love Language (and the specific dialects within it), the real transformation begins when they begin to understand each other's. When love becomes less about effort and more about impact. When clients stop asking, *"Am I doing enough?"* and start asking, *"Am I doing what actually matters most?"*

That shift—from self-awareness to relational attunement—is the heart of this chapter. As a coach, you become a translator and guide. You help each partner listen without defensiveness, speak with intention, and—perhaps most importantly—see the other person not as a puzzle to solve but as a story to understand.

In the pages ahead, you'll learn how to:

- Facilitate joint reflection using both partners' Premium Assessment reports
- Decode dialect differences that cause relational disconnect
- Support healthy conversations around missed needs and mixed signals
- Guide couples toward shared emotional fluency—one small practice at a time

Because love isn't enough when it's not understood. But when couples begin to hear each other clearly, love doesn't just return—it deepens.

Beyond Self-Awareness

Knowing your own Love Language is powerful—but knowing your partner's may be what saves the relationship. Many couples come into coaching having already taken a Love Language quiz or read about the concept. They can recite their top language and even talk about their dialect. But when you ask about their partner's needs, the clarity often fades. That's when the real work begins.

Research confirms what many couples intuitively know: Emotional connection is less about shared effort and more about felt attunement (Reis & Shaver, 1988; Gottman & Silver, 1999). Two people can be working hard in parallel, but unless they're aligned in how love is interpreted, their efforts often miss the mark.

In fact, studies on perceived partner responsiveness show that when individuals feel their partner "gets them," it significantly boosts emotional intimacy, commitment, and relationship satisfaction—even more than frequency of affection alone (Reis, Clark, & Holmes, 2004; Maisel & Gable, 2009).

As a coach, you help bridge that gap. You invite each partner to stop asking, *"Am I doing enough?"* and start asking, *"Am I doing what actually resonates with you?"*

Mutual insight isn't about agreement. It's about curiosity. It's about helping each partner become a student of the other's heart, not just a performer of good intentions. When couples move from self-knowledge to shared emotional fluency, a shift occurs. Defensiveness decreases. Tenderness increases. The emotional atmosphere changes.

As one client put it, after hearing their partner's dialect fully explained: "I've been speaking French, thinking it was helpful. Turns out they needed Spanish. And now I'm ready to learn."

Coaching Couples to "Compare Maps"

Once each partner has completed their 5 Love Languages Premium Assessment, a natural next step is for them to bring their reports into session—side by side. Think of it as inviting them to "compare emotional maps." The goal isn't to point out who's right or wrong, but to begin a new kind of conversation: one where understanding replaces assumption.

This is where the coach becomes a facilitator of mutual discovery—not a referee. Start by framing the session like this: "You've both spent time reflecting on what fills your emotional tank. Now let's take some time to explore what it looks like to pour into each other's—based on what actually matters most to each of you."

Then, walk through the two reports in parallel. Rather than jumping to problems or past misunderstandings, start with neutral observation:

- "What stands out to you about each other's top language?"
- "Are there any surprises?"
- "Do you see overlap—or areas where you're really different?"

This helps lower defensiveness and promote curiosity over critique—key elements of healthy relational dialogue (Gottman & Silver, 1999).

Use the Dialect Pages as Conversation Starters

Next, invite the couple to compare their dialects within each Love Language—even if they share the same primary one.

For example:

- One partner may rank high in Quality Time with a *Dreaming* dialect, longing for big-picture talks and "what-if" wonder.
- The other may prefer *Managing*, finding meaning in structured moments of presence and shared routines.

You might say: "It looks like you both value Quality Time—but the way you experience it emotionally is really different. How do you think that's played out in your connection?"

Encourage the partners to read their *own* dialect descriptors aloud in the session, then share some circled behaviors from the "Your Dialect" page (p. 13). These behaviors often bring clarity that labels alone can't.

Help Translate Intention Into Impact

In many cases, one partner will realize they've been "trying" in a way that hasn't quite landed. That can be vulnerable. It can also be healing. Use gentle, open-ended prompts like:

- "Has your partner tried to love you in this way before?"
- "What's one way they've shown love that you now realize meant more than you gave them credit for?"
- "Where might you have missed what they were trying to offer?"

This isn't about rehashing failure—it's about creating new pathways for empathy. When partners begin to see each other's *intentions* through the lens of emotional *preferences*, disconnection often gives way to compassion.

And that's the moment where mutual understanding begins to grow roots.

Coaching Through Emotional Disappointment

Even when two people love each other deeply, there can be a painful gap between effort and experience. One partner may feel they're doing everything they can. The other still feels unseen. This emotional mismatch—between intention and impact—is where Love Language coaching becomes most delicate, and most needed.

This section helps you guide couples through that tension with honesty, compassion, and forward movement.

When Love Is Offered, but Misses

One of the most heartbreaking dynamics in a relationship is when someone is genuinely trying, and the other doesn't feel it. That's not always because the effort is insufficient. It's often because the expression doesn't match the receiver's emotional blueprint.

You might hear:

- "I do so much, but it's like it doesn't count."
- "He's trying—I know that—but it still doesn't reach me."
- "It's like we're both working . . . just not on the same thing."

In these moments, your posture as a coach is everything. Slow the pace. Validate the pain. And name the gap without blame: "It sounds like the love is present—but the way it's being offered isn't matching the way it's most needed. That's something we can explore together."

Guide Honest, Specific Feedback—Without Blame

Often, a partner who feels emotionally disappointed isn't sure how to explain why. They know they feel empty—but not how to articulate the difference between "appreciated" and "truly seen." Use the "Your Dialect" and "Key Relationships" pages to anchor the conversation:

- "Can you share one specific behavior that fills your tank—and one that falls flat, even if well-intended?"
- "What do you hope your partner understands about *why* that expression matters to you?"

At the same time, help the "giver" feel safe enough to stay open. Defensiveness is common—especially when the effort feels invisible. Affirm the good intent, while gently redirecting the focus to impact.

Explore the Emotional Story Behind the Mismatch

Behind nearly every emotional misfire is a deeper story. Not just of what's happening in the present—but of *what shaped the need in the first place*. A partner who needs Physical Touch may have grown up in a family where affection was rare or conditional. Someone who thrives on Appreciation may carry the silent ache of being overlooked or undervalued as a child. A gift-oriented partner may have received thoughtful tokens from a caregiver and internalized those moments as tangible proof of love and intentionality.

These preferences don't come from nowhere. They're emotionally encoded—rooted in memory, meaning, and lived experience. And when couples begin to explore *why* their partner's Love Language matters—not just what it is—they start to experience a fundamental relational shift: curiosity replaces confusion, and compassion replaces critique.

"I rarely think about my husband's childhood when we're frustrated," one client said. "But when I finally heard the story behind his silence, I stopped being annoyed and started feeling protective."

As a coach, you can gently invite this level of insight with questions like:

- "When did you first notice this way of receiving love mattered to you?"
- "Was there a season when this kind of love felt scarce—or deeply meaningful?"
- "What does this expression of love *undo* or *affirm* in you?"

This practice deepens relational empathy. It also aligns with clinical literature on attachment history and emotional scripting, which shows that our expectations and sensitivities in adult relationships are often shaped by childhood relational environments (Mikulincer & Shaver, 2007; Johnson, 2008). These formative experiences create what psychologists call "internal working models"—mental templates of how love is given, received, or withheld.

Understanding these models doesn't mean excusing every emotional reaction or making a partner responsible for repairing childhood wounds. But it does allow couples to respond with greater tenderness and awareness. It frames a partner's need not as a demand but as a meaningful request shaped by emotional history.

This kind of narrative integration—connecting past and present—has been shown to increase both emotional intimacy and conflict resolution in romantic relationships (Kellas, 2005).

Ultimately, exploring each partner's emotional story brings relational depth. It gives context to needs, language to longings, and most importantly, a pathway to mutual healing through understanding.

Name What's Still Possible

Disappointment in love can make people feel like they're incompatible, or that nothing will ever be enough. Part of your role is to reframe emotional mismatch not as a dead end, but as a design flaw that can be reworked.

Let the couple know: "You're not broken. You're just operating with different defaults. And with intention and curiosity, those defaults can shift."

Help them choose a single dialect-based gesture to try that week. Not to fix everything, but to show, *"I hear you. And I'm learning."* That shift—from pain to practice—is the beginning of real repair.

Cultivating Mutual Responsibility for Connection

One of the greatest shifts you can help a couple make in coaching is from *"I need you to . . ."* to *"We are both responsible for keeping this connection alive."* That shift—from complaint to co-creation—marks a turning point in how partners relate, communicate, and care.

Don't allow Love Languages to be used as ammunition rather than insight:

"You're not speaking my language."

"I've been doing everything—what about you?"

This creates a power imbalance where one person becomes the "needy" one, and the other feels like they're constantly failing. Your job as a coach is to disarm that narrative and reframe emotional needs as shared relational stewardship.

From Scorekeeping to Shared Intentionality

When each partner focuses only on what they're giving—or not receiving—resentment builds. But when both partners take shared responsibility for *protecting the emotional climate*, connection becomes a team effort.

Coach them to ask:

- "What's one way I can speak your dialect this week?"
- "What would help you feel more emotionally connected to me right now?"
- "How can we each take one small step toward loving each other better this season?"

This doesn't require equal skill—but it does require equal investment. The Gottman Institute refers to this as a "culture of appreciation and responsiveness," which has been shown to predict long-term relationship satisfaction (Gottman & Silver, 1999; Driver & Gottman, 2004).

Set Collaborative Experiments, Not Just Individual Goals

When couples set mutual goals, the work becomes less about fixing and more about practicing together. Try assigning short, simple exercises they co-create, such as:

- "Each night this week, we'll take five minutes to affirm something we noticed in each other that day."
- "Let's each plan one small gesture in the other's dialect and do it without fanfare."

Invite them to reflect afterward: "How did that land for you?" and "What did you notice about how your partner responded?" These experiments foster both *accountability* and *discovery*, building a habit of curiosity that outlasts any specific task.

Give Language for Real-Time Repair

No couple gets it right all the time. That's why teaching micro-repair language is so important. Small phrases can reopen emotional connection before conflict takes root.

Offer couples scripts like:

- "That didn't land the way I meant—can I try again?"
- "I see that you tried, even if it wasn't exactly what I needed."
- "I appreciate the effort. Here's what might help even more next time."

These micro-repairs strengthen resilience, deepen emotional safety, and model grace over perfection. Research shows that couples who repair quickly and gently are more likely to stay connected over time—even in the face of recurring tension (Gottman et al., 1998).

It's Not Who's Right, It's Who's Reaching

At the end of the day, what matters most isn't whether partners always get it right—it's whether they're reaching for each other with open hands and open hearts.

Your role as a coach is to remind them: "Connection doesn't come from guessing perfectly. It comes from caring enough to keep trying." When both partners feel emotionally seen, empowered to ask for what they need, and willing to grow on purpose, they don't just understand each other's Love Language. They embody it. Together.

Summary

When couples begin coaching, they often come armed with effort but not understanding. They've been trying to connect, trying to show love, trying to repair—but it still feels like something's missing. More often than not, the missing piece is emotional clarity.

This chapter helped reframe Love Language work from individual self-awareness to shared emotional fluency. You learned how to:

- Walk through each partner's Premium Assessment side by side
- Use dialects to expose subtle mismatches and missed efforts
- Guide conversations around unmet needs with compassion and specificity
- Explore the emotional stories behind each partner's Love Language
- Shift the focus from blame to shared responsibility for connection

When couples stop asking, "*Why don't you see me?*" and start asking, "*How can I learn to speak what reaches you?*"—they begin to rebuild safety, intimacy, and mutual trust. And as their coach, you are the one holding the space for that healing to take root.

QUESTIONS TO PONDER

1. In my coaching with couples, do I prioritize understanding over behavior change—or do I rush to the "fix" too quickly?
2. How comfortable am I guiding couples into emotional backstories behind their Love Language preferences?
3. What's one way I could better coach a couple through mismatched efforts with greater empathy and clarity?
4. Do I emphasize mutual responsibility in sessions or unintentionally allow emotional labor to tilt toward one partner?
5. How can I better support couples in turning Love Language insight into regular, sustainable practice?

Chapter 17

Leveraging the "Love Tank"

They weren't in crisis.

They still laughed at each other's jokes. Still shared logistics and leftovers and the occasional hand on the lower back as they passed in the kitchen.

But something felt . . . flat.

Neither could point to anything obvious. No betrayals. No raised voices. Just the slow erosion of warmth—the kind of erosion that happens not because love is gone, but because it hasn't been checked on in a while.

This is the hidden cost of emotional disconnection: It's not always loud. Sometimes, it just hums along in the background—unspoken, unmeasured, and slowly widening the gap between two people who still care.

That's why the love tank metaphor has stuck. You've read about it in chapter 2 of *The 5 Love Languages*—a simple image with surprising emotional weight.

Simple, visual, and emotionally accessible, it gives people language for what so often goes unnamed. It offers a way to say, "Something feels off" without launching into blame. And more importantly, it invites repair before rupture.

As a coach, exploring the love tank metaphor can transform a couple's rhythm. It replaces guesswork with gentle inquiry, frustration with feedback, silence with small truths.

In the pages ahead, we'll explore how this metaphor can become one of your most effective tools for coaching emotional connection, maintenance, and growth.

What the Love Tank Represents—And Why It Matters

Before it was a coaching tool or a conversation starter, the "love tank" was an image—meant to make something invisible feel tangible. A way to describe emotional fullness or depletion in language even a child could grasp.

Where the Metaphor Comes From

While *The 5 Love Languages* popularized the love tank concept, the metaphor itself has roots that predate the book. Variations of the idea appeared in the mid-twentieth century in child development literature. For example, child psychologist Dr. Ross Campbell used similar language in the 1970s when talking about children's emotional needs, describing how kids thrive when their "emotional tanks" are full of love, attention, and affirmation (Campbell, 1977).

The 5 Love Languages brought the metaphor into mainstream adult relationships, helping people visualize emotional connection not as an abstract ideal but as something that requires regular attention—refilled or depleted by daily interactions.

The metaphor stuck because it speaks to a universal experience: the felt sense of being emotionally resourced . . . or emotionally running on fumes.

What It Actually Represents

The love tank is not just a measure of happiness. It's a living indicator of felt connection, security, and emotional support. It tells us how loved someone feels—not in general, but in this season, in this relationship, right now.

When full, the love tank often corresponds with:

- Greater relationship satisfaction
- Increased emotional generosity
- More resilience during conflict or stress

When empty, it shows up as:

- Irritability or defensiveness
- Withdrawal or shutdown
- Overreaction to minor slights
- Feeling unseen or uncared for—even if love is being expressed

Research on emotional availability and responsiveness confirms this: the perception of being emotionally cared for has significant effects on attachment security, conflict resolution, and long-term relationship stability (Collins & Feeney, 2004; Reis & Shaver, 1988).

In short, when someone says their love tank is low, they're often saying: *"I feel disconnected, and I don't know how to fix it."* That's where coaching can help.

Why It Matters in Coaching

As a coach, using the love tank metaphor offers people a shared emotional vocabulary—one that bypasses blame and centers on awareness. It helps them:

- Name what's hard to articulate
- Check in without escalating
- Move from abstract tension to specific need

The metaphor is disarming because it's familiar, non-clinical, and neutral. It's not "You're neglecting me"—it's "My tank feels low." That difference can determine whether a conversation leads to a fight or to repair.

Helping people adopt this tool isn't about sentimentality. It's about giving them a relational dashboard, a way to monitor the emotional quality of their connection and course-correct before disconnection becomes distance.

How to Use the Love Tank Check-In as a Coaching Tool

In a coaching session, few tools are as emotionally efficient—or as relationally illuminating—as a love tank check-in. It doesn't require a long story. It doesn't invite a debate. It simply asks: "On a scale from 0 to 10, how full is your love tank today?"

This deceptively simple question opens the door to emotional honesty that might otherwise stay buried. It gives people a shared language for naming their emotional state—without escalating into accusation or defensiveness.

As a coach, your job is to frame this tool wisely, use it regularly, and guide the conversation that follows with care and curiosity.

Framing the Check-In

When introducing the tool, begin with a tone of non-judgment: "This isn't about who's right or wrong. It's about staying connected to how loved you each feel—and how that changes over time."

Normalize fluctuation. A low number doesn't mean failure. It's not a verdict—it's a signal.

You can invite both partners to rate their love tank at the start of a session, or as part of a mid-session emotional check. In longer coaching relationships, it can become a routine anchor: "Before we wrap up today, let's check in on your tanks. Where are you sitting right now?"

Questions That Deepen the Check-In

The number is just a starting point. What makes the tool powerful is the curiosity that follows. You might ask:

- "What's been filling it lately?"
- "What's drained it—or kept it from filling?"
- "How long have you felt that way?"
- "What's one thing your partner has done recently that helped—or hurt?"

You can also guide partners to ask each other directly, fostering intimacy through shared inquiry:

- "What would help bring your tank from a 5 to a 6 this week?"
- "What does a '10' actually feel like for you?"

Over time, these check-ins increase emotional self-awareness, empathy, and trust—all qualities strongly associated with long-term relational satisfaction (Gable et al., 2006; Reis & Clark, 2013).

It's Not About the Number—It's About the Invitation

Some partners will give a 3. Others might say 6—but with a hesitant shrug. The number is only a clue. What matters more is how the couple *responds to the emotional vulnerability* behind it.

Teach them to hear it as a bid for connection: "When your partner says their tank is low, they're not criticizing you—they're letting you see what's underneath the surface."

And when the tank is full? That's a moment worth noticing too. A full tank is a reflection of care, consistency, and emotional presence. It deserves celebration.

The more this becomes a rhythm—not a rescue—the more the couple can move from emotional reactivity to emotional maintenance.

Teaching Couples to Use Love Tank Conversations at Home

The real power of the love tank metaphor isn't how well it works in your office—it's how well it travels home.

When couples integrate this check-in into their daily or weekly rhythm, they begin to track their emotional connection the way a good driver watches the fuel gauge. No panic. Just awareness. And when needed, they refuel.

Your role as a coach is to help them make this part of their relational routine: natural, normal, and safe.

Normalize the Practice, Not the Perfection

The goal isn't to have profound emotional revelations every week. It's to build a habit of asking and answering *before* disconnection takes root.

Coach couples to pick a simple, predictable time for a love tank check-in:

- Sunday night before the week begins
- Friday evening after work
- During a walk or coffee date
- As part of a monthly relationship review

Help them be specific and concrete. Have them set a reminder on their phone if that helps. Once a week is often enough. It's not the frequency that builds trust—it's the consistency. And, of course, this doesn't need to be rigid. The specificity is just to get them started on this weekly habit. It can evolve into a more relaxed approach as they get the swing of it.

Coach the Tone and Timing

Even good tools can be misused if delivered with edge or agenda. Help partners set emotional guardrails around the check-in:

- Don't do it in the middle of an argument.
- Don't weaponize it ("Well, your tank is probably low because you're too sensitive . . .").
- Don't interpret a low number as a failure—yours or theirs.

Coach them to approach the conversation with curiosity, not critique: "This is a check-in, not a scorecard. It's not about defending where we are—it's about exploring it together."

You might suggest using this kind of opening language: "Hey, I've been thinking about your tank. Where is it at these days?" Or: "I want to be more intentional. Is there something small I could do this week to move the needle?"

Equip Couples to Listen Without Defensiveness

A love tank check-in is only as helpful as the *emotional safety* surrounding it. Some partners will instinctively get defensive when their partner reacts with astonishment ("You're at a 4?"), even if it's not meant as criticism.

That's why it helps to coach the receiving posture too:

- "Thanks for telling me that. I want to understand more."
- "I appreciate your honesty—even if I didn't expect that number."
- "Let's talk about how I can show up for you better this week."

Remind couples: honesty isn't rejection. It's trust. And trust is the bridge to better connection. This posture echoes emotionally intelligent communication frameworks, such as the concept of *turning toward bids for connection* (Gottman & Silver, 1999), which predicts stronger attachment and emotional security over time.

Make It a Ritual, Not a Reaction

Once this becomes part of a couple's weekly rhythm, the check-in shifts from being a reactive crisis tool to a proactive connection ritual. That's when it starts to change the emotional climate of the relationship—not just in the low-tank moments, but in the ordinary weeks as well.

One couple described it like this: "It's not always deep. But it keeps us honest—and close. It's like emotional hygiene. We're less likely to drift."

That's the goal. You're not just teaching a metaphor. You're coaching a mindset: Connection doesn't have to be dramatic. It just has to be tended.

What to Do When a Love Tank Is Low

There will come a moment—maybe in session, maybe at home—when one partner finally says it out loud: "My tank is empty."

It may come out as frustration. Or quiet resignation. Or tears that surprise even the speaker. Regardless of how it surfaces, the emotional impact is often the same: one person feels vulnerable, and the other feels unsure what to do with it.

This is a turning point. Not a failure—but an invitation. As a coach, your task is to help both partners respond to the moment with emotional presence, mutual grace, and a clear path forward.

1. Slow the Reaction. Honor the Disclosure.

When a love tank is low, it's tempting for the partner hearing it to become reactive—defensive, ashamed, or dismissive.

"How can you say that? I've been trying!"

"But I thought things were better . . ."

"That's not fair."

These reactions are understandable. But they create distance. Coach the listening partner to pause the reaction and lean into reflection:

"Thank you for telling me that."

"I didn't realize you felt this way. I want to understand."

"It's hard to hear, but I'd rather know than not know."

Naming emotional depletion is an act of trust. Acknowledging it builds safety.

2. Avoid Framing One Partner as the Problem

The partner with the low tank is not "too needy." The other partner is not "doing everything wrong." This moment isn't about blame—it's about clarity.

Help them see the difference between *intention* and *impact*: "You may be putting in effort—and still missing what actually fills their tank. Let's get specific about what's working and what's not."

This moves the conversation from vague frustration to concrete insight. Use the **dialect page** from the Premium Assessment to anchor the discussion: "Which of these gestures do you wish you were receiving more often?" Or: "What's something your partner has done that filled your tank in the past?"

3. Reconnect Through Specific, Targeted Action

Generic efforts rarely move a low tank. Precision does. Coach the higher-tank partner to offer one small, specific act aligned with their partner's dialect—preferably within the next 48 hours. Not to "fix" things, but to say, *I see you. I'm responding.*

Examples:

- "I'll leave a handwritten note before work tomorrow."
- "I'll plan an hour this weekend to take a walk and talk with no distractions."
- "I'll handle bedtime solo on Thursday so you can rest."

These micro-acts can have outsized emotional effect, especially when done without pressure for reciprocation.

4. Draw on the Love Skills Page When Tanks Are Strained

When the gap feels especially wide, revisit the Love Skills section of the report: empathy, listening, curiosity. These are the relational muscles that help keep tanks full *even in seasons of stress or disconnection.*

Coach around questions like:

- "What would it look like to listen more fully right now?"
- "Where can you show curiosity instead of assuming?"
- "What helps your partner know you're emotionally present, even when things feel hard?"

These are the relational tools of repair—and they're often more impactful than any single loving gesture.

Low Tanks Are a Compass, Not a Crisis

It's easy to treat a low love tank as a red alert. But reframed well, it becomes something else entirely: a directional signal. A relational GPS. A sign that one person's heart is longing for connection and that the other now has a chance—not to be perfect, but to be present.

When couples begin to see these moments not as breakdowns but as invitations to draw near, the love tank check-in stops being just a metaphor. It becomes a practice of emotional repair.

Building Love Tank Awareness Into Long-Term Growth

The beauty of the love tank metaphor is that it scales. It works as a quick pulse check in a session—and as a long-term lens for helping couples develop emotional awareness, attunement, and shared responsibility for connection.

When couples begin to view their love tanks as dynamic and worthy of attention, they shift from reacting to disconnection to proactively sustaining closeness. The metaphor becomes not just a momentary diagnostic—but a framework for relational health.

Help Couples Revisit Tank Levels Over Time

Encourage couples to use the language of love tanks in everyday conversations—especially during transitions, stress, or emotionally vulnerable seasons.

Examples:

- "My tank's been low lately, and I just realized it's not about you doing more—it's about me needing more presence."
- "Your tank feels low to me. Is there something I can do this week that would help?"

This kind of language builds emotional literacy—the ability to name and respond to inner experiences in relationally healthy ways (Greenberg & Goldman, 2008). It's a skill that grows with practice.

Reinforce That Keeping a Love Tank Full Is Maintenance, Not Magic

Many couples fall into the trap of thinking love should be self-sustaining. But the truth is, emotional connection needs regular tending. Love tanks don't stay full by accident. They stay full because both people are paying attention.

This is especially important to remind couples during the plateau stage of coaching or marriage:

- "If your tank was full three months ago, what's kept it there?"
- "What small habits are contributing to that stability?"
- "What might shift as stress increases or circumstances change?"

By naming maintenance as success, you help couples stop chasing emotional highs and start cultivating emotional steadiness.

Expand the Framework: It's Not Just Romantic

Love tank awareness isn't just for couples. Many clients apply the metaphor to:

- Their relationship with their children[1]
- Their friendships
- Their work or caregiving roles
- Even their relationship with God or spiritual wellbeing[2]

1. For a more in-depth treatment, see *The 5 Love Languages of Children: The Secret to Loving Children Effectively* (Chapman and Campbell) and *The 5 Love Languages of Teenagers: The Secret to Increasing Joy and Trust with Your Teen* (Chapman).
2. For more on applying the Love Languages in a spiritual context, see *God Speaks Your Love Language: How to Enhance Your Relationship with God* (Chapman).

As a coach, you can affirm the versatility of the metaphor, and invite clients to reflect:

- "Where else in your life are you giving or receiving love that affects your tank?"
- "How does emotional depletion in one area bleed into another?"

This broadens the emotional self-awareness that supports relational growth across every domain of life.

Love Tank Awareness Is a Form of Relational Maturity

When couples become fluent in recognizing, discussing, and responding to emotional fullness and depletion, they build what psychologists call mutual emotional regulation—a shared capacity to maintain closeness and stability even in times of stress (Butler & Randall, 2013).

Love tanks aren't just about how we feel. They're about how we stay connected—on purpose, over time. When a couple knows how to check the gauge and refuel with care, they don't just love each other. They learn how to sustain each other.

Summary

The love tank is more than a metaphor—it's a relational mindset. It gives couples shared language to describe what is often hard to name: emotional depletion, unseen effort, unmet needs, and the quiet drift of disconnection.

In this chapter, you learned how to:

- Introduce the love tank metaphor as an emotionally safe and simple check-in tool
- Facilitate tank-level conversations in session to uncover unmet needs and deepen empathy
- Guide couples through low-tank moments without blame, and with targeted gestures of repair
- Equip partners to use the love tank metaphor at home, regularly and with mutual responsibility
- Reinforce long-term awareness through habits, reflection, and revisiting the Premium Assessment

When couples begin to treat emotional connection not as a mystery, but as something they can monitor, tend, and replenish—they stop guessing. They start caring with intention. And as a coach, you're helping them trade frustration for fluency. Resentment for rhythm. Silence for shared emotional stewardship.

QUESTIONS TO PONDER

1. How often do I check in with couples on how emotionally connected they feel, not just how they're functioning?
2. Do I use the love tank metaphor early and often—or only after problems emerge?
3. How do I help partners respond to low tank levels without taking it personally or becoming defensive?
4. What rhythms or rituals can I help couples implement that make love tank conversations feel normal, not loaded?
5. Am I using the Premium Assessment's "love tank" page as a strategic growth marker over time?

Chapter 18

The Love Language That Matters Most

For decades, *The 5 Love Languages* has helped millions of people unlock a simple truth: We don't all give and receive love the same way. What fills one person's heart might fall flat for another. That insight has changed marriages, friendships, families, and entire communities. It's foundational and transformative.

But it's not the finish line.

That's why we wrote *The Love Language That Matters Most*. It's the first true follow-up to the original book—not an adaptation for a specific group (like teens, children, or military couples) but a masterclass for every relationship ready to go deeper. For years, we've watched people gain clarity about their own Love Language . . . and still struggle. We've seen partners who could name their dialect with confidence, and yet still miss each.

Because knowing *your own* Love Language is only half the equation.

The next step—the one that takes emotional maturity, empathy, and commitment—is this: *The Love Language that matters most is the one that matters to the person you love.*

That simple sentence shifts the center of gravity from self to other. From awareness to action. From, "Here's how I want to be loved," to "How can I love you better?" It's where Love Languages move from insight to impact.

This chapter helps you, as a coach, walk people into that shift. It's about moving beyond self-awareness and helping them develop emotional fluency in the dialect that matters most: their partner's.

It's also where *The Love Language That Matters Most* becomes one of your most practical tools. It helps your clients deepen connection, build empathy, and sustain intimacy—even when good intentions still fall short.

From Self-Focus to Other-Focus in Love

It's a common breakthrough moment in coaching: a client realizes they've been working hard to show love, only to discover it hasn't been landing. Their gestures were sincere—thoughtful even—but they were filtered through their own preferences, not their partner's.

This is the hidden challenge of Love Languages: We often assume that what feels meaningful to us will feel meaningful to others.

And that's the trap.

Knowing your own Love Language is vital—but if the work ends there, people can unintentionally stay stuck in self-focused love. It's love offered with effort, but not always with empathy. The real transformation begins when partners turn their focus outward and ask a different question: "*What matters most to the person I love?*"

That's the heart of *The Love Language That Matters Most*. The book invites people to graduate from emotional intuition to emotional intentionality. It teaches that loving well isn't just about knowing your preferences, it's about mastering your partner's dialect, especially when it's different from your own.

This shift from self-awareness to other-awareness is what psychologists refer to as perceived partner responsiveness—the belief that one's partner "gets" them, sees their needs clearly, and responds in ways that feel attuned (Reis, Clark, & Holmes, 2004). Research shows that this single factor significantly predicts relationship satisfaction, emotional closeness, and long-term stability.

And it doesn't happen by accident. It requires curiosity. Adaptability. And a willingness to grow.

Your role as a coach is to guide this shift. To help clients understand that love isn't something they offer once, in the way that feels natural to them. It's something they learn, practice, and personalize. It's an ongoing invitation to discover what *actually reaches* the other person's heart. Because in the end, the most loving thing you can do isn't to express your love well. It's to make sure it's received.

The Empathy Gap—Why This Shift Is Hard

It's not that most people don't care. It's that they don't realize how deeply embedded their own emotional defaults are. The more you coach, the more you'll see this phenomenon show up in your office: a client who's genuinely trying to love well but keeps defaulting to their own preferences—because it's what feels right, familiar, or instinctive.

We tend to love from what we know. We reach for what would reach us. We assume that the gesture we'd appreciate—a well-timed compliment, an unsolicited errand, an extended hug—is what our partner would appreciate too. But love filtered through projection, no matter how sincere, can still fall flat.

Psychologists call this tendency *emotional egocentrism*—a subtle bias that leads us to overestimate how much others share our emotional preferences, interpretations, and responses (Keysar et al., 2003). In relationships, this often shows up as well-intended love that's mismatched, misread, or misunderstood.

Enter the empathy gap: the emotional blind spot between *what we give* and *what is truly needed*. Even when couples have learned each other's Love Languages, they can still get stuck here. A client might say:

- "That's just not how I'm wired."
- "I try, but it doesn't feel authentic."
- "Why can't they appreciate what I am doing?"

These are not signs of selfishness. They're signs of growth resistance—of love meeting the limits of comfort or comprehension.

As a coach, this is where you gently challenge the idea that love has to feel natural to be real. You help your clients see that *stretching* toward another person's emotional need is not performance—it's relational maturity. As we write in *The Love Language That Matters Most*, the goal isn't to abandon your natural style. It's to develop emotional bilingualism—to speak your partner's dialect even when it isn't instinctive.

Helping a partner move beyond "I don't get it" to "I want to understand it because it matters to you" is one of the most transformational moments in coaching. That's when love stops being about what feels easiest and starts being about what feels real.

Helping Couples Bridge the Empathy Gap

Ultimately, Love Language fluency isn't about mastering techniques. It's about practicing empathy as a lifestyle—daily, imperfect, and intentional. The most effective coaching doesn't just help clients understand what their partner needs. It helps them feel it. Not in theory, but in practice. That's how you close the empathy gap.

Empathy is the ability to temporarily set aside your own agenda so you can see through someone else's eyes, think with their mind, and feel with their heart (Parrott & Parrott, 2008). It's not agreement. Once again, it's attunement. And in love, it changes everything.

Because knowing someone's Love Language is knowledge, but speaking it—even when it doesn't come naturally—is empathy in motion. Here's how to help your couples do just that.

1. Help Them Set Aside Their Own Agenda

One of the greatest barriers to empathy is distraction—not always external, but internal. We all carry mental and emotional agendas: what we're hoping to say, what we're feeling frustrated about, what we want to defend or prove. These internal scripts can be so loud that they drown out what our partner is actually expressing—or needing.

That's why setting aside your own agenda is a crucial first step in developing empathy. It's not about erasing your needs or pretending your feelings don't matter. It's about choosing, momentarily, to shift the focus from self to other.

And that's not automatic. Our brains are wired for self-reference. Neuroimaging studies show that the brain's default mode network is engaged when people are thinking about their own thoughts, feelings, and goals—and that it takes *effortful mental redirection* to focus instead on the perspective of others (Lieberman, 2013).

In relationships, that means we don't become empathetic by default—we become empathetic by choice.

As a coach, this is a practice you can help couples strengthen. You might say: "Before you respond, take five seconds and do a quick internal scan. What's your agenda right now—what are you wanting to express, prove, or protect? Can you mentally place that aside, just for a moment, so you can fully tune in to your partner?"

Normalize this by naming common "agendas" that get in the way of real listening:

- Wanting to be understood before understanding
- Mentally preparing a defense while your partner is still speaking
- Reacting to past pain instead of present emotion
- Wanting to fix the problem instead of feel the feeling
- Needing to win, resolve, or move on—before your partner is ready

Sometimes our agendas are emotionally charged—like the need to be understood first, to fix what's broken, or to defend a position. But often, they're pragmatic and even mundane:

- Mentally finishing an email while your partner is speaking
- Worrying about picking up a prescription before the pharmacy closes
- Running through your next appointment or to-do list while nodding on autopilot

These internal distractions may seem harmless, but they drain the relational presence required for empathy. In fact, they make empathy impossible unless you set them aside. In other words, if your mind is still in motion—on what's unresolved, unsaid, or undone—you've left no space to *emotionally show up* for the person in front of you.

Research supports what you see in the coaching room: when individuals intentionally pause their own narrative and engage in active perspective-taking, they increase relational attunement and decrease interpersonal conflict (Galinsky et al., 2008; Zaki & Ochsner, 2012). In fact, *deliberate inhibition of self-focus* has been shown to be a predictor of long-term relationship stability and partner satisfaction (Reis et al., 2004).

Let your clients know: This is a skill. One they must practice again and again. And setting aside your agenda doesn't mean silencing your needs. It means prioritizing connection first. When that space is created, real empathy becomes possible. Because curiosity can't grow in a mind that's already full.

2. Teach the Cost of Assumption—and the Power of Curiosity

One of the most common Love Language breakdowns happens not because of malice or neglect but because of assumption.

In long-term relationships, partners often settle into familiar roles: "She likes gifts." "He's a Physical Touch guy." "We're just not words people." But people evolve. Contexts shift. What filled someone's tank in one season may miss the mark in another. Gestures that once delighted may now feel routine—or even irrelevant.

That's why curiosity is one of the most underused relational muscles. And as a coach, it's your job to help clients start flexing it.

The Cost of Assumption

Assumption may feel efficient—but it's relationally expensive. It breeds complacency, misunderstanding, and disconnection. In contrast, couples who maintain a posture of curiosity toward each other show greater empathy, satisfaction, and long-term engagement (Kashdan et al., 2011; Gordon & Chen, 2013).

Coaches should normalize this reality: "It's not that you don't love each other. It's that you stopped asking new questions."

Assumptions lead to stale patterns. Curiosity makes space for growth.

How to Coach Curiosity

Some clients are naturally inquisitive. Others are more emotionally reserved, pragmatic, or unaccustomed to introspection or asking thoughtful questions of their partner. For these individuals, curiosity needs to be modeled and made actionable.

You might coach them to:

- **Start small and specific.** Instead of "What are you feeling?" try, "What's something that felt good to you this week that I might've missed?"
- **Use a cue.** Pair the Premium Assessment dialect page with a prompt: "What's one thing on your list that feels especially meaningful this week?"
- **Reflect before reacting.** Teach them to pause before dismissing a partner's comment and ask themselves: *"What are they really asking for here?"*
- **Use structured rituals.** Encourage a simple weekly question like, *"How can I love you better this week?"* This not only opens dialogue—it helps clients practice attunement without needing to be naturally introspective.

You can say: "You don't have to be a naturally curious person. You just have to care enough to ask."

Why Curiosity Works

Relational curiosity fosters emotional safety. It signals to a partner, *"You matter enough for me to keep learning about you."* Research shows that curiosity increases responsiveness, reduces defensiveness, and leads to more satisfying romantic relationships (Kashdan & Roberts, 2004; Kashdan et al., 2011). It also buffers against conflict by reinforcing connection in times of relational strain.

Even more, curiosity is contagious. When one partner begins asking thoughtful questions, the other often softens—feeling seen rather than scrutinized. In *The Love Language That Matters Most*, we write that curiosity is how love stays fluent—not just at the start of a relationship but across the decades that follow. And it begins with a simple mindset shift: *"I don't want to stop learning about you."*

3. **Practice Empathy Exercises in Session**

Help clients actively trade places. Begin by creating a moment of emotional focus for the couple. Invite both partners to pause, slow their breathing, and gently close their eyes if they're comfortable. Then walk them through a simple exercise, framing it with care:

"Let's each take a moment to step into the other's experience. Not to judge it or fix it but to imagine it." Then prompt them:

- "What might your partner's last week have felt like emotionally?"
- "What stress did they carry that you may not have named?"
- "What do you think they hoped for from you but didn't ask for?"

Once they reflect silently, ask each to share what they imagined, while the other listens without interrupting or correcting. Then reverse roles. You can also center the exercise around the Premium Assessment's top Love Language, using a prompt like: "What does your partner's primary Love Language protect in them? What do they feel when it's not expressed? What seems to heal when it is?"

This builds what researchers call *perspective-taking empathy*—a specific form of cognitive empathy that allows one person to imagine another's thoughts, emotions, and needs without projecting their own. Perspective-taking is associated with reduced defensiveness, greater mutual care, and increased long-term relationship satisfaction (Longmire & Harrison, 2018).

These in-session practices work especially well in couple coaching because:

- They give both people equal voice and emotional airtime.
- They reframe frustration into shared understanding.
- They often create spontaneous moments of insight, softness, and gratitude.

Empathy doesn't have to be abstract. With the right environment and intentional guidance, it can become an experience couples share in real time—one that often reshapes how they speak, listen, and love.

4. Shift the Goal from Comfort to Connection

The empathy gap often widens when one partner feels awkward or uncomfortable trying to speak a non-native Love Language. They feel unnatural, inauthentic, or clumsy.

But the goal isn't comfort, it's connection. So don't let them stand on that excuse. Coach them gently this way: "Fluency in love isn't about it feeling easy. It's about it feeling real. And the more you try, the more authentic it feels."

Use reframing tools to help shift the internal dialogue:

- "This isn't about performing. It's about prioritizing."
- "I'm not losing myself—I'm learning to love with more intention."
- "This isn't how I instinctively show love, but it *is* how I want to show *you* love."

Empathy isn't always intuitive, but it's always worth it.

5. Assign Empathy-Building "Homework" Between Sessions

Real change happens between sessions, not just during them. That's why giving couples small, structured assignments is one of the most effective ways to build momentum. These empathy-based exercises reinforce what's been discussed and also invite couples to *practice* relational skills in the real world, where it matters most.

Homework fosters follow-through, creates new emotional habits, and extends the impact of coaching into the couple's daily rhythm. It moves insight into action—and that's where transformation begins.

Sample Assignments:

- Read a chapter from *The Love Language That Matters Most* together and discuss one idea that stood out, and bring your insights to the next coaching session.

- Use their personalized Dialect Pages from the Premium Assessment to identify one behavior to try—or one they now recognize and appreciate.
- Take turns sharing a moment during the week when they *felt* loved (because empathy was happening) and a moment when they *wished* they'd felt more seen (because empathy felt lacking).
- Set a timer and each share something you're carrying emotionally this week—with no fixing, just listening.

Research consistently shows that assigning homework in coaching settings enhances client engagement, learning retention, and overall outcomes and client satisfaction. In fact, clients who complete between-session tasks report significantly greater progress than those who don't (Kazantzis et al., 2000; Detweiler-Bedell & Whisman, 2005). Homework helps couples bridge the gap between insight and behavior—shifting empathy from an idea to a daily habit.

Practicing the Love Language That Matters Most

At the heart of every coaching strategy in this chapter is one guiding principle: Love only lands when it's spoken in the language (and dialect) that matters most to the person receiving it. That's why empathy isn't just a technique. It's a discipline of loving attention.

When couples begin to notice what their partner truly needs—not just what comes naturally to give—they're stepping into the sacred space of self-giving love. But this isn't a one-time insight or a fix-it formula. It's a lifelong pursuit. No one checks empathy off a to-do list. No one ever fully arrives. We just keep showing up, practicing, flexing the muscle of attunement until it becomes stronger, more reflexive, more wholehearted.

Helping couples learn their partner's primary Love Language is powerful. But helping them attune to the subtle nuances—the dialects—is where transformation really happens. That's the work of coaching: moving from assumption to awareness, from autopilot to intention, from a generic version of love to the customized expression that says, *I see you.*

That's the Love Language that matters most.

Summary

Love is never one-size-fits-all. And it's never one and done. The heart of great coaching is helping couples not just identify each other's Love Language but learn to speak it fluently, with nuance, empathy, and intention. That means moving beyond insight into action, beyond awareness into practice. Whether it's assigning simple between-session homework, guiding reflective listening, or encouraging daily habits of attunement, the goal is progress, not perfection. Empathy is a muscle, and love is a language we keep learning. Coaches don't hand out quick fixes. We help couples build lifelong rhythms of connection, one small act at a time.

QUESTIONS TO PONDER

1. How am I helping couples move from understanding their partner's language to truly *speaking it—dialect and all?*
2. In what ways can I support couples in making empathy a daily habit rather than a reactive response?
3. What simple, tailored assignments could help each couple I coach strengthen their emotional reflexes?
4. Am I helping couples embrace the idea that love is a practice—not something to master, but something to keep working at?
5. How can I model the same kind of curiosity and attunement I want couples to build with each other?

PART 5

COACHING SPECIAL CASES

"There is no greater agony than bearing an untold story inside you."

—MAYA ANGELOU

Not every coaching session fits a neat mold—and not every client walks in with the same story. Part 4 equips you to adapt. Whether you're working with singles, parents, or couples in crisis, this section helps you navigate complexity with clarity and care. You'll learn how to flex the 5 Love Languages framework in high-stakes moments, hold space when emotions run hot, and offer tailored strategies for clients facing unique relational challenges. This is where coaching goes from effective to masterful—where nuance matters, and your ability to meet people in their mess becomes your greatest strength.

Chapter 19

Coaching Singles with the 5 Love Languages

Riley sat back on the couch and gave a half-smile that didn't quite reach her eyes.

"I've read the book. I know my Love Language is Quality Time. But honestly?" she sighed and then paused. "Sometimes it feels like knowing that just makes me lonelier. I don't have a partner. I don't have someone to *give* that to—or get it from. So what do I even do with that?"

It's a familiar moment for many coaches working with single clients. The insight is there. The language is helpful. But without a romantic relationship to apply it to, it can feel more theoretical than transformational.

That's where coaching steps in to reframe things. To help singles see their Love Language not as something waiting for a relationship, but as something already shaping every connection in their life—starting with how they see themselves.

It's easy to assume the 5 Love Languages only come into play once someone is in a committed romantic relationship. But that couldn't be further from the truth. The need to give and receive love—to feel emotionally connected, seen, and valued—is universal. And the ability to speak love in a way that lands is just as important in friendships, family dynamics, workplace relationships, and faith communities as it is in marriage.

Coaching single clients through the lens of the 5 Love Languages offers a powerful opportunity. It's not about preparing for "someday." It's about showing up fully for *today*—with greater self-awareness, emotional confidence, and relational wisdom. When a single client gains clarity about how they're wired to experience love, they become more courageous in expressing it, more perceptive in recognizing it, and more intentional in offering it to others.

That's the reason I (Gary) wrote *The 5 Love Languages: Singles Edition*. It's a framework that applies far beyond marriage. Singles can deepen relationships with friends and family, heal from past hurts, and date with more insight and success. More than anything, they can stop waiting to be loved and start living out love in meaningful, affirming ways right now.

Your role as a coach is to help them see that this season isn't a waiting room—it's a training ground.

The Single Client's Coaching Journey

The single person who comes to see you arrives for a variety of reasons. Some are healing from heartbreak. Others are navigating long seasons of singleness. Some feel emotionally ready for a partner but relationally stuck. Still others simply want to grow in self-awareness and relational intelligence.

For many singles, the core emotional need is not all that different from those in a relationship: to feel seen, safe, and loved. But the absence of a romantic partner can bring a unique kind of ache—especially when the culture around them seems to equate love with coupledom. Research confirms that single adults often report lower social support and higher levels of loneliness than their partnered peers, despite being just as capable of forming emotionally meaningful relationships (Adamczyk & Segrin, 2015). In other words, it's not capacity that's lacking—it's connection.

This is where the coach's perspective matters deeply. A healthy coaching posture resists the urge to treat singleness as a problem to solve or a phase to rush through. Instead, it frames it as a meaningful chapter—one filled with opportunity for personal growth, emotional depth, and relational refinement.

Helping a single client explore their Love Language can unlock powerful insight, but it must be tethered to something bigger than future romantic success. This work is not about *preparing* for love, it's about *practicing* love—now, in real time. In friendships. In family systems. In their faith communities. And perhaps most importantly, in how they show care for themselves.

According to research by Chopik (2017), individuals who invest intentionally in close friendships experience increased wellbeing, resilience, and life satisfaction. That means as coaches, we're not just helping singles "wait well." We're helping them live fully.

Their story is already in motion. Your job is to help them recognize they're not missing a chapter; they're writing one.

Applying the 5 Love Languages to Single Life

One of the most valuable shifts a coach can facilitate for single clients is helping them realize that Love Languages don't require a romantic partner to matter. They are woven into every relationship, and every day. Friends, family, coworkers, and even the way a person cares for themselves all become arenas for Love Language expression and growth.

As I (Gary) noted in *The 5 Love Languages: Singles Edition*, these principles are just as relevant for individuals outside of romantic partnerships. They help people better understand themselves and others, deepen existing relationships, and communicate care with greater confidence and clarity.

Here are practical ways each of the 5 Love Languages can show up in a single person's life, along with ways a coach might help clients explore and apply them:

Words of Affirmation

- **Inward:** Identifying and challenging harsh inner criticism; intentionally speaking to oneself with the same encouragement one would offer a friend or journaling expressions of gratitude
- **Outward:** Offering verbal encouragement to friends or family, texting someone a specific appreciation, speaking blessing over others
- **Coaching Cue:** Ask your client to keep a "words bank" of life-giving things others have said or that they wish someone *would* say

Quality Time

- **Inward:** Prioritizing soul-filling solitude or intentional rest (e.g., taking yourself on a "solo date")
- **Outward:** Scheduling meaningful time with a close friend, joining a small group or community activity

- **Coaching Cue:** Help clients recognize the difference between *isolation* and *intentional alone time*—and where meaningful connection still fits

Receiving Gifts

- **Inward:** Honoring milestones with small, symbolic gifts to oneself; creating beauty in one's space
- **Outward:** Thoughtfully choosing gifts that reflect someone else's values or needs
- **Coaching Cue:** Help the client reflect on what kinds of gifts they've received that made them feel seen—and why

Acts of Service

- **Inward:** Taking care of one's physical and emotional needs (e.g., preparing meals, managing health, asking for help)
- **Outward:** Volunteering, helping a neighbor, doing something thoughtful for a friend without being asked
- **Coaching Cue:** Invite the client to complete one intentional act of service this week for someone they're close to—and one for themselves

Physical Touch

- **Inward:** Practicing somatic awareness, engaging in activities that promote healthy touch (yoga, massage, petting a dog), tending to physical wellness
- **Outward:** Appropriate touch in friendship (hand on the shoulder, hugs), touch-based hobbies (dancing, physical play with nieces/nephews)
- **Coaching Cue:** Ask your client where they feel safe receiving physical connection—and where they've felt that boundary disrespected in the past

Many single clients may not realize how richly their lives already reflect their Love Language—just not in the ways they'd initially expected. Your coaching can help them connect those dots, offering new insight into their own relational patterns, unmet needs, and opportunities to love and be loved right where they are.

Coaching Toward Dialect Discovery

Helping single clients recognize their dialect—the personalized, behavioral expression of their language—is where coaching becomes transformational. This is especially important for singles, who may already have some awareness of their Love Language but haven't explored the *how* and *why* of how it's playing out in their everyday life.

In coaching terms, dialect discovery moves clients, including singles, from category awareness to behavioral precision. That means asking not just *What's your Love Language?* but *How does it actually look when you feel loved?*

The 5 Love Languages Premium Assessment, again, offers a huge advantage here. The personalized Dialect Pages reveal specific behaviors, wordings, and expressions that matter most to the individual—not just the general concept. For example, a client might score high in Quality Time, but what fills their tank is side by side activity (e.g., running errands or doing a project together), not deep conversation or eye contact over coffee. That distinction matters.

For single clients, dialect work can be profoundly healing. Many have experienced relationships—romantic or otherwise—where they were "loved" in someone else's language, not their own. Helping them name what has felt fulfilling versus frustrating creates self-clarity and can reduce unnecessary shame. It also empowers them to communicate more clearly in the future.

Coaching Prompts for Dialect Discovery

- Think of a time when someone made you feel truly loved or cared for. What exactly did they do or say?
- What kinds of gestures tend to *miss the mark* for you, even if well-intended?
- What do you long for in your close relationships but hesitate to ask for?
- How have you tried to express love to others, and how has it landed?
- What behaviors have you wrongly labeled as "needy" that may actually reflect your core dialect?

This process often uncovers deeper relational narratives. For instance, a client might say, "I thought I didn't like gifts. But when someone gives me something that shows they *really know me*—that hits deep." That's not just Receiving Gifts—it's the dialect of sentimental customization.

Research on relational attunement supports this idea. Reis and Shaver's (1988) foundational work on intimacy emphasizes that feeling understood and cared for in specific, personal ways is a critical driver of closeness and wellbeing. Helping singles identify their own responsive patterns sets the stage for healthier connections in all areas of life.

Growth Goals for Singles

Once a single client begins to identify their Love Language and unique dialect, the natural next step is applying that insight through action. But this isn't about performance, it's about presence in other people's lives. The goal is to create a life where love is actively practiced, not passively awaited.

Growth goals help clients integrate their emotional awareness into everyday behaviors. Whether they're seeking deeper friendships, preparing for a future relationship, or simply hoping to feel more whole in their current season, these goals are about becoming more intentional, attuned, and emotionally courageous.

As a coach, you're not just helping your clients "work on themselves." You're helping them live more relationally—even when a romantic relationship isn't currently in view.

Sample Growth Goals by Love Language

These goals aren't about fixing something that's broken. They're about strengthening what's already good—and building habits that reflect a deeper understanding of how love flows in and out of your client's life. One helpful way to approach this is by aligning growth goals with your client's primary Love Language. Here's how that might look:

Words of Affirmation

- Keep a daily journal of one self-affirming statement and one compliment offered to someone else.
- Record a voice memo of encouraging truths you want to internalize, and play it when negative self-talk creeps in.

Quality Time

- Schedule two "presence appointments" per week: one with a friend, one with yourself (no phone allowed).
- Attend one new group activity or small gathering where meaningful connection is possible.

Receiving Gifts

- Start a small ritual of "symbolic gifting" (e.g., buying a postcard, flower, or token that reflects something meaningful).
- Reflect on one gift you've received that made you feel seen, and express gratitude to the giver if possible.

Acts of Service

- Choose one weekly act of service for yourself (e.g., prepping healthy meals, taking a relaxing walk, or even splurging at a spa).
- Do something thoughtful for a friend, neighbor, or colleague—unprompted and unannounced.

Physical Touch

- Add a body-based mindfulness practice (e.g., stretching, walking, grounding touch like placing your hand on your chest while breathing deeply).
- Schedule touch-positive experiences: a massage, a petting session with a dog, or a movement class.

Growth goals should feel invitational, not obligatory. Encourage your client to pick one or two goals per week that feel meaningful—and then reflect together on how those actions felt.

Also, normalize that these goals may bring up grief, vulnerability, or unexpected joy. This isn't just behavior change—it's identity growth.

In fact, research on behavior activation therapy shows that small, intentional actions—especially those aligned with a person's values—create momentum toward emotional wellbeing and connection (Dimidjian et al., 2011). Helping singles practice love in these bite-sized, personalized ways increases their capacity to connect—without needing to "have it all together."

Common Pitfalls to Avoid in Coaching Singles

Coaching singles through the lens of the 5 Love Languages is deeply rewarding—but it comes with its own set of landmines—both subtle and systemic. A good coach stays attuned not only to what they're teaching but also to what they're *implying*—in tone, posture, and unspoken assumptions.

Here are several common pitfalls to avoid:

1. Reducing the Coaching Goal to "Getting Ready for a Relationship"

It's easy to drift into a preparation mindset, subtly treating the single client's growth as a means to an end. But the goal isn't to become more datable—it's to become more whole. Coaching must honor the *present* moment, not just the imagined future.

2. Treating Singleness Like a Problem to Solve

Even with good intentions, coaching can unintentionally reinforce the idea that singleness is a deficit. Stay alert to any language that implies "something is missing." Instead, normalize singleness as one valid expression of human flourishing, and highlight the relational richness already in their life.

3. Ignoring the Client's Broader Relational World

Love Languages are not confined to romantic partnerships. Overlooking the client's friendships, family dynamics, faith community, or workplace relationships means missing the full scope of where love is both needed and offered.

4. Over-Spiritualizing (or Under-Spiritualizing) the Experience

If faith is part of your client's worldview, avoid dismissing their longing for connection—or overinterpreting it as spiritual immaturity. Likewise, if faith isn't central for them, avoid framing content in a way that feels disconnected from their values. Attunement here is key.

5. Underestimating Grief, Shame, or Loneliness

Some clients carry unresolved sorrow from past relationships or internalized shame from not "having someone." Resist the urge to cheerlead too quickly. Instead, hold space for what's real. As one client said, "I'm not sad every day. But I do wish someone would choose me. And that's hard to say out loud."

When these dynamics are navigated with care, coaching becomes a space of safety and empowerment. Your posture communicates just as much as your process. The goal isn't to get your client partnered; it's to get them rooted.

The Coach's Role: Naming, Normalizing, Nurturing

Your posture as a coach carries more weight than any insight you deliver. For singles, especially those who have felt overlooked, pitied, or pathologized by culture or community, your presence can be profoundly healing. You have the opportunity to name what's good, normalize what's hard, and nurture what's growing.

Naming means helping clients put language to their needs, patterns, and strengths—especially those that may have gone unnoticed or unnamed. It means calling out emotional courage when they voice a longing, or affirming their progress when they try something new, even if imperfectly.

Normalizing means helping clients feel less alone in their experience. When a client admits they're lonely or uncertain, they don't need a fix—they need to know they're human. You get to reframe emotional struggles as normal, understandable responses to real relational dynamics—not as evidence of failure.

Nurturing is about fostering growth over time. That might mean introducing a new practice, encouraging a small risk, or simply holding a steady presence while they untangle an old narrative. Great coaches don't rush growth—they make space for it. You don't need to be flashy or profound. You just need to be faithful to the slow work of love.

Done well, coaching singles isn't about filling a relational gap. It's about helping them discover that love is already available to them—within themselves, around them, and through the choices they make every day.

Bringing It Back to the Love Language That Matters Most

Whether partnered or single, every person wants to feel seen, safe, and loved. The work of coaching singles is not about helping them prepare to love "someday"—it's about helping them love well today. And that begins with empathy.

The Love Language that matters most is always the one that matters to the person in front of you. It means identifying their needs without shame, expressing love without reservation, and offering kindness without waiting for someone else to go first.

This is not a detour from the real work of love—it *is* the work. When singles grow in their fluency to love others in their dialect, they cultivate emotional courage and relational clarity that will serve them in every future connection. More importantly, they come to see that love doesn't begin with a partner. It begins with a posture.

Empathy is a practice. Self-awareness is a strength. Love is a language we never stop learning. And that learning matters—whether you're single, married, or somewhere in between.

Summary

Singleness is not a season to be bypassed or fixed—it's a season to be honored and inhabited. Coaching single clients through the lens of the 5 Love Languages offers a unique opportunity: to deepen emotional self-awareness, cultivate empathy, and strengthen relational habits that will serve them in every part of life, not just romance.

With thoughtful coaching, singles can learn to recognize how love already shows up around them, how their personal dialect shapes their needs and offerings, and how to live relationally in every sphere of their world. Your role isn't to prepare them for "someday"—it's to help them flourish today.

QUESTIONS TO PONDER

1. Do I approach coaching singles as its own valid path of growth, or do I treat it as a holding pattern for a future relationship?
2. How well do I help clients explore the richness of their relational world beyond romance?
3. Am I helping singles identify and practice their Love Language in friendships, family, and self-care?
4. What subtle messages might I be sending—through my tone, language, or assumptions—about the value of singleness?
5. How can I better equip single clients to name their needs without shame and love others with intentionality?

Chapter 20

Coaching Parents with the 5 Love Languages

I just don't get it," Jason said, rubbing his forehead. "I show up. I drive her to practice, I help with homework, I'm at every game. But my daughter says she doesn't feel close to me anymore. I don't know what else to do."

His wife, Andrea, added quietly, "She says I'm always busy. But I'm doing everything *for* her. And then she shuts down. We're trying, but . . . something's missing." Their daughter is thirteen—right at the edge of adolescence—and the gap between effort and connection is growing wider by the week.

Tasha, a single mom of a six-year-old boy, described something harder to name. "He's always sweet and I know he's had a good time when he comes back from his dad's," she said. "But lately, he's been clingy for days afterward. Like he doesn't want me to leave the room."

She sighed. "I hug him, I read to him, I tell him I love him . . . but something feels off. He's just quieter than usual. I can't tell if he's sad, or mad, or just adjusting." She paused and looked up. "Sometimes I wonder if I'm missing something he's trying to say—but doesn't have the words for."

Then there's Miguel and Sara, parents of a seventeen-year-old. "He used to tell us everything," Miguel said, his voice quieter than before. "Now it's one-word answers. Shrugs. We try to talk to him, but he barely looks up from his phone."

Sara nodded. "We used to feel close. But now it's like . . . we don't know how to reach him. Things have changed."

These are not disconnected or disinterested parents. They're showing up, sacrificing, doing what they know how to do. Their love is real—and often relentless. But when a child doesn't *feel* that love, the result can be confusion, guilt, or quiet heartbreak. Parents ask: *Why isn't what I'm doing enough? Why don't they feel it?*

The 5 Love Languages framework offers a powerful shift. It gives parents a way to decode what each child needs to feel emotionally seen and secure. As I (Gary) and Ross Campbell note in *The 5 Love Languages of Children* (2012), "What makes one child feel loved won't necessarily work for another." That's not a flaw—it's a feature of personhood. Every child is wired differently.

Coaching parents through this framework isn't about prescribing the right behavior. It's about helping them to pay better attention. To notice. To adapt. To learn how their child is already showing them what they need—and to respond with love that truly lands.

Your job isn't to question whether parents love their kids. It's to help them translate that love into a form their child can actually receive. This chapter will show you how.

Coaching the Shift—From Loving Intuitively to Loving Intentionally

Most parents love deeply and instinctively. It's not effort they're lacking—it's alignment. They often give the kind of love they *know*, the kind that feels natural to them or mirrors how they were raised. And sometimes, it lands beautifully. But when it doesn't, parents can feel blindsided (Reis & Shaver, 1988). The child pulls away, acts out, or simply seems unaffected. And the parent is left wondering, *Why isn't this working?*

That's where your role as a coach becomes powerful. You're not there to critique their love—you're there to help them understand it through the eyes of their child.

This requires reframing love from something we *feel* or *intend* to something we learn to *express effectively*. It's the difference between speaking a language fluently and just shouting louder in your native tongue, hoping the other person finally gets it.

Helping parents make this shift means inviting them to:

- Step back from their own assumptions about what love *should* look like
- Reflect on what kind of love expression comes most naturally to them—and how that may or may not match their child's needs
- Tune in to the behaviors, preferences, and emotional bids their child is already offering

This move from intuitive to intentional love requires humility, curiosity, and adaptability. And it's often a stretch—especially when a child's Love Language feels foreign to the parent. A Words of Affirmation parent might struggle to give hugs to a child whose primary language is Physical Touch. A parent who thrives on Acts of Service might miss their child's desire for one-on-one time. Helping parents see these gaps without shame, and adjust without defensiveness, is at the heart of this work.

I (Gary) and Campbell (2012) note that when a child's love tank is full, behavior improves, connection strengthens, and resilience grows. And that's not because parents are doing *more*—it's because they're doing what matters *most* to that child.

Understanding and Discovering a Child's Love Language

One of the most meaningful shifts you can facilitate as a coach is helping parents become curious observers of their child's emotional world. While some children clearly express what they want or need, most communicate in subtler ways—through behavior, repetition, tone, or even complaints. Discovering a child's Love Language begins not with labeling, but with noticing.

As I (Gary) and Campbell (2012) emphasize in *The 5 Love Languages of Children*, every child has a Love Language, but it may not emerge clearly until around age five or six—and even then, it continues to develop with age, personality, and life experience. That's why coaches must guide parents away from rigid typing and toward open, ongoing discovery.

You can help parents tune into their child's Love Language by asking questions like:

- "What does your child complain about most often?"
- "When do you see them light up?"

- "What do they request from you when they want to feel close?"
- "What do they do to express love to *you*?"

For example:

- A child who constantly says "Watch me!" or asks for one-on-one activities may be craving **Quality Time**.
- A child who creates drawings or crafts for others might be expressing **Gifts** as a way to connect.
- A child who offers spontaneous hugs, wrestles playfully, or curls up next to a parent on the couch might speak **Physical Touch** most fluently.
- A child who beams at praise—or wilts under criticism—may be especially tuned to **Words of Affirmation**.
- A child who loves to help, clean, or be part of a task might be looking to connect through **Acts of Service**.

Parents are often surprised to realize they've been "speaking love" all along—just in a dialect their child doesn't fully register. Or they may recognize that their own childhood patterns shaped how they default to showing care. Coaching invites reflection: *Am I loving them in the way that's easiest for me or in the way that's most meaningful to them?*

It all comes down to the parent: watching, listening, adjusting, and trying again.

Again, a child's Love Language isn't static. What fills their tank at six might look different at sixteen. That's why discovery is never one and done; it's a relationship posture. You're helping parents move from guessing to attuning. From assuming to learning. And from doing what they've always done to offering what their child truly needs now.

As a coach, your role is to normalize this process, guide without over-defining, and encourage parents to stay in the humble position of *student*, not expert. Your job is to guide that empathy into action. You're helping parents become students of their child's emotional world—not to fix them, but to truly know them.

Applying Each Love Language with Children

Once parents begin to discover their child's Love Language, the next step is learning how to speak it intentionally. This is where coaching becomes deeply practical—and deeply personal. You're helping parents build a toolkit of behaviors and habits that reflect their child's emotional wiring, while also coaching them through what may feel unfamiliar or uncomfortable.

Each Love Language offers a different opportunity for connection. Below is a coaching guide to help parents implement each one in everyday life.

Words of Affirmation

Children who crave Words of Affirmation flourish when they feel noticed, encouraged, and emotionally named.

Coaching cues:

- Encourage parents to affirm *character* more than performance: "I love how kind you were to your sister," not just "Great job on the test."
- Suggest making affirmations visual or tangible—lunchbox notes, sticky notes on the bathroom mirror, or "mailbox" folders where kids find occasional kind words.
- Help parents notice how tone impacts these children. Affirming children are often especially sensitive to criticism or sarcasm. One harsh word can undo days of positive input.

Developmental nuance: Young kids may light up at simple phrases like "I'm so proud of you." Older kids might respond more deeply to honest, vulnerable encouragement—especially when spoken in private.

Quality Time

For these children, love is spelled T-I-M-E. They want presence, not just proximity.

Coaching cues:

- Help parents identify small windows for one-on-one connection—ten minutes after school, a short walk after dinner, or tech-free "kid dates."
- Emphasize that undivided attention matters more than duration. A distracted hour isn't as powerful as a focused fifteen minutes.
- Invite parents to ask their child, "What do you love doing with me?" Their answers often point directly to Quality Time needs.

Developmental nuance: Toddlers may just want eye-level play. Tweens and teens might prefer parallel presence—watching a show together, running errands, doing art side by side. Follow their lead.

Receiving Gifts

This language is often misunderstood. For children with this wiring, it's not about materialism—it's about *meaning*.

Coaching cues:

- Help parents think symbolically: a shell from the beach, a keychain that reflects an inside joke, a book that says, "I thought of you."
- Coach parents to mark moments—firsts, losses, transitions—with small tokens that say, "This mattered, and you matter."
- Encourage letting the child give gifts too—it's often how they express love back.

Developmental nuance: Young children with this language may treasure handmade crafts or stickers more than store-bought toys. Older children may prefer meaningful surprises: "I saw this and thought of you."

Acts of Service

These children feel most loved when others take time to help them with what feels hard, overwhelming, or unspoken.

Coaching cues:

- Invite parents to identify one regular task their child dislikes—and occasionally join in without being asked.
- Suggest offering small, surprise gestures of support: laying out clothes, helping organize their backpack, fixing a broken toy without fanfare.
- Encourage language like, "I noticed this was hard for you, so I wanted to help."

Developmental nuance: For younger kids, Acts of Service can look like help with tying shoes or making their sandwich just right. For older kids, it may mean emotional service: helping them prep for a test or giving them a ride when it's inconvenient.

Physical Touch

Touch-based kids feel safest and most secure when love is felt physically.

Coaching cues:

- Offer a wide range of ideas: hugs, hair ruffles, piggyback rides, hand squeezes, high-fives, wrestling, or simply sitting close during story time.
- Help parents create predictable moments of safe touch: a morning snuggle, a secret handshake, or a bedtime back rub.
- Gently explore if parents are uncomfortable with this language. Some weren't raised in touch-positive environments and may need coaching to become more expressive.

Developmental nuance: Young kids thrive on physical closeness. As children age, Physical Touch needs often shift toward brief, public-safe expressions (e.g., fist bumps, pats on the back). Always emphasize consent and comfort.

As a coach, remind parents that none of this requires perfection. It's about showing up, noticing, and adjusting. Even small shifts can build trust and fill a child's emotional tank. The goal isn't to perform love—it's to make it *felt*.

Next, we'll explore how to support parents when they realize they've missed the mark—or feel overwhelmed by the gap.

Coaching Through Parental Guilt and Growth

It's not uncommon for parents—especially highly invested, emotionally aware ones—to feel a wave of guilt once they begin discovering their child's Love Language. They might say things like:

"I think I've been loving them in my own language this whole time."

"No wonder they've been pulling away."

"How could I have missed this?"

As a coach, this is a tender moment. Your posture matters more than your precision. These parents need to know that awareness is a form of love, too.

And in fact, guilt often shows up because they care so deeply. Research confirms this: parents who score high in emotional attunement and conscientiousness often experience more parenting-related guilt, not less (Liss et al., 2013). Guilt isn't a sign of indifference. It's often the emotional signature of love meeting its limits.

The temptation is to jump in and help parents "fix" what they now see. But the real coaching opportunity lies in helping them reframe this moment—not as failure, but as *formation*. This isn't evidence of falling short. It's evidence of showing up differently now.

You might gently say:

"What matters is that you're seeing it now. That kind of awareness is love in action."

"You didn't do it wrong. You were speaking the language you knew. And now you know more."

Guilt most often surfaces in two forms:

1. **Regret over the past**—*"I wish I'd known this sooner."*
2. **Overwhelm about the future**—*"What if I can't change enough now?"*

Both are coaching moments. Your role is to help parents understand that Love Languages are not about perfection but about *progress*. That shift is essential. As I (Gary) and Campbell (2012) remind us, children whose emotional love tanks are filled consistently—even if imperfectly—are more resilient to stress, better able to regulate their behavior, and more open to correction.

And perhaps even more importantly, research in child development confirms that strong parent-child bonds are not built on flawless connection but on what developmental psychologist Edward Tronick (2007) describes as *rupture and repair*. In healthy relationships, disconnection is inevitable—but reconnection is powerful. When a parent misses the mark and then moves toward the child with empathy and intention, trust is built.

Encourage parents to start where they are. One gesture. One adjustment. One moment of trying again. Love is a long game, and the willingness to keep learning is what gives it strength.

Building Family Rhythms Around Love

Once parents begin to understand their child's Love Language—and take small steps toward expressing it more intentionally—the next invitation is to create *rhythms* that keep love flowing naturally. Coaching parents toward consistent, sustainable practices is far more effective than encouraging occasional grand gestures.

Why rhythms? Because they:

- Remove decision fatigue
- Build emotional security through predictability
- Normalize love as something woven into everyday life
- Offer multiple, low-pressure opportunities for connection

You can help parents think in terms of *repeatable touchpoints*—not more to do, but more meaning in what they already do. The more they do them, the more they become loving habits. Below are sample practices for each Love Language, framed as ideas you can customize with the families you coach:

Words of Affirmation

- End each day with one sentence of spoken encouragement: "One thing I noticed and appreciated about you today is . . ."
- Slip a short note into their backpack or leave it by their toothbrush on hard days
- Use a dry-erase marker to write affirming words on their bathroom mirror

Quality Time

- Schedule a rotating "kid date"—even thirty minutes of undivided attention once a week
- Create rituals of connection: morning walks, bedtime chats, baking Saturdays
- Share a hobby together: puzzles, playlists, sports, or journaling side by side

Receiving Gifts

- Keep a small "gift stash" (stickers, bookmarks, shells, mini-notes) and use it to mark moments: "First day back," "I noticed your effort," "I'm proud of how kind you were"
- Encourage shared gifting—invite your child to choose something meaningful for a family member or friend
- Wrap up small items creatively, not expensively—a leaf in an envelope can mean everything if it says "I saw this and thought of you"

Acts of Service

- Help them with a task they usually do alone—organizing Legos, folding laundry, packing lunch
- Invite them into your own service: "I'm making cookies for Grandma—want to help?"
- Occasionally do something unexpected that lightens their load: lay out their clothes, fix a loose toy, quietly refill a water bottle

Physical Touch

- Create consistent rituals of safe touch: morning hugs, bedtime snuggles, a hand squeeze before school
- Offer spontaneous physical affection: a back rub during homework, a playful wrestling match, a couch cuddle during a show
- Tune into signals—some kids want touch at home but not in public; others crave closeness but don't ask for it

Help parents see that love doesn't have to be *loud* to be *lived*. Rhythms make love accessible, repeatable, and less dependent on mood or energy. They also give children something to look forward to—a form of emotional scaffolding that builds resilience and belonging.

And remind parents: These rhythms aren't about perfect follow-through. They're about showing up, again and again, in ways their child can count on.

Bringing It Back to the Love Language That Matters Most

At its core, this chapter isn't about parenting techniques—it's about empathy. The Love Language that matters most is the one that most helps a child feel known, safe, and deeply loved.

For parents, that often means letting go of what feels most natural and choosing what feels most *meaningful* to their child. It means trading instinct for intention. Familiar habits for focused attention. Assumptions for attunement.

As a coach, your job isn't to hand parents a formula. It's to walk with them as they become students of their children's emotional world. To help them notice what fills their child's tank—and what drains it. To gently name when they're loving on autopilot and celebrate when they begin to love with purpose.

Most of all, remind them: No one gets it right all the time. Love is not about perfection—it's about pursuit. And every time a parent leans in, tries again, adjusts the way they give, or learns a little more about who their child is becoming, they are speaking the Love Language that matters most.

Summary

Every child longs to feel loved—but not every child feels it in the same way. That's why the 5 Love Languages can be such a powerful tool in parenting. They help parents move from loving by instinct to loving with intention.

As a coach, you have the privilege of guiding that shift. You help parents discover their child's emotional wiring, name the subtle ways love can be misunderstood, and build rhythms of connection that fill emotional tanks daily. Whether it's a hug, a note, a shared moment, or a quiet act of service, your coaching invites parents to speak love in a way their child can *actually receive*.

And when they do? Behavior often improves. Connection deepens. And both parent and child begin to feel more secure. The Love Language that matters most is the one that meets the child right where they are—with empathy, presence, and grace.

QUESTIONS TO PONDER

1. Am I helping parents tune in to how their child *receives* love, not just how they give it?
2. How can I support parents in shifting from loving on autopilot to loving with empathy?
3. What tools or language might help parents become students of their child's emotional world?
4. How do I respond when parents express guilt or overwhelm in this process?
5. What rhythms or rituals could I suggest that would make love more visible in everyday family life?

Chapter 21

Coaching Love Languages in Crisis and Conflict

"We've tried everything," Michael says, jaw tight, arms crossed like a shield. "I read the five languages book—or whatever it's called. I've been doing it. Brought home flowers, got her a massage gift card. But nothing's changing. It's like none of it even counts."

Danielle doesn't look up. Her hands are clasped in her lap, knuckles white. "He's not lying," she says quietly. "He's doing the things. But it feels like he's checking boxes. There's no heart in it. No real emotion. Definitely not love. Truth is, I just don't know if I can trust him—or his motives."

Michael lets out a slow sigh and does a quick eye roll.

Danielle presses on. "He knows I need Quality Time. But he won't sit with me. Not really. He talks, but he won't *go there*. He won't talk about what we need to talk about. So yeah, I got the gift card. But what I really want is to *feel* him with me. I don't need something you order off Amazon."

Their marriage was still standing, technically. But after years of slow emotional erosion—and one recently revealed betrayal—small acts of care felt empty. They weren't just missing the mark. They were hitting a nerve.

So they find their way to you, a Love Language Coach. Are you prepared? Do you know what to do?

Are you prepared? Do you know what to do when "I brought her flowers" is met with silence? When a massage gift card feels more like a bribe than a bridge? When one partner is trying hard to reconnect and the other no longer feels safe enough to respond?

This is where coaching shifts from simple skill-building to soul-level discernment. It's no longer about what to say or do—it's about what *not* to rush. Because in a relationship cracked by crisis, love can't land until emotional safety returns.

As a coach, you may hear a story like this and feel the tension; both partners are trying, but nothing seems to be working. One gives effort, the other receives it like a stranger's gesture. The Love Languages framework—so often a bridge to connection—feels more like a list of unmet expectations.

This is when coaching must take a different shape.

You know that the 5 Love Languages can be a powerful tool for connection. But it's not magic. It's not designed for trauma therapy. It's not about conflict resolution. And it's not a shortcut around deep emotional pain.

In times of relational crisis, you don't start with Love Languages. You start with emotional safety.

This chapter is about helping coaches use the Love Languages *gently*—as a framework for healing, not a formula for fixing. It's about learning when to pause, when to offer small gestures without demand, and how to coach couples through the long work of rebuilding trust before rushing to express affection.

Because when a relationship is in crisis, the message that matters most is often the one that says: *I see your pain. I respect your boundary. I'm still here.*

What Love Languages Can't Fix

A relationship that's been through betrayal, burnout, or long-term neglect needs more than a little coaching in the 5 Love Languages.

When deeper crisis or conflict is occurring, the Love Languages will likely *backfire*. Why? Because couples in crisis need *emotional self-protection*. When trust has been fractured, gestures of love can feel confusing, even manipulative. A surprise gift may land like a guilt offering. A thoughtful act of service may feel transactional. A hug might trigger a memory of past hurt rather than comfort.

In other words: the expression of love won't land when the foundation of emotional safety has fractured or crumbled. That groundwork has to be rebuilt. Otherwise, Love Language efforts may feel like empty theatrics—nice on the surface but disconnected from the emotional reality underneath.

As a coach, your role is to slow the couple down. To help them understand that Love Languages were never meant to fix a broken foundation—they're meant to build on one. In moments of crisis, love needs to be redefined not as *doing the right thing* but as *showing up with empathy, accountability, and care for the pace of the other person.*

Because when safety is gone, even the most fluent expression of love will sound like noise.

Rebuilding Emotional Safety

Before a couple can reconnect emotionally—let alone reintroduce the 5 Love Languages—emotional safety has to be restored. Without it, even the most thoughtful gesture can feel hollow or threatening. A love note may trigger suspicion. A gift may be received as a guilt offering. A hug may bring up past pain instead of present comfort.

That's because in the wake of betrayal, chronic disconnection, or emotional volatility, the nervous system is in protection mode. The brain reads subtle signals—tone, timing, eye contact—as either cues of connection or signals of threat. When a relationship has been through crisis, love doesn't feel safe until trust begins to reemerge.

As attachment researchers have shown, emotional security is the foundation of all healthy intimacy (Johnson, 2008; Mikulincer & Shaver, 2007). Without it, couples can't fully engage emotionally or interpret gestures of love accurately. According to numerous studies (Porges, 2011), our ability to receive connection depends on whether we feel safe enough to let our guard down. If one or both partners are stuck in a state of hypervigilance, "speaking their language" won't land—it will feel like noise, or worse, pressure.

As a coach, this is where your role becomes delicate—and vital. You are not there to fix the wound. You are there to slow the pace, reduce pressure, and help the couple name what still feels unsafe. You create a space for honesty, not performance.

For coaches with limited experience in relational trauma or high-conflict dynamics, this is also the point to **consider referral**. Rebuilding emotional safety often requires clinical skills—especially when there's been infidelity, emotional abuse, trauma histories, or unprocessed grief. That doesn't mean you can't continue to work with the wounded couples as their coach. But it does mean you may need to come alongside, not lead the repair.

A good referral sounds like: "This is meaningful work we're doing here. And I want to help you do it in the most supportive way possible. I'd love for us to continue this coaching journey while you also work with a licensed therapist who can guide you through the emotional rebuilding piece."

The goal in these moments isn't quick connection, it's slow stabilization. You're helping the couple reenter shared emotional space—not with romantic gestures, but with honesty, presence, and patience.

Coaching questions that support safety might sound like:

- "What still feels emotionally risky for you in this relationship?"
- "When you try to connect, what do you fear the most?"
- "What's one way your partner could signal, 'You're safe with me'—without needing anything back?"

You're teaching them that love is not just expressed in Love Languages—it's felt in *consistent signs of emotional safety*. It's in a softened tone. A well-timed pause. The willingness to listen without defense. The humility to say, "I didn't realize that still hurts. I want to understand."

Because emotional safety isn't the result of a technique. It's the outcome of trust slowly being rewoven, moment by moment—until love has space to land again.

Using Love Languages Gently in Times of Pain

Let's make this abundantly clear: The practices in this section are meant for couples who are **already in the process of rebuilding emotional security**—ideally with the support of a licensed therapist, in addition to your coaching. If safety has not been reestablished or major breaches of trust remain unaddressed, this is *not* the time to use Love Language strategies. Focus instead on emotional regulation, boundaries, and outside referral.

Once a couple has begun to stabilize—when honesty is returning, emotions are being expressed safely, and trust is regrowing—you can begin to gently reintroduce the language of love. But the key word is *gently*. In crisis recovery, Love Languages shouldn't look like grand gestures or prescribed routines. They should look like invitations.

"Would it feel helpful if I made time just for us this weekend?"

"I don't know if you're open to it, but I'd love to bring you coffee tomorrow morning."

"I'm here if you ever want to talk . . . no pressure."

It's about making small, attuned efforts that honor the other person's *readiness to receive.* Even something as simple as folding laundry or a kind word can carry meaning—*if* it's offered with openness and no strings attached.

What does it look like to speak a Love Language gently?

Words of Affirmation

- "You don't have to respond. I just want you to know I see how hard you're working."
- Avoid over-apologizing or using flattery to smooth things over. Focus on truth, not polish.

Quality Time

- Invite low-pressure connection: a walk, shared silence, sitting together during a routine task.
- Let the other person set the pace or end the time early without penalty.

Receiving Gifts

- Small, symbolic, no-pressure gifts—like a shared photo, a comfort item, or a meaningful quote.
- Make sure it's about *them*, not your effort to be appreciated or reduce guilt.

Acts of Service

- Offer specific help: "Would it ease your day if I took that off your plate?"
- Don't expect recognition; do it because you're choosing kindness.

Physical Touch

- Ask before initiating: "Would a hug feel okay right now?"
- Respect their cues. Sometimes just sitting near them, without touch, is the most loving thing you can do.

The guiding questions in this phase are:

What expression of love might help (not pressure) this person toward healing?

Am I offering this from a place of empathy, not expectation?

Because in pain, what we need most isn't effort—it's attunement.

As a coach, remind couples that they're not restarting the Love Languages to "get back to normal." They're practicing new rhythms that reflect greater empathy, emotional awareness, and humility. These aren't just gestures. They're small acts of rebuilding. And every gentle gesture says: *I see you. I'm re-learning you. I'm here.*

Coaching Toward Repair, Not Just Reconnection

It's tempting—for both couples and coaches—to aim for reconnection as the ultimate goal. A returned smile. A gentle touch. A moment of shared laughter. These glimpses of warmth are meaningful. But if you stop there, you may miss what matters most: the deeper emotional repair underneath.

Reconnection is a spark. Repair is what makes it sustainable.

In many cases, the couple's current pain is tethered not just to emotional distance but to a specific rupture—something said or done (or left unsaid or undone) that left one partner feeling unseen, unsafe, betrayed, or alone. In those moments, gestures of love aren't enough. The wound needs to be named, and the hurt needs to be disclosed.

As a coach, you are not a therapist (unless you're both). But you can create space for repair by gently guiding the couple into meaningful emotional accountability. This doesn't mean rehashing every fight or excavating trauma. It means helping them speak honestly about *what still hurts—and what it would take to begin rebuilding trust.*

You might ask: "What's one thing you wish your partner understood about your pain?" Or "What expression of care feels safe to receive right now—and what doesn't?" Or "What do you need to hear or see that would help you start believing things could change?"

A common misstep is for the "offending" partner to jump into action too quickly—trying to "make up" for the past through Love Language behaviors. But this often skips over the emotional truth that *hasn't yet been heard.* The hurt partner may begin to feel like their healing is being rushed for the sake of comfort or optics.

Instead, guide couples to practice a different rhythm:

1. **Slow down.** Don't treat gestures as shortcuts to closeness.
2. **Name the injury.** Not to dwell but to validate.
3. **Take responsibility.** Without justifying or minimizing.
4. **Offer repair.** Not through gifts or touch alone but through humility, presence, and empathy.
5. **Invite connection.** Only when the other is ready—not when you need reassurance.

When Love Languages become part of that process, they can support healing. A carefully chosen word. A gentle service offered without expectation. A gift that says, *I remember who you are, even in the hurt.* That's repair—not as performance, but as a posture. And it's how a couple begins not just to feel close again, but to feel safe.

Love as a Long Game in Crisis Recovery

Crisis tempts urgency. Couples want to feel normal again, fast. Coaches want to help. And practical tools like the 5 Love Languages can feel like the perfect fix. But love isn't a sprint back to safety. It's a long walk through discomfort and disorientation to eventually reach deeper connection. In crisis recovery, the timeline isn't linear or short.

Your job as a coach is to set expectations gently and clearly. Let couples know that recovery isn't about getting back to who they were before. It's about learning how to love each other again from where they *actually are now.*

Here's what that often means:

- **Gestures may go unacknowledged**—not out of spite, but self-protection.
- **Progress may feel invisible**—because emotional safety builds quietly.
- **Misfires will still happen**—but don't mean recovery isn't working.
- **Love may look quieter than ever before**—and still be healing.

In these moments, the 5 Love Languages aren't tools for behavior management. They're small, daily offerings that support what Sue Johnson (2008) calls *emotional responsiveness*—the ability to signal, "I see you, I care, I'm here," even when it's hard.

As trust slowly returns, coaches can help couples track progress not by how warm things feel, but by how safe they're becoming. You'll need to ask questions like: "When you're hurt, do you still turn away—or are you willing to reach out?" Or "When your partner offers love, do you brace—or breathe?" Or "What feels different now compared to a month ago—not better, just different?"

These are the questions of someone playing the long game. Someone who understands that love isn't earned back in a weekend getaway or through a checklist of dialect-perfect actions. It's restored when care is *consistent* enough, *honest* enough, and *patient* enough to be trusted again.

That's what you're helping couples build—not just reconnection, but resilience.

How to Know When to Pause

In emotionally charged seasons, couples often crave reconnection more than anything. Love Language efforts can seem like the obvious path: Do the gestures, speak the dialect, and hope the spark returns. But if you're speaking their Love Language when emotional wounds begin to reappear or remain raw, it's time to put a bookmark in the Love Languages. Continuing to express love in any of the 5 Love Languages without truly restoring *safety* first can become a form of avoidance on the part of the couple. And truth be told, it may be an unconscious or conscious attempt to short-circuit the arduous work of first getting emotionally stable and safe. Deeper work is still needed.

Know this: Pausing is not a retreat—it's a repair strategy.

In emotionally distressed couples, slowing down the pace of reconnection can actually enhance outcomes. Research in emotionally focused therapy shows that lasting relationship repair depends more on how emotionally available and responsive each partner is—not just on what they *do* (Johnson, 2008). Similarly, Gottman's work on conflict patterns shows that rushing back into affectionate behavior before trust has been reestablished can trigger further withdrawal or reactivity (Gottman & Gottman, 2015).

Here's the point: You must be honest, as a coach, and learn to notice when Love Language efforts are being used to bypass the deeper emotional work that's needed before the Love Languages do what they do best: connect.

So as you do your work and you begin to realize that the emotional foundation still needs strengthening, the most compassionate coaching move is to *name it—and pause*. You might say:

- "I'm noticing that these gestures are starting to feel more like pressure than care. Can we step back for a moment and focus on how safe it feels to receive love right now?"
- "Sometimes even kind acts land wrong when there's still unresolved hurt. That's okay. Let's spend some time there first."
- "You're doing the actions, but what would it look like to check in emotionally before offering them?"

Pausing the Love Language work isn't failure. It's discernment. It signals that you're attuned to the emotional climate, not just the coaching structure. And it gives the couple space to return to the work later—with more empathy, more honesty, and more readiness to receive.

Summary

In seasons of relational distress, the Love Language that matters most isn't always the one listed at the top of an assessment report. It's the one that says, *I see your pain, and I'm not trying to rush it away.*

Crisis has a way of stripping love down to its core. It reveals whether affection is being offered as an escape hatch or as a steady hand. In these moments, Love Languages lose their meaning if they aren't grounded in empathy, emotional presence, and timing.

That's what your coaching is meant to offer—not a toolkit to fix a broken connection, but a framework to help couples move slowly, tenderly, toward repair. You help them name what still hurts, notice what still feels unsafe, and offer small gestures of love *only when those gestures can be safely received.*

Because when trust is fragile, even fluent love needs translation. And that translation begins with emotional safety. So what's the language that matters most in a season of conflict or crisis? The one spoken with humility. The one received with consent. The one offered without pressure. The one that says: *"I'm here. I'm listening. I'm not giving up."*

QUESTIONS TO PONDER

1. Am I helping couples prioritize emotional safety over behavioral progress?
2. Do I know how to recognize when Love Language efforts are backfiring—and how to guide couples to pause?
3. When coaching couples in distress, do I lead with empathy or urgency?
4. How comfortable am I referring clients to therapy when deeper healing work is needed?
5. What signs tell me if a couple is ready to gently reintroduce the 5 Love Languages—and what signs tell me they're not?

PART 6

BUILDING A THRIVING LOVE LANGUAGE COACHING PRACTICE

"Don't ask what the world needs.
Ask what makes you come alive, and go do it."

—ATTRIBUTED TO HOWARD THURMAN

Coaching isn't just a calling—it can be a sustainable, life-giving vocation. In this final section, you'll shift from theory to traction, learning how to build a practice that's both meaningful and resilient. Whether you're launching your first sessions or scaling a growing client base, these chapters offer practical strategies for finding your niche, cultivating referrals, setting boundaries, and staying energized for the long haul. Because coaching isn't just something you ***do***—it's something you ***build***. And when you bring your voice, your values, and the power of the 5 Love Languages into the world with intention, your impact doesn't just grow. It multiplies.

Chapter 22

The Business of Love Language Coaching

You've done the online training. You've studied the resources. You've got the tools. You believe in this work. But now what?

For many new coaches—especially those coming from ministry, caregiving, or volunteer backgrounds—this part can feel disorienting. You're motivated, maybe even called, but you're unsure how to translate that calling into a clear path forward.

Maybe you're a stay-at-home parent, a pastor, small group leader, wanting to do some coaching on the side. Or maybe you're a newly certified coach ready to launch a full-fledged practice—but have no idea where to begin: how to set prices, schedule sessions, draw boundaries, or even explain what you do when someone asks.

Whatever your situation, here's the good news: There's room for all of it.

Not every Love Language Coach will build a business. Some will serve informally in churches, marriage ministries, or nonprofit spaces—equipped with new tools, language, and confidence to walk with others more effectively. Others will build a coaching practice, whether part-time or full-time, and want to do it with clarity, professionalism, and sustainability.

This chapter is for both. It will help you build a practice—or a presence—that reflects the very things you coach others toward: intention, empathy, consistency, and impact.

If you're brand-new to business concepts, we'll walk you through the basics—gently, clearly, and practically. If you're already coaching but need better structure, we'll help you think about pricing, systems, and scalability. And if you're coaching inside a church or organization, you'll still find guidance here for managing your time, setting boundaries, and showing up well.

Because whether you're coaching one couple a month or launching a full-time practice, this work matters. And the way you structure it—ethically, clearly, and sustainably—helps you do it even better.

Let's walk through what it takes to turn purpose into practice.

Starting Smart—Legal and Ethical Foundations

Before you print business cards or schedule your first session, there's one crucial truth to settle: Coaching may feel personal, but it's still a professional relationship. Whether you're charging for your services or offering them as part of a ministry or mentoring role, the moment someone trusts you with their emotional world, you step into a space that requires clarity, boundaries, and responsibility.

This doesn't mean you need to hire a lawyer—but it does mean you need to understand what it takes to protect your clients, your practice, and yourself.

Here are the foundational pieces every Love Language Coach should consider:

1. Choose Your Structure

If you plan to charge for your services—or even accept donations—it's important to consider how your coaching is legally structured. This protects your work, your time, and your peace of mind.

Most new coaches choose one of three paths:

- **Sole Proprietorship**
  This is the simplest option and may not require formal registration in your state. You report your coaching income on your personal taxes. However, it offers no personal liability protection, meaning your personal assets aren't separated from your business obligations.

- **Limited Liability Company (LLC)**
  An LLC adds a layer of legal and financial protection, separating your personal and business finances. It also allows you to open a business bank account, create more formal contracts, and appear more professional in your communications. Many part-time coaches opt for this once they begin accepting regular payment.

- **Nonprofit Organization**

  Some coaches, especially those working in ministry contexts, choose to form a nonprofit. This can make sense if your coaching is part of a larger mission—like offering relationship support through a church, community outreach, or donor-funded initiative.

  With nonprofit status, you can still charge for services, but you'll likely operate on a different financial model: grants, donations, or program fees.

  Becoming a 501(c)(3) nonprofit requires formal filing with the IRS, board formation, and compliance with nonprofit law. If you go this route, consider consulting an attorney or nonprofit advisor.

Note: You don't need to make this decision right away. But within your first year of coaching for pay, it's worth exploring—especially if you're seeing multiple clients.

2. Clarify the Coaching Relationship

Whether you coach professionally or as part of a church role, your clients need to understand what coaching is—and what it isn't. You are not providing therapy, mental health treatment, or legal advice. Even if you're licensed in another field, when you're functioning as a Love Language Coach, you must stay within the boundaries of that role. This is echoed by the International Coaching Federation (ICF), which emphasizes the importance of defining the coaching relationship, establishing boundaries, and clearly distinguishing coaching from clinical care (ICF, 2021).

To help with this:

- Use a Coaching Agreement or intake form, even in informal settings. It doesn't need to be fancy—just clear. We've included an example you can use in the Appendix.
- You'll note that it uses language like: "This coaching relationship is focused on helping individuals or couples apply the 5 Love Languages for greater connection. It is not a substitute for mental health counseling, medical care, or professional therapy."

3. Stay in Your Lane—And Know When to Refer

There will be times when a client's needs stretch beyond what coaching can or should address—addiction, abuse, unprocessed trauma, crisis, infidelity, or a history of severe mental health challenges.

Your job is not to diagnose or dive into crisis; it's to notice when deeper help is needed and refer with compassion.

It's okay to say: "This is important work, and I want to make sure you're supported at the right level. I'd encourage you to consider working with a licensed counselor while we continue coaching the skills and strategies that support your relationship."

You don't lose credibility when you refer. You gain trust.

4. Keep Your Notes Professional (or Don't Keep Them at All)

If you choose to take notes, keep them brief and factual. Don't write anything you wouldn't feel comfortable being seen in court or shared with your client. Alternatively, you can opt not to keep session notes at all—especially if you aren't operating in a regulated clinical capacity.

5. Consider Liability Insurance

If you coach for pay, even just a few clients a month, it's wise to explore general and professional liability coverage. It's surprisingly affordable—often under $200/year for coaches—and gives you peace of mind if a misunderstanding arises.

6. If You're Coaching Online, Learn the Rules

Coaching across state lines (or internationally) is common—but you need to be clear that:

- You are not practicing therapy
- You are not governed by licensing boards
- You are working under a private coaching relationship by consent

You should always state that in writing and, where appropriate, include your governing business address and terms of service.

Bottom Line: Coaching is a relationship built on trust. And that trust begins with how you structure the work—even behind the scenes. When clients know you're clear, ethical, and professional, they're more likely to relax, open up, and do the work. So don't let this part intimidate you. Take it one step at a time. Clarity protects everyone and creates a foundation you can build on.

Designing a Coaching Package That Works

One of the most common mistakes new coaches make is offering open-ended, session-by-session coaching with no clear process or structure. It feels flexible, but in reality it creates uncertainty for both you and your clients.

People don't just need support. They need a path.

A coaching package gives your clients clarity. It helps them know what they're saying yes to and gives you a clear arc to guide them through. Whether you're coaching professionally or offering services in a ministry or nonprofit context, packaging your coaching helps create structure, momentum, and value. In fact, research on coaching outcomes suggests that structured programs with consistent arcs lead to stronger client satisfaction and perceived value than open-ended or one-off sessions (Bachkirova, Cox, & Clutterbuck, 2014).

Why Packages Work Better Than One-Off Sessions

- They create a clear beginning, middle, and end
- They reduce drop-offs and no-shows
- They give people time to build trust and traction
- They help you manage your calendar and energy
- They communicate that coaching is a *process*, not a quick fix

What's Included in Your Package?

When you design a coaching package, you're not just selling your time—you're curating a relational growth experience. That experience includes your sessions, yes, but it also includes the tools, resources, and guidance that support transformation between sessions. What you include brings clarity and added value to your clients, and it reinforces that your coaching is built on a well-supported process.

We strongly recommend that you build key resources directly into the price of your package so that every person you coach has access to the most helpful tools.

Include the following:

- **The 5 Love Languages Premium Assessment**—This gives people a personalized, detailed view of their Love Language *and* their dialects, giving you a common language and framework to work from. This is more in-depth and actionable than the free quiz many people have seen.

- ***The 5 Love Languages* (Classic Book)**—A foundational reference that reinforces the core ideas you'll be coaching around. It's especially helpful for clients who are new to the framework.
- ***The Love Language That Matters Most***—This book takes the concept deeper, guiding people toward empathy and attunement—not just matching actions to a profile. It also introduces the idea of dialects, which can often explain why "speaking their language" sometimes doesn't land.

Including these resources up front does three things:

1. **It gives your coaching structure and depth**—you're not just talking, you're guiding. Clients have materials to engage with between sessions, which reinforces learning and keeps momentum strong.
2. **It prevents surprises around cost**—clients know exactly what's included and what it's worth. Bundling the materials into your package price avoids nickel-and-diming and feels cohesive.
3. **It strengthens your value proposition**—your coaching package now includes approximately $100 worth of trusted resources. This not only benefits your clients, it becomes a compelling part of how you communicate your offering. You're not just selling time, you're offering a complete, well-equipped experience.

We'll talk more about how to leverage this built-in value when we get to the next chapter on marketing—but for now, just know this: What you include reflects what you believe your clients deserve. So when you're pricing your package, be sure to calculate not only your time but also the value of the resources you're offering.

How Many Sessions Should You Offer?

There's no one-size-fits-all, but here are a few proven models:

1. Intro Package – 3 Sessions

Great for discovery, education, and getting started

- Session 1: Assess each partner's Love Language and relational goals with the Premium Assessment
- Session 2: Identify barriers and misfires in communication
- Session 3: Teach practical strategies and create a short action plan

2. Core Package – 6 Sessions

Ideal for people who want to apply the Love Languages with support

- Covers dialects, communication patterns, and real-time practice
- Allows for deeper reflection and growth
- Often used as the standard coaching package

3. Premium Package – 8–10 Sessions

Designed for deeper transformation and accountability

- Includes deeper work on empathy, dialect fluency, and patterns of disconnect
- Allows space for growth, relapse, reengagement, and sustained application
- Ideal for people in mild distress or post-crisis rebuilding

Session Frequency

- **Weekly sessions** work well for building momentum—especially early on
- **Biweekly** is often ideal for longer packages, once foundational trust is built
- **Monthly check-ins** can be offered as a follow-up or maintenance option

In-Person vs. Online

- Virtual coaching allows flexibility, comfort, and reach beyond geography
- In-person sessions work well if you're embedded in a church or local community
- Hybrid models (e.g., start in-person, then continue virtually) also work well

Clarity Builds Confidence

When people know what to expect, they engage more fully. Be up front about:

- What's included (e.g., number of sessions, access between sessions if any, materials like books and assessments)
- What's not included (e.g., emergency support, therapy, long-term marriage counseling)
- The goals of your work together—and how they'll know if it's working

And always make it clear that this is a partnership, not a rescue mission. Coaching works when both people show up, stay engaged, and practice what they learn.

Pricing with Integrity and Confidence

Few things trip up new coaches more than the question: *"What should I charge?"*

If you're coaching through a church or nonprofit, you may not be charging at all—or you may be offering services by donation. But if you're launching a formal coaching practice or even doing part-time work on the side, setting clear and confident pricing is essential.

And here's the truth: You can care deeply about people and still charge for your time. Compassion and compensation are not in conflict.

Common Mindset Traps

- "I'm not licensed, so I shouldn't charge much."
- "I just want to help—I feel weird asking for money."
- "What if they can't afford it?"
- "Am I really worth that yet?"

These are *normal* thoughts for new coaches. But they often lead to underpricing or emotional exhaustion. Remember, coaching is valuable when it's consistent—and it can't be consistent if it's unsustainable. Undervaluing your services doesn't just affect your sustainability—it can actually diminish how clients perceive your value. Research shows that pricing too low can erode credibility and lead clients to engage less fully with the experience (Nagle, Hogan, & Zale, 2016).

How to Think About Your Rates

Consider these factors when setting your fees:

- **Your experience** (ministry background, related certifications, years in coaching or caregiving roles)
- **Your location and audience** (urban vs. rural, church-based vs. private practice)
- **Your coaching format** (virtual, in-person, group vs. individual)
- **Your financial needs and goals** (part-time income vs. full-time business)

You don't have to get it perfect from the start. Begin where you feel honest, then adjust as your confidence grows.

Suggested Ranges (USD)

These are ballpark figures—your rates may fall outside of these depending on your market and model:

Ccoach Level	Session Rate	6-Session Package
New Coach (0–1 yr)	$50–$90/session	$300–$540
Developing Coach (1–3 yrs)	$90–$150/session	$540–$900
Seasoned Coach (3+ yrs)	$150–$250/session	$900–$1,500+

Tip: Offering a *slight* discount on packages (vs. per-session rates) can encourage clients to commit and give structure to your coaching arc.

Should I Offer Sliding Scale or Scholarships?

You can—especially if you're serving in ministry or feel strongly about accessibility. But set clear boundaries:

- Offer a set number of reduced-fee spots
- Require an application or short conversation
- Reassess every 6–12 sessions

Important: Don't discount your value so much that you begin to resent the work. A coach who feels drained or taken advantage of won't be helpful to anyone.

How to Talk About Pricing Without Flinching

When you believe in the value of what you offer, it's easier to communicate it clearly. Try this:

"I offer a 6-session coaching package focused on helping people identify and apply their Love Languages in a way that works. The full package is $600, which includes materials and tools. If you're ready to move forward, I'll send over next steps."

Speak with warmth and clarity. Don't overexplain. Let your tone match your conviction.

Payment and Scheduling Systems

You became a coach to help people—not to manage calendars, chase invoices, or wrestle with email threads. But here's the truth: The systems you put in place are part of the client experience. When your scheduling is seamless and your payments are clear, clients feel safe, respected, and well cared for—even before the session starts.

And if you're coaching on the side or just getting started, the right systems will save your energy and your time.

Scheduling: Let Technology Do the Heavy Lifting

You don't need a fancy website to start—just a reliable booking tool that lets clients:

- View your availability
- Schedule (or reschedule) their own sessions
- Receive automatic reminders
- Avoid back-and-forth email tag

Some popular and trusted options include **Calendly** (a clean, user-friendly platform that integrates with Google and Outlook calendars), **Acuity Scheduling** (which also includes built-in payment options), and coaching-specific platforms like **PracticeBetter** or **CoachAccountable**, which offer added features like intake forms.

Pro tip: Set clear boundaries on your availability (e.g., "Coaching sessions available Tuesdays and Thursdays from 3–7 p.m."). This prevents overscheduling and burnout.

Payments: Make It Easy, Safe, and Professional

Whether you're charging clients directly or receiving donations for your time, the goal is to make payment friction-free. That means:

- Clients know when payment is due
- They can pay easily (ideally online)
- There's no awkwardness or confusion

When it comes to collecting payments, keep things simple, secure, and easy to manage. **Stripe** and **Square** are excellent options for sending invoices and accepting credit card payments directly. Many clients are also familiar and comfortable with **PayPal**, making it a widely trusted choice. For more informal or nonprofit settings, **Venmo Business** can be convenient, though it may feel less professional if you plan to scale your practice. If you're using platforms like **Acuity** or **PracticeBetter**, you can also integrate payment directly into your booking process so clients pay at the time of scheduling—streamlining the entire experience.

Set Clear Policies—and Stick to Them Kindly

Even if you're a "heart person," you still need a few policies to protect your time and energy:

- **Cancellation policy:** e.g., "Sessions canceled within 24 hours may be forfeited or charged."
- **Refund policy:** Clarify up front whether packages are refundable or transferable.
- **Rescheduling:** Give clients a clear way to move sessions—ideally through your scheduling system, not by text.

Put these policies in writing—in your coaching agreement, confirmation emails, or intake forms—and revisit them briefly in your first session.

Bottom Line: You don't need a complex setup. But you do need systems that serve you and your clients well. Start simple. Automate what you can. Make it easy for clients to work with you—and easy for you to keep showing up with full presence and professionalism.

Building an Exceptional Client Experience

Great coaches don't just offer insight—they offer an experience. From the moment someone reaches out for help, they're not only evaluating your coaching—they're evaluating your presence, your clarity, and your care.

An exceptional client experience isn't about fancy materials or elaborate onboarding. It's about building trust through every interaction—before, during, and after the work you do together. Whether you're coaching in a church setting, through your own business, or online with couples you've never met in person, this part of your work matters deeply.

Here are four core areas to focus on:

1. The First Contact Matters

Whether a couple is referred to you by a pastor or finds you online, their first impression often comes from your tone in an email or your clarity in a brief discovery call. Aim to be warm, prompt, and clear. You don't need to "sell" yourself—just communicate that you're trustworthy, focused, and here to serve.

Sample language: "Thanks so much for reaching out. I'm honored you're considering coaching. Here's what I offer and what a first step might look like."

2. Set the Stage with Thoughtful Onboarding

Coaching starts before the first session. You might send:

- A short **welcome message** explaining what to expect
- A brief **intake form** (including contact info, goals, and what drew them to coaching)
- Your **coaching agreement** and scheduling/payment info

Even if you're coaching informally or through a church, it's still wise to offer structure. It builds safety and minimizes confusion.

3. Be Clear About What Coaching Is—And Isn't

Clients will sometimes expect therapy, advice, or conflict resolution. Use your first session to explain:

- That coaching is goal-oriented, future-focused, and grounded in emotional insight
- That your role is to **guide**, not to diagnose, rescue, or mediate
- That the 5 Love Languages are a tool for greater empathy and connection but not a solution for deep psychological trauma or crisis

Setting these expectations clearly builds trust and prevents future frustration.

4. Use Loveology.org to Extend Your Coaching Voice

Your coaching doesn't need to stop when the session ends. In fact, what you do between sessions can quietly reinforce connection, momentum, and trust—without adding hours to your workload.

One of the simplest, highest-impact tools for between-session connection is **Loveology.org**. It offers free and brief, research-informed videos, from over a hundred leading relationship voices (including Gary Chapman and Les & Leslie Parrott)—all accessible without a login or paywall.

Loveology is designed especially for this purpose. So it's quick and easy to send a link to your clients with a note: *"This underscores what we talked about yesterday—give it a watch."*

It takes you just thirty seconds, and gives them something rich to reflect on.

You're not assigning homework—you're giving an echo. A reminder. A soft nudge to stay engaged. And this isn't about constant access or hand-holding. It's about thoughtful, low-effort moments that remind clients they're supported and still on the path.

These small touch points build continuity and presence. They signal, "*You matter. I didn't forget.*"

Going Virtual: Building an Online Practice

Let's be clear: Online coaching is not a fallback. It's not what you do when you can't meet in person. For many Love Language Coaches, virtual coaching *is* the plan—and a highly effective one at that.

Meeting over Zoom or Google Meet doesn't lessen the impact of your work. If anything, it increases your reach, lowers overhead, and allows couples to connect with you in the comfort of their own space. And for some couples, it actually helps them open up faster—because they're more relaxed in their own environment. Studies show that virtual coaching—when done with presence and professionalism—can be just as effective as in-person work in producing meaningful learning and performance outcomes (Jones, Woods, & Guillaume, 2016).

Whether you're looking to coach from home, serve clients in other states, or simply reduce the logistical burden of back-to-back appointments, building an online practice can be one of the most sustainable ways to grow.

Why Online Coaching Works

- **Comfort:** Clients are in a familiar setting—this often leads to deeper conversations sooner.
- **Accessibility:** You're not limited by zip code. You can coach couples across your state—or even the country.
- **Flexibility:** You can schedule with less commute, more rhythm, and fewer logistical complications.
- **Affordability:** No office rental, no overhead.

And perhaps most important: It meets clients where they already are—digitally. Today's clients are used to learning, connecting, and growing online. Coaching this way aligns with how they already engage the world.

What About Coaching Across State Lines?

Because you're not providing therapy or clinical services, most states do not restrict coaching across borders—as long as you're clearly operating as a coach. You don't have to know the legal code of every state, but you do need to stay in your lane by making it clear that you are coaching, not counseling.

Don't think of online coaching as a workaround. Think of it as a modern, flexible, and deeply effective way to deliver what matters most: connection, empathy, and growth. And for many clients, the fact that they can do it from their living room, between kid drop-offs, or during their lunch hour *is what makes coaching possible in the first place.*

Summary

Coaching isn't just about meaningful conversations—it's about offering those conversations within a clear, professional, and sustainable structure. Whether you're building a side practice, coaching through your church, or pursuing this work full-time, the way you set up your coaching matters.

In this chapter, you learned how to choose a business structure that aligns with your goals and responsibilities, and how to create coaching packages that give your work clarity, rhythm, and value. You explored how to set prices with integrity and confidence—reflecting both your time and your impact—and how to use systems for scheduling, payment, and communication that support you and serve your clients. We covered how to offer thoughtful between-session touch points, including curated resources like Loveology.org, and how to build an exceptional client experience from the first email to the final session. You also learned how to launch and grow a coaching presence virtually, with professionalism and warmth. And perhaps most importantly, you were reminded that this work doesn't require perfection—it begins with humility, clarity, and a deep belief that what you're offering truly matters.

You don't have to be fully formed to get started. Just stay grounded in your why, clear on your boundaries, and open to learning as you go. Coaching is both service and stewardship—and you're building something that lasts.

QUESTIONS TO PONDER

1. Do I know what kind of coaching structure fits my goals (volunteer, ministry-based, or business-focused)?
2. What kind of client experience do I want to offer—and is my current process aligned with that?
3. Am I pricing my services in a way that honors my time, effort, and impact?
4. What systems do I need to put in place to make my coaching simpler and more professional?
5. How might I use simple tools (like Loveology.org) to extend my care without exhausting myself?
6. Where do I need to build more clarity—about what I offer, who I serve, or how I show up?
7. Am I giving myself permission to grow at my own pace—with excellence but without pressure?

Chapter 23

Marketing Your Coaching Services

Let's get one thing straight: Marketing is not a dirty word.

If that word makes you cringe a little, you're not alone. Many coaches, especially those coming from ministry, caregiving, or volunteer backgrounds, feel conflicted about marketing. It can seem self-promotional, gimmicky, or at odds with your deeper "why." You got into this to help people, not to talk about yourself. Right?

But here's the truth: Marketing isn't about convincing people. It's about clarifying your value so the right people can find the help they're already looking for. It's service through communication. Visibility through empathy.

In fact, research shows that people are far more likely to trust and engage with services that feel human, relevant, and clearly articulated (Kotler, Kartajaya, & Setiawan, 2017). Effective marketing isn't about volume—it's about resonance. When you clearly communicate who you are and how you help, you build trust before the first session even begins.

Marketing researcher Bernadette Jiwa puts it this way: "Marketing is the generous act of helping people solve a problem. Their problem" (Jiwa, 2019). That's exactly what you do as a coach. So why wouldn't you communicate that well?

In this chapter, we'll reframe marketing as a natural extension of your coaching practice. You'll learn how to:

- Clarify what you offer and who it's for
- Communicate your value in ways that feel honest and unforced

- Use the tools already at your fingertips (like Loveology.org and the 5 Love Languages brand)
- Set up simple, sustainable ways to make your coaching findable and easy to say yes to

Marketing done right doesn't feel like a pitch. It feels like an invitation. Let's start by asking the question at the heart of every great coaching offer: What problem do you solve?

Clarify Your Message—What Problem Do You Solve?

Before you build a website, post on social media, or ask for referrals, there's one essential question every coach must answer: *What problem do you help people solve?* It sounds simple, but most new coaches skip straight to describing what they *do*.

You might find yourself saying things like:

"I help couples understand their Love Languages."
"I offer six-session coaching packages."
"I'm certified in relationship coaching."

Those are fine descriptions—but they don't speak to what your potential clients are actually looking for. People aren't searching for a methodology. They're searching for hope. They want to feel heard. They want to feel better. What they're really asking is, *"Do you get what we're going through—and can you help?"*

Effective marketing flips the focus from your process to their pain point. Instead of describing your approach, describe what's going wrong in the relationship that coaching can make right:

- "You love each other, but you're not feeling connected."
- "You keep trying, but nothing seems to land."
- "You've read the book, but the spark still isn't there."
- "You're tired of having the same argument over and over."

These are the kinds of phrases couples actually use. When they see or hear them in your messaging, they feel seen. It's that simple—and that powerful.

One of the most important mindset shifts in marketing is learning to position yourself not as the hero but as the guide. Donald Miller, in *Building a StoryBrand*, teaches that every good brand plays the role of a guide helping someone else win their story. Your clients are the heroes—they're the ones doing the hard work. You're the one who helps them find a way forward.

So instead of saying, "I'll help you master the 5 Love Languages," you might say, "Many couples try to show love—but still miss each other. I help you get it right." It's not about impressing them. It's about making them feel understood.

If you need help getting started, try this simple message formula:

"Many couples feel ________________, even though they ____________________.

I help them ________________, so they can ____________________."

Here are two quick examples: "Many couples feel disconnected, even though they genuinely care about each other. I help them speak love in a way that finally lands—so they can feel seen, supported, and closer again." Or "Many couples read *The 5 Love Languages* and still struggle to apply it. I help them take it from 'we tried' to 'this actually works.'"

Your message doesn't need to be clever. It needs to be clear. When people hear your words and say, *"That's us,"* your marketing has already done its most important work.

Know Who You Serve (and Who You Don't)

One of the biggest fears new coaches have around marketing is that they'll narrow their message too much. "But I could help all kinds of couples!" And it's true—you probably could.

But here's the paradox: When you try to speak to everyone, you usually end up reaching no one. Your message becomes vague, forgettable, and hard to connect with. But when you speak directly to the *kind* of couple you most understand and feel called to help, those people hear you more clearly—and are far more likely to respond.

That's what it means to know your niche.

You don't need to box yourself in. You're not turning anyone away. You're simply focusing your message so it *resonates*. Think of it like tuning your signal. You want the right people to hear, *"This coach gets us."*

Ask Yourself: Who Am I Uniquely Equipped to Serve?

- Do you connect especially well with newlyweds or engaged couples?
- Do you have experience walking alongside blended families?
- Are you drawn to faith-based couples, military or first-responder families, second marriages, or long-distance relationships?

You don't have to choose forever. But start where your voice feels natural and your empathy runs deep.

Create a "Client Snapshot"

Imagine one couple that's a perfect fit for your coaching. Who are they? What are they struggling with? What are they hoping for? How might they describe their pain—and what do they wish someone would help them with?

Now test your marketing language against that snapshot. If it wouldn't grab *that* couple's attention, refine it.

Knowing your audience is the difference between broadcasting and connecting. When you get specific, your message goes from generic to personal.

Make It Easy to Say Yes—Your Offer at a Glance

Once someone is interested in working with you, don't make them dig for the details. Clarity builds confidence. Confusion stalls decisions.

Your job is to make the "yes" feel simple, informed, and low-pressure. That starts with communicating your offer in plain, compelling language.

What Should You Include?

When someone lands on your website, reads a brochure, or talks with you during a consultation, they should quickly understand:

- What you offer
- What's included
- What it costs
- What they can expect to experience or gain

Avoid vague phrasing like "relationship coaching packages tailored to your needs." Say what it is: "I offer a 6-session coaching experience that helps couples understand each other's Love Language, apply it in ways that work, and reconnect emotionally—using trusted tools that are personalized to their relationship."

Position the Package, Not Just the Sessions

We've already discussed the merits of offering preset packages in the last chapter. Here's an example of how to highlight the value of the package and make it attractive and easy to say "yes" to:

The Connection Package

6 sessions over 8 weeks

Includes the 5 Love Languages Premium Assessment

Two bestselling books (*The 5 Love Languages* and *The Love Language That Matters Most*)

Check-ins between sessions

Total value: Over $100 in resources + 6 hours of personalized coaching

Package Price: $595

Don't be afraid to name the value. When people see what's included, they're more likely to perceive your coaching as a meaningful investment, not just an expense.

Preview the Journey

Give a snapshot of what working with you feels like. A short arc helps potential clients picture the process:

- Session 1: Discovery – identify each partner's Love Language and dialect
- Session 2–4: Application – address disconnects, practice empathy, build fluency
- Session 5–6: Integration – strengthen connection, develop habits, plan for growth

This reassures clients: *"There's a path here—we're not just winging it."*

Make the Next Step Obvious

End with a warm, clear invitation:

- "Schedule your free 20-minute consult."
- "Book your first session today."
- "Have questions? I'd love to hear from you."

Link directly to your calendar or contact form—no hoops, no hard sell. People often reach out at vulnerable moments. Your clarity gives them courage to take the next step.

Leveraging the Power of the 5 Love Languages® Brand

When it comes to trust and name recognition, you're not starting from scratch. As a Certified Love Language Coach, you're aligned with one of the most recognizable relationship frameworks in the world.

This isn't a niche concept or a trend. The 5 Love Languages has become a global phenomenon—translated into more than fifty languages, with over twenty million copies sold, and still a consistent bestseller decades after its release. It's referenced in sermons, counseling offices, corporate training, military chaplaincy, TikTok videos, and even sitcom punchlines. It's on nightstands, book club lists, and wedding registries. It's ubiquitous and carries a lot of cultural capital.

For many couples, *The 5 Love Languages* was their first exposure to the idea that love isn't just about intention—it's about communication. Even if they read it years ago, the language has stuck. When people hear "Love Languages," they immediately understand the category—and many already know their own.

That's your advantage.

As a certified coach, you're not introducing a foreign concept. You're offering something instantly familiar, and then taking it deeper. You get to say, "You've heard about Love Languages. I'll help you make them work."

The 5 Love Languages® Coaching Marketing Kit

To make it easy for you to spread the word about your services, we've created the 5 Love Languages Coaching Marketing Kit—a complete bundle of promotional tools you can personalize and use right away once you become a Certified Love Language Coach.

Inside the online kit, you'll find things like:

- A customizable one-page flyer for workshops or coaching promotions
- Sample emails and social media posts to help you announce your services
- Pre-written descriptions of your role as a Certified Love Language Coach
- A simple brand-aligned slide deck for presentations or info sessions
- Graphics and banners for social media and websites
- A PDF overview you can send to churches, counselors, or referral partners

All of it is professionally designed, message-aligned, and easy to edit with your name, photo, and contact info. No need to become a marketer overnight—we've done the heavy lifting so you can focus on what you do best: helping couples connect.

Being aligned with the 5 Love Languages brand gives you visibility, trust, and instant resonance. But more than that—it gives you a platform to serve. People are already talking about Love Languages. With the right message and tools, you can be the one who helps them move from knowing the concept to *living it well.*

Where to Begin

You don't need a social media team, a slick video campaign, or a dozen lead funnels to start getting clients. What you *do* need is a clear offer, a little consistency, and the confidence to let people know you're here to help.

Marketing doesn't have to be overwhelming. In fact, the most effective marketing strategies are often the simplest—the ones that fit your life and reflect your voice. Here are five reliable ways to start:

1. Begin with Referrals and Relationships

Your best first clients will likely come from people who already trust you. Reach out to:

- Friends or family who know couples in transition or growth seasons
- Past or current clients who might share their experience
- Therapists or counselors who want to refer couples for coaching (not therapy)
- Pastors or small group leaders looking for premarital, marital, or enrichment help

Don't overthink it. A simple message like: "Hey, I'm now offering coaching for couples using the 5 Love Languages framework. If you know anyone who might be interested, I'd love to offer a free consultation."

2. Host a Free Workshop

Teaching a short workshop (online or in-person) is a great way to introduce your voice, your style, and your value—without pitching. Partner with a church, library, or counseling center—or host it virtually. Don't worry about the size of the group. Start small. At the end, simply say: "If this resonates and you want more personalized help, I offer coaching for couples and individuals. Come talk to me or grab a card."

3. Create a Simple, Clear Website

Your website doesn't have to be fancy, but it should answer three questions fast:

1) Who are you?
2) What do you offer?
3) How can I get started?

Include:

- A short bio and warm photo
- A clear description of your coaching package(s) and what's included
- Your pricing (or a general range)
- A booking link for a discovery call or session
- A contact form

You don't need to hire a developer or have a degree in design. There are plenty of online tools that make building a basic website easy and even fun. Whether you use a template-based platform or enlist the help of a motivated high school student in your life, the goal is simple: Create a clean, welcoming space where people can learn who you are, what you offer, and how to get started.

4. Use Social Media (Only If You Want To)

You don't need to be an influencer to use social media effectively. But if you enjoy the platform, consider sharing short, helpful posts that reflect your voice and values. You might offer a quick reflection on something common in couples work, a quote or takeaway from a recent coaching theme, or a behind-the-scenes glimpse into what a session feels like. Keep your tone warm, wise, and personal—think *encouragement meets invitation, not a sales pitch. It's less about performing, and more about building trust one honest moment at a time.*

5. Follow Up Thoughtfully

When someone expresses interest, don't disappear. Respond in a timely way with warmth, clarity, and direction: "I'd love to connect. Here's a link to book a free twenty-minute consult. I can walk you through what coaching looks like and answer any questions."

Even if they don't sign up right away, a kind and clear follow-up leaves a lasting impression—and may bring them back later.

Bottom Line: Marketing isn't about reaching *everyone*. It's about connecting with the *right people* in the right way. Start where you are. Be consistent. And trust that small steps, taken with heart, are enough to grow something meaningful.

Authenticity Over Hype

Let's be honest: Most people can spot "sales-y" from a mile away. Over-polished, overly confident messaging might work for products, but it doesn't work for people. And definitely not for relationships.

That's why your best marketing tool is the one you already have: your voice.

Your coaching is grounded in empathy, presence, and trust—and your marketing should reflect the same. You don't need to hype results or promise transformation in three easy steps. You just need to sound like a human who cares.

Your goal is never to impress; it's to *invite*.

So be the voice you'd trust if you were struggling. Imagine you're in a relationship on the edge of disconnection. You're not looking for flash. You're looking for someone who feels real. Someone who knows what they're doing and who genuinely cares. That's who you are. Let your marketing reflect that.

Play the Long Game—Trust Builds Slowly

You won't build a thriving coaching practice overnight. And that's okay. Most people don't say yes the first time they hear about you. They notice. They scroll. They forget. Then they hear about you again—maybe from a friend, a post, or a workshop. Eventually, something lands. And *then* they reach out.

That delay isn't disinterest; it's human nature. Especially when it comes to relationships. Couples are often hesitant, busy, or unsure whether their issues are "big enough" to warrant help. Your consistent, trustworthy presence over time helps quiet that hesitation.

You don't need a perfect campaign. You need a steady voice:

- A workshop every few months
- A post every week or two
- A follow-up email that says, "Still here when you're ready."

The coaches who make the biggest impact aren't the loudest; they're the most consistent.

So don't obsess over numbers. You don't need thousands of followers or a full calendar every week. You just need a handful of couples who are ready for what you offer. Serve them well. Word will spread.

Summary

Marketing isn't about pressure—it's about clarity. When you can clearly communicate what you offer, who it's for, and why it matters, you make it easier for the right people to say yes. In this chapter, you learned how to reframe marketing as an act of service, not self-promotion, and to focus your message on the real problem you help people solve.

You explored how to identify your ideal clients and speak to their needs in ways that feel natural and human. You also learned how to present your coaching offer with clarity, warmth, and value—highlighting not just your sessions, but the transformation they support. By leveraging the strength of the 5 Love Languages brand, you gain instant recognition and trust. And by using simple tools like referrals, free workshops, and a clear website, you can begin growing your presence in ways that fit your life and reflect your voice.

Most importantly, you were reminded that marketing is not about being everywhere or doing everything. It's about being findable, authentic, and consistent—so that when someone is ready for help, they know exactly where to turn.

QUESTIONS TO PONDER

1. What problem am I most passionate about helping people solve?
2. Who do I feel especially equipped to serve, and what language would make them feel seen?
3. Is my current message focused more on what I *do* or who I *help*?
4. Am I presenting my coaching in a way that's clear, warm, and easy to act on?
5. Have I identified a few simple marketing rhythms I can stick with over time?
6. Where might I be holding back because of fear or perfectionism—and what's one small way I can show up more consistently this month?

Chapter 24

Partnering with Churches and Organizations

You don't have to build your coaching practice on your own.

Across the country, churches, counseling centers, schools, and nonprofits are looking for meaningful ways to support relationships—but many of them are under-resourced, overwhelmed, or unsure of where to start. That's where you come in.

As a Certified Love Language Coach, you bring something these communities already recognize and trust. You're not a stranger with a pitch. You're a partner with a purpose. And when you position yourself that way—with humility, clarity, and shared vision—you open the door to powerful, mutually beneficial collaboration.

This chapter isn't about cold calls or polished proposals. It's about building relationships. It's about showing up as someone who can help extend a mission already in motion. Because when you step into a space like a church, school, or nonprofit with the heart of a servant and the strength of a proven tool, your work multiplies.

You don't need to sell yourself. You just need to show how your coaching can support the people they already care about.

Why Churches and Organizations Are Looking for Relationship Help

Many churches, counseling centers, and community organizations care deeply about relational health—but few feel fully equipped to address it (American

Association for Marriage and Family Therapy, 2015). Pastors are stretched thin. Counselors often have waitlists. Nonprofits focus on urgent needs and may not have the bandwidth for proactive relational programming. That's where a coach can step in—with focus, flexibility, and tools that work.

In churches, couples often turn to their pastor when they're struggling. But most pastors, while deeply compassionate, aren't trained in relationship dynamics (Pargament, 2007). They may offer encouragement or Scripture—but not the skills-based guidance couples often need. And while some churches have marriage ministries, many lack structure, trained leaders, or consistent resources. The desire is there. The infrastructure often isn't.

In counseling centers, therapists may prioritize clinical needs—crisis, trauma, or diagnosable conditions. But what about the couple that's "just a little stuck"? Or the pair who is post-therapy but still wants to grow? These couples don't always need counseling—but they do need support. As a coach, you fill that gap with something deeply valuable: relational guidance that's proactive, hopeful, and rooted in empathy.

Even schools, universities, and family-focused nonprofits are recognizing that healthy relationships fuel healthy communities. Whether they're supporting parents, young adults, or underserved populations, many are open to offering skills-based enrichment that doesn't feel clinical or overwhelming.

In other words, organizations are already looking for what you provide—they just don't know who can do it. When you offer yourself as a trusted coach, certified in a framework they already recognize, you become a solution to a felt need.

What You Bring as a Certified Love Language Coach

When you approach a church, counseling center, or nonprofit, you're not showing up empty-handed. You're bringing a powerful combination of credibility, clarity, and compassion—anchored in one of the most recognizable relationship tools in the world.

Here's what makes your role uniquely valuable in a partnership setting:

Credibility Through Familiarity

You're not introducing an obscure framework or experimental approach. The Love Languages are already widely known and trusted, especially in church and familyoriented environments. When you say you're a Certified Love Language Coach, there's instant recognition. That familiarity builds trust from the start.

Practical, Actionable Help

While pastors and counselors often handle crises or spiritual concerns, you offer something different: a pathway forward. You guide people through tangible, structured steps to improve their relational connection—whether that's speaking their partner's Love Language more fluently or rebuilding daily habits of emotional safety.

A Safe, Non-Clinical Option

Many couples aren't looking for therapy—they just want something to help them get unstuck. You provide a middle ground: not as intense as counseling, not as casual as a book study. Your work is accessible, strengths-based, and focused on growth, not diagnosis. That makes it a great fit for couples who are hesitant about therapy or simply want to invest in their relationship before things get worse.

Flexibility in Format and Delivery

You can meet in person or online, with one couple or several. You can coach one partner at a time, offer group workshops, lead team trainings, or support a specific ministry. You can show up for premarital couples, young families, empty nesters, or volunteers. That kind of flexibility makes you a high-value partner to any organization trying to meet diverse needs with limited staff.

In short, your presence fills a real gap—and you do it with a toolset that's already been welcomed into thousands of churches, schools, and homes. You're not asking for a place at the table. You're offering to serve the people already seated there.

Ways to Partner

Partnerships don't have to be formal, complicated, or time-consuming. Often, they start with a simple conversation: *"How can I support what you're already doing?"* The goal isn't to insert yourself; it's to come alongside.

Below are some of the most effective, flexible ways to partner with churches, counseling centers, and nonprofits—plus real-world examples to help you see the possibilities.

Partnering with Churches

Churches are natural allies. They care about marriage, family, and spiritual connection—but they often lack the tools or time to support couples with ongoing, practical help (Frame, 2003; Olson & Olson-Sigg, 2000). As a coach, you can fill that need.

Examples:

- Host a Love Languages workshop as a one-time event or offer a 4-week series for couples.
- Provide coaching for staff couples, who often face unique ministry pressures.
- Collaborate with a church's small group ministry to offer training for lay leaders or marriage mentors.

Partnering with Counseling Centers

Therapists are often glad to have someone they trust for non-clinical referrals or aftercare. Coaching is a perfect complement to counseling—especially for couples who've moved past a crisis and want to grow.

Examples:

- Create a relationship with a local counseling practice and offer to support couples with post-therapy growth coaching.
- Serve couples who are "not quite therapy clients"—they may not meet clinical thresholds but still need help.
- Run skills-based workshops for clients waiting for an available therapist.

Partnering with Nonprofits, Schools, and Community Organizations

Family-focused nonprofits, parenting networks, and college ministries often want to provide relationship enrichment but don't have the staff to develop it. That's where you come in.

Examples:

- Offer a session on Love Languages in Parenting to a local parent group.
- Partner with a high school or college ministry to host a talk on healthy dating habits.
- Volunteer to run a couples' connection workshop for clients in a transitional housing or recovery program.
- Provide coaching for newly married or co-parenting couples in a faith-based nonprofit.

You don't have to pitch a big program. Often, just offering a single workshop, a small coaching package, or your availability for referrals is more than enough to begin. The best partnerships aren't transactional. They're built on mutual mission and a shared desire to help people thrive.

Introducing Yourself Without Selling Yourself

One of the biggest hesitations coaches have when approaching churches or organizations is the fear of sounding too self-promotional. And it's a fair concern—especially in ministry or nonprofit settings, where humility and trust matter more than polished pitches.

The good news? You don't need a pitch. You need a posture.

Lead with service, not a sales script. Start by identifying with the mission of the organization or church. Speak from shared values: supporting families, helping marriages thrive, offering hope before couples hit a crisis. When people sense that your heart is aligned with theirs, walls come down.

Focus on the Need You Can Help Meet

Instead of saying, "I'm a certified coach and I'd love to offer my services here," try something like:

"I know a lot of couples in churches feel stuck or disconnected, but they're not sure if they need counseling. I'm certified as a Love Language Coach, and I work with couples in that space—helping them connect better using a framework they already recognize. If that's a need in your community, I'd love to support what you're doing."

This shows humility, clarity, and relevance.

Bring Something Tangible to the Conversation

Rather than just letting them know what you do, offer something specific:

- "Would it be helpful if I led a free 60-minute workshop for your small group leaders?"
- "I have a one-page overview of my coaching services if you'd like to share it with your care team."
- "I'd love to offer a few free consults to couples you think might benefit."

You're not asking them to promote you. You're offering to help.

The goal is never to convince—it's to connect. When you show up with the mindset of *how can I serve your people better*, you don't have to sell anything. You just have to mean it.

When to Formalize (and When You Don't Need To)

Not every partnership needs a contract. In fact, many great collaborations start with a handshake, a conversation, or a shared cup of coffee. But as your relationships with churches and organizations grow—and especially if money, space, or repeated referrals are involved—it helps to define expectations on paper.

Formality doesn't signal distrust; it signals professionalism. And most churches and nonprofits will appreciate your clarity and care.

A free workshop, a casual referral, or an invitation to coach one couple from a congregation rarely requires formal documentation. These early-stage opportunities are often built on trust, shared vision, and word-of-mouth.

In these cases, a friendly email follow-up confirming your conversation (date, time, audience, purpose) may be all that's needed to keep everyone on the same page.

When the work becomes ongoing or operational, you'll want something in writing when:

- You're being listed as an official partner or resource on the church's website
- You're using the church's space regularly or offering coaching on-site
- You're receiving payment or donations in connection with the partnership
- You're providing group coaching, speaking to multiple ministry teams, or leading events that carry expectations for outcomes

This doesn't need to be a legal contract. A Memo of Understanding (MOU) works well—a simple, mutual agreement outlining what you're offering and how often, who you're serving (e.g., members, staff, community), any compensation or expectations around donations, space, or promotion, and so on. You can easily create a one-page MOU that feels warm, clear, and collaborative.

Follow Through with Professionalism and Gratitude

Partnerships are built on trust, but they're sustained by follow-through. When you show up dependably, communicate clearly, and express sincere appreciation, you not only build your coaching credibility—you build relational equity that opens doors for years to come.

Respond Promptly to Referrals

When a church or organization sends someone your way, they're extending part of their reputation. Treat every referral as a vote of confidence. Respond promptly and warmly. Even if the individual or couple decides not to move forward, thank the referring party and, when appropriate, let them know you followed up. You can simply say something like: "*Thanks again for connecting me with Sam and Joanna. We had a great first conversation—I'll keep you posted as appropriate.*"

Respect Confidentiality, Honor Trust

If you're coaching someone connected to the organization—whether a couple in the church or a member of staff—guard their privacy closely. Don't share personal details unless you've been given written permission to do so. Churches and nonprofits will trust you more when they know you're trustworthy with the people they care about.

Keep Key Leaders in the Loop (When Appropriate)

If you're partnering on an event, workshop, or ongoing coaching program, check in with a short progress note or update now and then. Letting them know it's going well reinforces that their decision to partner with you was a good one. Something like: "*Just a quick note—really enjoying the couples group from your Wednesday night crew. They're engaged, thoughtful, and leaning in.*"

Always Say Thank You

Whether they gave you space, referrals, or simply shared their platform, never underestimate the power of gratitude. A handwritten thank-you note. A kind email. A public thank-you at the end of a workshop. These small gestures leave a lasting impression.

You don't need flashy materials or a formal pitch. You just need a good reputation—and the follow-through to match.

Summary

You don't need to build your coaching work alone. Churches, counseling centers, nonprofits, and community organizations are actively looking for trusted, practical ways to support relationships—and your role as a Certified Love Language Coach uniquely positions you to help. In this chapter, you explored why these partnerships matter, what specific value you bring, and how to approach them with clarity and humility. You learned simple ways to begin—through workshops, referrals, or one-on-one conversations—and how to follow through with professionalism, gratitude, and trust. Some collaborations may remain informal; others may require a clear agreement. But either way, your ability to build honest, mutual relationships with organizations can greatly expand your reach and impact.

QUESTIONS TO PONDER

1. Who in my community might already be looking for relationship support but doesn't know where to find it?
2. What kind of organization aligns best with my values and the clients I most enjoy serving?
3. How can I introduce myself and my services in a way that feels helpful, not self-promoting?
4. Am I clear on the difference between coaching and counseling when explaining my role?
5. Do I have a simple, professional overview of what I offer that I can share with potential partners?
6. What's one small partnership I could initiate or reengage this month—with no pressure, just presence?

Chapter 25

Continuing Education and Growth as a Coach

Coaching isn't something you master once and for all. It's something you grow into over time—with every person you meet, every challenge you navigate, and every insight that reshapes your perspective. The best coaches aren't the most credentialed or confident. They're the ones who stay curious, humble, and committed to the process.

That's because coaching isn't just about what you know; it's about how you show up. And how you show up gets better when you keep learning.

The good news? You don't need a graduate degree or a packed calendar of professional development to grow. You just need a posture of openness. Whether you're reading a new book on emotional resilience, reflecting on your latest session, or joining a conversation with fellow coaches—you're doing the work.

This chapter isn't about pressure to keep proving yourself. It's about staying rooted, sharp, and sustainable in a field that demands presence, empathy, and wisdom. Because your growth isn't separate from your coaching—it's what makes it credible, compassionate, and lasting.

Ongoing Learning—Stay Curious and Informed

The most impactful coaches aren't those with all the answers—they're the ones who stay curious. Ongoing learning isn't about accumulating certifications or checking boxes. It's about cultivating a mindset that's open, engaged, and willing to grow. When you keep learning, you don't just sharpen your skills—you deepen your empathy, broaden your perspective, and stay relevant to the real lives your clients are living.

While revisiting the 5 Love Languages material is always helpful, your growth shouldn't stop there. Great coaches read widely—from books on communication, conflict, and attachment to memoirs, leadership studies, and research on emotional intelligence. Expanding your input makes you more versatile, more relatable, and more attuned to the subtle dynamics couples bring into the room.

It's also important to stay culturally aware. Relationships are shaped by shifting norms, generational expectations, and changing language around topics like emotional safety, mental health, gender, and commitment. You don't need to become an expert on every trend, but staying informed allows you to meet clients where they are—with insight and credibility. Whether you're learning from a podcast, a parenting article, or a social science study, let your curiosity guide you. If something keeps surfacing in your sessions—a dynamic you don't fully understand, a theme that challenges your assumptions—make it your mission to explore it.

Growth doesn't just enhance your coaching; it honors the people you serve. When you become a coach who says, "Let me learn more about that," and then actually does, you're modeling the very kind of openness and growth you're inviting your clients into.

Grow From the Work Itself

Some of your best education as a coach won't come from a book or a workshop—it will come from the room you're already in. Every coaching session is an opportunity to learn, not just about the client, but about yourself. Reflection is what turns experience into growth. As Donald Schön (1983) emphasized, professionals don't just learn from doing—they learn by thoughtfully reflecting on what they do in action and after the fact. When you take time to pause, process, and ask, *"What just happened in that session?"* you begin to develop not only insight but instinct.

Reflection can be simple. After a session, jot down what stood out. What felt stuck? What moved the conversation forward? Were there moments when you felt especially effective—or especially unsure? Instead of rushing to the next appointment, give yourself space to name your reactions and patterns. Over time, these reflections will help you notice your blind spots, clarify your strengths, and sharpen your intuition.

It's also worth regularly revisiting your own "why." Coaching can become routine if you let it, but reflective practice keeps your work anchored in purpose. Ask yourself: *Why do I do this? Who am I becoming through it? Where do I sense joy, resistance, or growth happening in me?* These aren't indulgent questions—they're essential to your sustainability.

Lastly, don't be afraid to invite feedback. A trusted mentor, a fellow coach, or even a brave client can offer you insight that strengthens your presence. You're not aiming for perfection. You're aiming for awareness. Because the more aware you are of your own emotional landscape, the more skilled you become at navigating someone else's.

Supervision, Mentoring, and Peer Support

Coaching can sometimes feel like solitary work, but it shouldn't be. Even if you meet with clients one-on-one or couples in private sessions, you're not meant to grow alone. Every great coach needs a few safe, trusted spaces where they can process challenges, ask honest questions, and receive feedback without fear or shame.

One of the most powerful tools for growth is peer connection. Whether it's an informal group of fellow coaches who meet monthly, an online forum where ideas are exchanged, or a small circle of colleagues who support one another in the work—you'll grow faster and feel less isolated when you're in conversation with people who get it. These relationships can provide practical wisdom, emotional encouragement, and even referrals when you need them.

Mentoring and supervision are also worth pursuing—especially as you encounter more complex relational dynamics. A seasoned coach or therapist can help you think through a difficult session, debrief emotional responses, or point you toward resources you didn't know you needed. Supervision isn't a sign of weakness—it's a marker of professionalism. As Carl Rogers (1961) noted, personal growth and self-awareness are essential for anyone working in a helping role—and that includes regularly stepping back to reflect with others. Even the most experienced coaches benefit from a trusted voice who can ask, *"What's yours to carry in this dynamic—and what's not?"*

Over time, the most sustainable coaches are those who create rhythms of connection. Whether that means reaching out to one mentor quarterly or joining a monthly coaching huddle, your growth accelerates when you stop doing this work in isolation. Because the same thing you're encouraging in your clients—honest support, mutual challenge, and safe connection—is what you need, too.

Formal Continuing Education Opportunities

While reflective practice and peer support are essential, there's also a place for structured, skill-based learning that expands your knowledge and deepens your impact. Formal continuing education can help you stay sharp, grow your confidence, and extend the range of people you're equipped to serve.

There's no single path you have to follow—but depending on your goals, you might explore online courses, coaching certifications, or specialized training in areas that complement the 5 Love Languages framework.

For example, some coaches pursue certification in SYMBIS (Saving Your Marriage Before It Starts) or Prepare/Enrich, both of which align well with premarital and marriage coaching. Others take advanced training in communication models, conflict resolution, trauma-informed practice, or emotional intelligence. Even one high-quality course a year can dramatically expand your ability to support the couples who come your way.

If you're drawn to group settings, then events such as workshops, live trainings, and conferences can be energizing and connective. They offer the added benefit of hearing fresh voices, asking questions in real time, and stepping outside your regular rhythm to focus on development.

As you continue learning, always stay mindful of your scope of practice. Education should enhance your ability to serve, not tempt you to take on roles you're not trained for. Coaching is not therapy, and expanding your skill set should never replace the humility to refer out when needed. That's part of what keeps your work safe, trusted, and respected.

Self-Care

The most effective coaches aren't just well-trained—they're well-rooted. You can be skilled, insightful, and fully booked, but if you're depleted, distracted, or disconnected from your own emotional and spiritual center, your coaching will eventually suffer. Your presence is your most powerful tool—and presence requires inner strength.

Self-care isn't a luxury in this work. It's a necessity. That means tending to your physical energy, your emotional resilience, your relational boundaries, and your soul. It means knowing when you need rest, not just productivity. It means having rituals of renewal—whether that's journaling, walking, worship, therapy, or simply being off the clock with your phone out of sight. When you coach from overflow instead of emptiness, your clients feel the difference.

For those who coach from a place of faith, spiritual grounding becomes even more essential. It's easy to drift into performance mode—to show up for others while neglecting the very source that fuels your compassion. But the work is too sacred, and too demanding, to be done in your own strength alone. Make space for stillness. Anchor yourself in practices that remind you of who you are and why this matters. Let your identity as a beloved child of God hold more weight than your identity as a coach.

And protect your boundaries. The better you are at loving people well, the more likely they are to want more of you. But more isn't always better. Healthy coaches say "no" with kindness, pause with purpose, and create space not only for their clients to grow—but for themselves to breathe.

Sustainability in coaching isn't just about systems and education. It's about tending to the well you draw from. Because the health of your coaching often mirrors the health of your inner life.

Ultimately, formal learning isn't about collecting certificates. It's about stewardship—of your gifts, your credibility, and the people who trust you with their stories.

Growing the Work That Grows You

By now, you've learned the structure, tools, and strategies that form a solid coaching practice. But more than that, you've been reminded that this work is deeply personal. Coaching with the 5 Love Languages isn't just about helping others connect. It's about showing up with clarity, humility, and love in a world that's often starved for all three.

Yes, you'll refine your message. Yes, you'll grow your referral network and lead workshops and navigate tricky conversations. But the soul of this work is quieter—and far more powerful. It's in the sacred moments when a couple looks at each other differently than they did before. When someone feels seen, maybe for the first time in a long time. When the right question at the right time becomes a turning point they'll never forget.

That's the real business you're building. And it's built not just on your skill but on your willingness to keep growing. The more you develop—not just as a coach, but as a person—the more meaningful, lasting, and life-giving your impact will be.

So take care of your practice. But more than that, take care of your presence. Because who you are is the most important tool you bring into any coaching space.

Keep learning. Keep showing up. Keep growing the work that is, little by little, growing you.

Summary

Great coaching isn't about mastering a script; it's about becoming a person of increasing depth, clarity, and care. In this chapter, you explored how growth happens over time, not only through formal training but through curiosity, reflection, community, and self-awareness. Ongoing learning keeps you sharp. Reflective practice helps you grow from your own experience. Supervision and peer connection keep you grounded and supported. And continuing education—when aligned with your scope and calling—can expand your impact. But at the core of all of this is something deeper: your own wellbeing. When you care for your body, mind, and spirit, you're able to offer others the kind of presence that heals and transforms. Growth isn't a side note to the coaching journey. It *is* the journey.

QUESTIONS TO PONDER

1. What's one area in your coaching where you feel the most confident—and one where you'd like to grow?
2. What learning rhythms can you build into your month or year to stay fresh and curious?
3. How often do you pause to reflect after a session—and what helps you find meaning in those moments?
4. Who do you go to when you need wisdom, perspective, or accountability in your coaching?
5. Is there a training, ccrtification, or area of study you've been putting off but sense would serve you (and your clients) well?
6. What does healthy, honest self-care look like for you right now, and what needs to shift to protect your sustainability?

Coaching That Lasts

You've walked through every dimension of what it means to coach with the 5 Love Languages—how to listen, how to guide, how to grow. You've learned the frameworks, explored the dialects, navigated the pitfalls, and stepped into complex territory like crisis, co-parenting, and singleness. You've seen how coaching isn't about delivering answers but cultivating insight. And most of all, you've been reminded of what brought you here in the first place: a belief that love matters—and that helping people give and receive it well is holy, vital work.

This handbook wasn't designed to give you a script. It was built to give you a foundation. Because while the Love Languages are simple to grasp, they're endlessly nuanced in practice. They're shaped by personality, history, culture, trauma, attachment, and season of life. What looks like a missed cue on the surface may actually be a cry for safety, or a silent plea for tenderness in a language the other person never learned to speak.

That's where you come in. You're not just a translator. You're a presence, a guide who helps people slow down, tune in, and discover what empathy really looks like in practice.

Throughout this journey, we've returned again and again to one central idea: The most important Love Language is the one that matters to the person in front of you. Not the one that feels easiest to give. Not the one that makes the most sense to you. Not even the one you think they "should" need.

That's why coaching through the 5 Love Languages isn't just about helping someone learn the five categories. It's about helping them practice attunement—the ability to notice what their partner is feeling, needing, and hoping for . . . and to respond with intentional, self-giving love.

Sometimes that means helping a couple rediscover connection through a shared moment of laughter. Sometimes it means sitting in the tension of unhealed hurt. Sometimes it means saying, "Let's pause the Love Languages until safety is rebuilt." In every case, you're pointing them toward love that listens.

And that's where transformation happens.

You may never get public recognition for this work. You might coach someone who never fully circles back to say thank you. And that's okay. Because coaching isn't about outcomes you control—it's about space you hold. The trust you build. The insight you offer. The nudge that comes at the right moment and changes the tone of a conversation or the trajectory of a relationship. You're not here to fix people. You're here to remind them of what they're capable of. What they may have forgotten. What they still long for.

Next Steps

You've reached the end of this handbook, but in many ways, your work is just beginning.

If you are already enrolled in the 5 Love Languages Coaching Network, your next step is to complete the final certification quiz and begin applying what you've learned with clients. Don't overlook the opportunity to take the 5 Love Languages Premium Assessment yourself using your complimentary credit. Experiencing the assessment firsthand will deepen your personal insight and strengthen your confidence in guiding others through it.

If you have not yet begun the certification process, now is the time. Completing the official certification allows you to represent yourself as a Certified Love Language Coach, display the certification indicium, and serve clients with the credibility and training this role requires. Certification equips you with the structure, tools, and confidence to help others translate love into meaningful action.

Wherever you are in the process, take the next step forward. People are searching for clarity, connection, and hope. With the right training and commitment, you can be the guide who helps them find it.

Learn more or continue your certification journey at:

Coaching.5LoveLanguages.com

When you sit with a couple or an individual, you are offering them something many people rarely receive: undivided attention and gentle accountability in a world that too often rushes, shames, or disconnects. That kind of presence doesn't just support relationships; it restores dignity.

This handbook may be complete, but your formation as a coach is ongoing. You're going to keep learning. You're going to stumble. You'll have sessions that energize you, and others that leave you questioning whether you made any difference at all. That's part of the calling.

The most important thing you can offer your clients is not expertise. It's integrity. A commitment to keep showing up. To keep learning. To stay humble. To ask better questions. To hold space for the messy middle, not just the shiny resolution. If you do that—if you keep growing into the kind of person whose presence brings calm, curiosity, and care—you'll already be ahead of most.

You may never know the full ripple effect of your coaching. A softened tone in a conversation. A handwritten note left on a nightstand. A dad who hugs his daughter more often. A wife who finally feels like her needs aren't "too much." These small shifts—these quiet moments where love finally lands—add up to something bigger than you'll ever see.

You're not just coaching couples. You're planting seeds of connection in families, churches, and communities. You're offering people the tools—and the courage—to love more intentionally, more effectively, and more meaningfully.

And that's world-changing work.

As you close this book, don't close your hands. Stay open. To the next client. The next insight. The next lesson you didn't see coming. Stay open to being surprised, stretched, and sometimes even undone. Because that's how you'll know this work is still forming you too.

Let your coaching be an extension of who you are becoming. And let your becoming be rooted in love—the kind that listens, adjusts, perseveres, and tells the truth with tenderness. You don't have to be perfect. You just have to be present.

And that's more than enough.

Appendix 1: Sample Coaching Agreement

(Customize as needed for your practice)

Coaching Agreement: 5 Love Languages Relationship Coaching

Welcome! I'm honored to partner with you in this coaching journey. This agreement outlines the nature of our work together and helps ensure we're aligned on expectations, boundaries, and goals.

1. Purpose of Coaching

Relationship coaching is a forward-focused, goal-oriented process designed to help couples improve connection, communication, and emotional expression—particularly through the 5 Love Languages framework. Coaching is not counseling, therapy, or mental health treatment.

2. Scope of Services

We will focus on helping you (individually or as a couple) develop greater awareness, insight, and relational skills. Sessions may involve assessment results, Love Language strategies, goal-setting, and guided conversation.

3. Confidentiality

All information shared in coaching sessions will be kept confidential, with the following exceptions:

- If I believe you or someone else is at risk of serious harm.
- If I am required by law to disclose information (e.g., in cases of abuse or imminent danger).
- With your written permission to consult with another professional.

4. Session Format and Logistics

- Sessions will last approximately ____ minutes and be conducted via [Zoom / in-person / phone].
- We will meet [weekly / biweekly / monthly], starting on ______________.
- You may reschedule with at least 24 hours' notice.
- Coaching investment: $_______ per session (paid via __________).

5. Referrals and Limits of Practice

If it becomes clear that therapy or another professional service is better suited to your needs, I will recommend a qualified provider and pause coaching until appropriate support is in place.

6. Ending the Coaching Relationship

You may discontinue coaching at any time. I simply ask that you let me know in advance so we can bring closure to the process respectfully.

7. Agreement and Signature

By signing below, we acknowledge that we have reviewed this agreement together, understand the nature and boundaries of coaching, and are entering this process with mutual respect and clarity.

Client Name(s): ______________________________

Signature(s): ______________________________

Date: ______________________________

Coach Name: ______________________________

Signature: ______________________________

Date: ______________________________

Appendix 2: Code of Ethics for Certified Love Language™ Coaches

Ethical coaching doesn't happen by accident. It happens by design—through clear boundaries, thoughtful practices, and a deep respect for the people we serve. That's why this *Code of Ethics for Certified Love Language Coaches* exists: to offer a shared standard for integrity, professionalism, and relational care.

This code is more than a checklist—it's a compass. It provides guidance when the path feels unclear, language when tough decisions arise, and a structure that protects both coach and client. Whether you're coaching in a ministry, a private setting, or as part of a larger organization, these principles can serve as the foundation of your credibility and care.

Use this Code of Ethics as both a personal commitment and a professional guide. Review it regularly. Share it with clients when needed. And know that honoring these standards isn't just about doing what's right—it's about creating the kind of coaching relationships where real transformation can take root.

As a Certified Love Language Coach, I commit to practicing with integrity, humility, and professionalism. This Code of Ethics serves as a guide for my conduct, a safeguard for my clients, and a standard by which I hold myself accountable. These commitments reflect both the values of the broader coaching profession and the relational wisdom embedded in *The 5 Love Languages*.

1. Confidentiality

I will protect the confidentiality of my clients to the fullest extent permitted by law. I will clearly communicate the limits of confidentiality—particularly in cases involving harm to self or others, abuse, or legal requirements for disclosure.

2. Informed Consent

Before coaching begins, I will ensure that clients understand the nature of the coaching relationship, the boundaries of my role, the goals of the process, the expected duration, and any associated fees or policies. I will provide written or verbal consent agreements that reflect these terms.

3. Scope of Practice

I will coach within my training and experience. I will not offer services or advice that require clinical licensure (such as diagnosing mental health conditions or treating trauma). If concerns arise that are beyond the scope of coaching, I will make appropriate referrals to licensed professionals.

4. Role Clarity

I will maintain clear boundaries between coaching and other roles I may hold (e.g., therapist, pastor, mentor, friend). I will avoid dual relationships that could impair objectivity or lead to conflicts of interest, and I will disclose any potential role conflicts to my clients.

5. Nonjudgment and Respect

I will approach each client with curiosity, empathy, and unconditional positive regard. I will respect cultural, spiritual, relational, and individual differences without imposing my personal values or beliefs.

6. Voluntary Participation

I will ensure that all coaching is entered into willingly. If working with a couple or family system, I will make every effort to maintain a balanced alliance and avoid taking sides.

7. Professional Integrity

I will represent my training, qualifications, and coaching services truthfully. I will not promise outcomes I cannot guarantee or market myself in a misleading manner. I will give credit where credit is due and avoid plagiarism or misuse of proprietary materials.

8. Responsible Referrals

When a client presents issues beyond my scope, I will refer them to appropriate professionals and, where possible, assist them in locating trusted care. I will not continue coaching when it would be more ethical or effective to refer.

9. Ongoing Growth and Supervision

I will seek regular feedback, mentorship, or supervision to grow in competence and character. I will pursue continuing education to stay current with best practices in coaching, communication, and relational dynamics.

10. Accountability

I welcome feedback and take responsibility for my actions. If a client or colleague raises a concern about my conduct, I will engage the conversation with openness and a commitment to resolution. I will report ethical violations where appropriate and uphold the reputation of this certification with integrity.

I affirm this Code of Ethics as a reflection of my values, a safeguard for my clients, and a commitment to the integrity of the Love Language coaching community. I recognize that ethical practice is not a one-time decision, but a daily responsibility—and I will seek to uphold these standards with humility, courage, and care.

Name: ____

Signature: ____________________________________

Date: ____

Appendix 3: Sample Intake & Discovery Form

To be completed prior to or during the first coaching session.

Client Information

- Name:
- Email:
- Phone:
- Preferred Contact Method:
- Date of Birth:
- Occupation:

Relationship Status

☐ Single

☐ Dating

☐ Engaged

☐ Married

☐ Separated

☐ Divorced

☐ Widowed

Other: ____________

Brief Relationship History (if applicable)

When did your current relationship begin?

Is this your first committed relationship?

Have you received coaching or counseling before?

Coaching Goals

What brings you to relationship coaching?

What would a successful coaching experience look like for you?

Are there any specific issues or topics you hope to address?

Personal Values or Faith Background (Optional)

How do your personal values or beliefs influence your relationships?

Would you like your coach to integrate these into your sessions?

☐ Yes ☐ No ☐ Not sure yet

Assessment Notice

As part of the coaching process, you will be invited to take the 5 Love Languages Premium Assessment. This personalized tool will provide a deeper understanding of how you give and receive love. You'll receive your link after the first session and we'll review your results together soon after.

Signature: ______________________________________

Date: ____

Appendix 4: Session Planning Template

Designed for use by the coach to prepare and document each session.

Client Name:

Date:

Session Number:

Coach Name:

Today's Focus / Client Goal:

____

Love Language(s) Identified or In Progress:

____

Client's Self-Reported Love Tank Level (0–10):

____

Key Insights from Session:

____

Client Action Steps / Homework:

____

Coach Notes for Follow-Up:

____

Next Session Date: ______________

Appendix 5: Love Tank Tracker

A tool for clients or couples to reflect on their emotional connection between sessions.

Instructions:

Use this simple tool once a week to reflect on how full your love tank feels and why. Discuss it together if desired.

Week of	My Love Tank (0–10)	What filled my tank this week?	What drained it?

Note: A rating of 7–10 generally suggests emotional connection is strong. A rating under 5 may be a cue to express needs and reconnect.

Appendix 6: Referral Decision Grid

A checklist for determining whether coaching is the appropriate path or if referral to a licensed therapist is needed.

Use this grid when intake reveals deeper concerns or coaching is not progressing.

Mark any that apply:

☐ Signs of abuse (physical, emotional, verbal, or sexual)

☐ Current or past trauma that remains unresolved

☐ Suicidal thoughts or self-harming behavior

☐ Untreated mental health diagnosis or addiction

☐ Severe communication breakdown or hostility between partners

☐ Fear, control, or emotional manipulation present in relationship

☐ Coaching is repeatedly triggering distress without resolution

☐ One partner is unwilling or unable to engage in healthy dialogue

If two or more boxes are checked, pause coaching and gently recommend a therapeutic referral. You might say: *"I want to honor how much courage it takes to seek help. From what you've shared, I believe a licensed therapist may be better equipped to help you right now. If you'd like, I can recommend someone I trust or help you explore options."*

Appendix 7: Coaching Agreement with the Client

Before any coaching relationship begins, it's wise to create a simple, clear agreement between coach and client. This isn't about legal protection or red tape—it's about setting the tone for trust, clarity, and professionalism from the very first session.

The Coaching Agreement Serves Several Purposes:

- It defines the nature of the relationship and scope of your role.
- It sets boundaries around confidentiality, scheduling, and expectations.
- It helps your client feel safe, informed, and respected.
- It gives you language to fall back on when questions arise—about cancellations, scope, or when a referral is needed.

In the pages that follow, you'll find two versions of the Coaching Agreement: one general and one tailored for Christian or faith-based settings. You are encouraged to adapt either version to reflect your style, structure, and the unique context in which you coach. You can also format it for digital signature, use it as a conversation guide in your first session, or incorporate it into your intake process.

Whether you're coaching individuals, couples, or families, this simple agreement can become one of your most valuable tools—not only for protecting your boundaries, but for honoring your client's trust.

Below is a sample agreement you can adapt for your setting. It's written to be clear, respectful, and easy to personalize—giving you a strong foundation for every new coaching relationship.

---

1. Nature of the Coaching Relationship

Coaching is a collaborative, goal-oriented relationship that focuses on helping clients improve their relationships through skills, insight, and intentional practice. As your coach, I will not diagnose, treat, or attempt to resolve mental health issues. Coaching is not therapy, and it is not a replacement for therapy or other clinical services.

2. Confidentiality

Everything shared in our sessions will remain confidential unless you disclose:

- Intent to harm yourself or others,
- Abuse or neglect (particularly involving a minor or vulnerable adult),
- Any situation that legally requires disclosure.

If you are participating as a couple or family, I do not keep secrets between individuals. What is shared with me privately may be brought into the coaching conversation if it is relevant to the goals of our work together.

3. Scope and Limitations

Our coaching will focus on relational growth and skill-building using the 5 Love Languages framework, as well as other proven tools and practices. If deeper emotional or psychological issues arise, I may recommend referral to a licensed mental health professional. This is not a sign of failure, but a commitment to your wellbeing.

4. Sessions and Scheduling

- **Number of sessions:** ____________ (or "open-ended")
- **Length of sessions:** ____________ minutes
- **Frequency:** ____
- **Location / Platform:** ______________________________________

Cancellations require ____________________ notice. Missed sessions without notice may be billed or forfeited.

5. Fees and Payment (if applicable)

- **Rate per session:** $__________________
- **Package options (if any):** ________________________________
- **Payment method:** ____

Note: If you are receiving coaching through a ministry or volunteer setting, this section may not apply.

6. Commitment to Growth

Coaching works best when approached with openness, honesty, and a willingness to try new things. My role is to walk alongside you—not to fix you, judge you, or take sides. Your role is to show up with curiosity and commitment.

7. Questions or Concerns

If at any point you feel uncomfortable or confused about our work together, please speak up. I welcome your feedback and want this experience to feel safe, respectful, and meaningful.

Appendix 8: Love Language Lexicon

The Love Language Lexicon is a shared vocabulary designed to equip Certified Love Language™ Coaches with precision, clarity, and consistency in their work. Coaching accelerates when both coach and client can name relational dynamics accurately. These terms provide conceptual anchors for common patterns, misalignments, growth strategies, and assessment insights. Rather than relying on vague language like "we're disconnected" or "we just argue," this lexicon gives structure to what is happening beneath the surface. Used well, it sharpens listening, strengthens intervention, and helps translate insight into intentional relational action.

This lexicon is not intended to be memorized, recited, or imposed on clients. It exists to support your thinking, not to dominate your sessions. You are not required to use every term or even most of them. Instead, think of this as a professional toolkit you can draw from when clarity is needed. Some clients benefit from shared terminology; others simply need you to internalize these concepts so you can guide the conversation skillfully. Your role is not to impress with vocabulary, but to create insight, safety, and forward movement. Use these terms when they serve the relationship—not when they serve you.

Acts of Service

Expressions of love through helpful actions that ease a partner's burden or meet practical needs. For individuals whose primary language is Acts of Service, completed tasks communicate care more powerfully than verbal assurances. Reliability, follow-through, and initiative are central.

Agenda Set Aside

A coaching posture in which a client intentionally releases personal preferences and defensiveness in order to focus fully on loving their partner in the partner's language. It requires humility and emotional maturity. Setting aside one's agenda does not mean self-erasure; it means prioritizing relational connection over being right or comfortable.

Agenda-less Presence

Intentional time together without correction, problem-solving, distraction, or hidden expectations. This type of presence communicates emotional safety and attentiveness, particularly for those whose primary language is Quality Time. It reassures a partner that they are valued for who they are, not merely for what they accomplish or resolve.

Attachment Style

A relational pattern shaped by early bonding experiences that influences how individuals pursue closeness, respond to perceived threat, handle conflict, and regulate emotional distress. Secure, anxious, avoidant, or disorganized attachment tendencies often affect how Love Languages are expressed, interpreted, and prioritized. For example, an anxious partner may seek frequent reassurance through Words of Affirmation, while an avoidant partner may under-express needs altogether. Coaches remain attentive to attachment dynamics, recognizing that Love Language misalignment may reflect deeper attachment strategies rather than simple preference differences.

Building Trust and Connection

The foundational aim of Love Language™ coaching. Trust grows when expressions of love are consistent, predictable, and emotionally accurate. Connection deepens as partners feel seen and valued in their preferred language. Without trust, even well-intended gestures may be questioned or dismissed.

Compensatory Language

When someone overexpresses love in a secondary language as a substitute for not receiving love in their primary one. For example, a partner may give excessive gifts while quietly longing for Quality Time. This pattern often reveals unmet needs and emotional depletion beneath outward generosity.

Conflict Crossover

When a couple argues about a surface issue—such as chores, parenting, or finances—but the deeper wound involves unmet Love Language needs. Coaches learn to listen for emotional undercurrents and redirect the conversation toward connection rather than content alone.

Default Language

The Love Language a person naturally gives because it is how they themselves most strongly experience love. Operating from default feels effortless but can create unintended disconnection when partners differ. Coaching helps clients move from instinct to intention.

Dialect

The personalized expression within a broader Love Language category. For example, within Words of Affirmation, one partner may crave simple compliments, while another longs for detailed encouragement tied to behaviors or character traits. Within Physical Touch, one may value playful touch, while another prefers reassuring contact. Understanding dialect within the Love Language prevents well-meaning gestures from missing their emotional target. Coaches help clients move beyond category-level awareness to the specific forms of expression that create the greatest emotional impact.

Dialect Disconnect

When partners attempt to express the correct Love Language but miss the preferred dialect. An act of service that emphasizes care may fall flat if saving time is the most desired dialect. Precision and personalization determine emotional impact.

Distracted by Default

A pattern of offering love casually, inconsistently, or while multitasking. Though not malicious, distraction weakens emotional impact. Coaching encourages mindful, intentional expressions that communicate presence rather than obligation.

Effective Communication Techniques

Structured relational skills such as reflective listening, validation, clarification questions, and emotional labeling. These tools enhance Love Language accuracy and reduce misinterpretation. Communication competence supports sustained fluency.

Emotional Bid

A subtle invitation for connection—such as a passing comment, lingering glance, playful joke, sigh, touch, or question—that signals a desire for emotional engagement. Bids are often small and easily overlooked, yet they carry significant relational weight. Consistently turning toward a partner's bids builds emotional safety, trust, and intimacy over time. Repeatedly ignoring or dismissing bids, even unintentionally, can gradually erode connection. Coaches help clients recognize bids in real time and respond with attentiveness rather than distraction or defensiveness.

Emotional Echo

The lingering emotional impact of a loving, neutral, or neglectful interaction that continues shaping a person's internal experience long after the moment itself has passed. Positive echoes reinforce security, warmth, and goodwill, often softening future conflict. Negative echoes, however, can amplify insecurity, doubt, or defensiveness, especially when repeated over time. Because echoes accumulate, small interactions matter more than people often realize.

Empathy Lens

The intentional decision to interpret a partner's behavior through curiosity rather than assumption. An empathy lens softens defensiveness and increases relational insight. It is foundational to speaking a partner's language accurately.

Fluency

The ability to consistently and naturally express a partner's Love Language with confidence and accuracy—especially in the person's most desired dialect within their Love Language. Fluency develops through awareness, repetition, feedback, and adjustment. It moves love from theory to embodied practice.

Fluent in All Five

A developmental goal in which individuals can competently express all 5 Love Languages, regardless of their own preference. This flexibility enhances relational resilience across life stages and stressors.

Fuel Type

A metaphor describing a person's primary Love Language as the emotional fuel that powers connection and security to fill their love tank. When fueled appropriately, individuals are more generous, patient, and responsive.

Full-Focus Zone

A distraction-free environment intentionally designed for undivided relational attention. Phones, screens, and competing demands are minimized to strengthen Quality Time and emotional presence.

High Love Tank

A state of emotional fullness marked by security, generosity, and relational warmth. When tanks are high, couples feel connected, navigate stress more constructively and recover from conflict more quickly.

Insight-to-Action Gap

The space between understanding a partner's Love Language and consistently practicing it. Many people stall here—mistaking awareness for transformation. Insight may create clarity, but practice creates change. Coaching bridges this gap through accountability, structure, and measurable habits that convert good intentions into observable behaviors. Closing the gap is less about motivation and more about disciplined follow-through.

Intake & Discovery Form

A structured coaching tool used to gather relational history, assessment results, goals, and areas of concern. It provides clarity and direction for strategic session planning.

Intent vs. Interpretation

The difference between what one partner means and how the other experiences it. Love Language misalignment often widens this gap. Clarifying intent and adjusting delivery reduces misunderstanding.

Language Calibration

The intentional process of refining how a Love Language is expressed so that it aligns precisely with a partner's emotional preferences, timing, and context. Calibration moves beyond simply choosing the correct category (e.g., Acts of Service) and focuses on how often, in what form, and under what circumstances love is most deeply received.

Language Discrepancy

A noticeable difference between partners' primary or secondary Love Languages that creates recurring misunderstanding or emotional imbalance. Discrepancy itself is not a problem; unmanaged discrepancy is. Coaching helps couples recognize the gap, normalize the difference, and build adaptive behaviors that prevent chronic frustration or emotional neglect.

Language Dialect

A specific and personalized expression within a broader Love Language category. Dialects reflect individual history, personality, and emotional wiring. For example, within Physical Touch, one partner may prioritize reassuring touch while another prioritizes playful touch. Identifying dialects dramatically increases relational precision and emotional impact.

Language Mapping

A structured coaching exercise that visually identifies each partner's primary, secondary, and default Love Languages, along with their preferred dialects. Mapping clarifies relational patterns, highlights areas of mismatch, and provides a practical roadmap for intentional growth and accountability over time.

Leveraging the Love Tank

The strategic use of periods of strong emotional connection to address sensitive conversations, behavioral adjustments, or long-standing concerns. When a partner's love tank is full, defensiveness decreases and receptivity increases. Coaches teach couples to time important discussions wisely, using emotional strength as relational leverage.

Lost in Translation

A dynamic in which love is sincerely expressed but not emotionally received due to language mismatch, dialect confusion, or poor timing. This experience often leads to discouragement and the false belief that love is absent. Coaching reframes the issue as miscommunication rather than lack of care.

Low Love Tank

A condition of emotional depletion in which a partner feels unseen, undervalued, or disconnected. Symptoms may include irritability, withdrawal, heightened sensitivity, or increased conflict. Recognizing low tank levels early allows couples to intervene intentionally before resentment solidifies.

Love Impact

The emotional effect created when a Love Language expression is accurately delivered and genuinely received. Impact is measured not by effort or intention, but by the receiver's experience. Coaches continually redirect clients toward behaviors that produce consistent, measurable emotional return.

Love Intention

The internal motivation or desire to express affection, appreciation, or commitment. While intention is foundational, it does not guarantee connection. Effective coaching bridges the gap between heartfelt intention and skillful execution in a partner's preferred language.

Love Language Drift

A gradual shift in the relative importance of a Love Language due to life transitions, stress, aging, parenthood, or unmet needs. Drift can be temporary or enduring. Coaches help people reassess periodically rather than assuming preferences remain static over time.

Love Language Mismatch

A common dynamic in which partners' primary languages differ significantly, leading each to express love in ways the other does not naturally prioritize. Mismatch requires intentional adaptation rather than criticism. Awareness reduces blame and increases empathy.

Love Language Premium Assessment

A comprehensive evaluation tool designed to identify not only primary and secondary Love Languages but also dialect nuances and personality patterns. The Premium Assessment provides deeper insight and actionable data that guide targeted coaching interventions.

Love Language Shift

A noticeable change in language priority prompted by crisis, transition, burnout, or relational strain. Unlike drift, a shift is often more sudden. Coaches assess whether the shift reflects temporary stress or a deeper emotional recalibration.

Love Leaks

Recurring behaviors, tone patterns, or omissions that gradually drain a partner's love tank and weaken emotional security over time. Leaks may include criticism, chronic distraction, broken promises, sarcasm, dismissive responses, emotional withdrawal, or inconsistent follow-through. They are often subtle and unintentional, which makes them especially dangerous. They compound quietly until resentment builds. Unlike a single conflict, a leak represents a pattern. Naming the leak shifts the focus from isolated incidents to sustainable relational repair.

Love Tank

A metaphor describing an individual's subjective sense of emotional security and connection within a relationship. When the tank is full, generosity, patience, and resilience naturally increase; partners interpret each other more charitably and recover from conflict more quickly. When depleted, even small frustrations can feel amplified, leading to reactivity, defensiveness, or withdrawal. Because tank levels fluctuate over time, wise couples learn to monitor them intentionally. Coaching often centers on helping partners recognize early warning signs of depletion and make consistent emotional deposits before resentment accumulates.

Love Tank Gauge

A reflective question or structured tool used to assess current emotional connection levels. Gauging the tank encourages early intervention rather than crisis response. It builds self-awareness and relational transparency between partners.

Love Tank Tracker

A structured system—daily habits, check-ins, or measurable commitments—designed to maintain emotional connection over time. Tracking reinforces consistency and accountability in Love Language practice.

Mismatch Fatigue

Emotional exhaustion that arises when one partner repeatedly expresses love in ways that go unnoticed or unreciprocated. Fatigue often masquerades as apathy or irritability. Coaching reframes fatigue as a solvable alignment issue.

Multilingual in Love

The capacity to competently and intentionally express multiple Love Languages, regardless of personal preference. Multilingual individuals demonstrate relational flexibility and resilience, especially during seasons when a partner's needs intensify in specific areas.

Neuroplasticity

The brain's ability to reorganize and strengthen neural pathways through repeated behavior. Consistent Love Language practice literally rewires relational habits, making new patterns more automatic over time.

Partner's Love Language

The primary Love Language that matters most to one's partner. Effective love requires prioritizing their emotional framework over one's natural tendencies. Coaches continually redirect attention toward this outward focus.

Physical Touch

Love expressed through appropriate physical closeness—such as holding hands, hugs, reassuring contact, or affectionate gestures. For some, touch communicates safety and belonging more powerfully than words or actions.

Premium Assessment Results

Personalized interpretive data generated from the Premium Assessment, including prioritized languages, dialect insights, and coaching recommendations. Results become the foundation for measurable growth planning.

Primary Love Language

The dominant way an individual most deeply experiences love, emotional security, and relational affirmation. While all five languages may hold meaning, the primary language carries disproportionate emotional weight.

Progress, Not Perfection

A coaching philosophy emphasizing steady improvement over flawless performance. Sustainable relational growth depends on consistency, humility, and course correction rather than dramatic gestures. People often sabotage momentum by expecting immediate mastery; this mindset reframes growth as incremental and realistic. Small, repeated behaviors create relational stability over time. Coaches reinforce the idea that forward movement—even imperfect effort—builds far more trust and connection than waiting to "get it right."

Progress Summary

A structured review of relational development, habit formation, and assessment insights across coaching sessions. Summaries reinforce momentum and clarify next steps.

Quality Time

Love expressed through undivided attention, shared experiences, meaningful dialogue, and intentional presence. For Quality Time individuals, distraction can feel like rejection, while focused engagement builds deep emotional security.

Referral Decision Grid

A framework guiding coaches in determining when issues exceed the scope of coaching and require licensed therapeutic intervention. Ethical clarity protects both client and coach.

Refill Before You Withdraw

A relational principle encouraging partners to make emotional deposits before requesting change, offering correction, or expressing frustration. Emotional safety increases receptivity to feedback, while depletion heightens defensiveness. When a love tank is low, even constructive input can feel like criticism or rejection. Coaches help people become intentional about timing—prioritizing connection before confrontation. Consistent deposits of love create the relational margin necessary for honest dialogue without unnecessary escalation.

Relationship Coaching

A structured, goal-oriented process focused on strengthening relational skills, enhancing connection, and improving communication patterns. Coaching emphasizes growth and accountability rather than clinical diagnosis or trauma treatment.

Relationship Dynamics

Recurring interaction patterns shaped by personality, attachment history, communication style, and Love Language alignment. These dynamics often operate beneath conscious awareness, creating predictable cycles of pursuit, withdrawal, defensiveness, or repair. Without insight, couples may blame isolated incidents rather than recognize the broader pattern at play. Coaching brings these dynamics into focus, helping partners interrupt reactive cycles and replace them with intentional, emotionally responsive behaviors that strengthen long-term connection.

Results Mapping Worksheet

A visual coaching tool that connects assessment findings to specific action steps and measurable relational goals. Mapping transforms insight into structured implementation.

Role of a Relationship Coach

To guide clients toward clarity, intentional behavior change, and improved emotional connection through structured conversation, assessment insight, and accountability. Relationship coaches help clients translate relational awareness into practical, repeatable action steps that strengthen trust and responsiveness. While coaches facilitate growth, skill development, and forward momentum, they do not diagnose, treat, or provide therapy for mental health disorders. Ethical coaching includes recognizing scope limits and making appropriate referrals when clinical issues arise.

Secondary Love Language

A meaningful but less dominant language that still contributes significantly to emotional fulfillment. Neglecting secondary languages may not wound deeply, but honoring them strengthens overall connection.

Session Planning Template

A structured outline used by coaches to organize objectives, exercises, assessment review, and measurable commitments within each session. Planning increases clarity and continuity.

Slow Practice

The intentional repetition of specific Love Language behaviors at a manageable pace in order to build comfort, consistency, and neurological reinforcement. Mastery grows gradually, not instantly.

Speak What They Hear

A coaching reminder that love must be expressed in the form a partner actually receives, not merely how it feels natural to give. Communication effectiveness is determined by reception, not intention. Many couples assume that sincerity guarantees impact, yet love that is not translated into a partner's emotional language often goes unnoticed. Coaches help clients shift from self-expression to emotional attunement, ensuring that what is offered aligns with what is most deeply felt.

The Love Language That Matters Most

The Love Language that matters most is the one that matters to the person in front of you—whether a spouse, child, friend, or family member. Effective love requires setting aside ego, agenda, instinct, and personal preference in order to prioritize the emotional experience of the other. *The Love Language That Matters Most* is also the title of a book that explores this principle in depth, emphasizing empathy as the foundation of meaningful connection.

Trading Places

An empathy exercise in which one partner imagines and articulates the emotional experience of the other. This perspective shift often precedes meaningful behavioral change and increased compassion.

Words of Affirmation

Love expressed through verbal encouragement, appreciation, gratitude, and meaningful acknowledgment. For those who value this language, words have lasting emotional resonance and shape their sense of worth and connection.

References

Preface

International Coach Federation. (2023). *2023 ICF global coaching study: Executive summary.* https://coachingfederation.org/research/global-coaching-study

Stober, D. R., & Grant, A. M. (2006). *Evidence-based coaching handbook: Putting best practices to work for your clients.* John Wiley & Sons.

Williams, P. (2017). *Becoming a professional life coach: Lessons from the Institute for Life Coach Training* (2nd ed.). W. W. Norton & Company.

Introduction

Gottman, J. M., & Silver, N. (2015). *The seven principles for making marriage work: A practical guide from the country's foremost relationship expert* (Rev. ed.). Harmony Books.

Pett, R. C., Lozano, P. A., & Varga, S. (2022). Revisiting the languages of love: An empirical test of the validity assumptions underlying Chapman's (2015) five love languages typology. *Communication Reports, 36*(1), 54–67. https://doi.org/10.1080/08934215.2022.2113549

Stanley, S. M., Rhoades, G. K., & Markman, H. J. (2006). Sliding versus deciding: Inertia and the premarital cohabitation effect. *Family Relations*, 55(4), 499–509. https://doi.org/10.1111/j.1741-3729.2006.00418.x

Williams, P. (2017). *Becoming a professional life coach: Lessons from the Institute for Life Coach Training* (2nd ed.). W. W. Norton & Company.

Chapter 1: The Role of a Relationship Coach

American Psychological Association. (2017). *Ethical principles of psychologists and code of conduct.* https://www.apa.org/ethics/code

Arredondo, P., Toporek, R., Brown, S. P., Jones, J., Locke, D. C., Sanchez, J., & Stadler, H. (1996). Operationalization of the multicultural counseling competencies. *Journal of Multicultural Counseling and Development, 24*(1), 42–78. https://doi.org/10.1002/j.2161-1912.1996.tb00288.x

Boyatzis, R. E., Smith, M. L., & Beveridge, A. J. (2013). Coaching with compassion: Inspiring health, well-being, and development in organizations. *Journal of Applied Behavioral Science, 49*(2), 153–178. https://doi.org/10.1177/0021886312462236

Chapman, G. (2024). *The 5 love languages: The secret to love that lasts* (Updated ed.). Northfield.

Dweck, C. S. (2006). *Mindset: The new psychology of success.* Random House.

Goleman, D. (1995). *Emotional intelligence: Why it can matter more than IQ.* Bantam.

Gollwitzer, P. M. (1999). Implementation intentions: Strong effects of simple plans. *American Psychologist, 54*(7), 493–503. https://doi.org/10.1037/0003-066X.54.7.493

Gottman, J. M., Driver, J. L., & Tabares, A. (2002). Building the sound marital house: An empirically derived couple therapy. In A. S. Gurman & N. S. Jacobson (Eds.), *Clinical handbook of couple therapy* (3rd ed., pp. 373–399). New York, NY: Guilford Press.

Gottman, J. M., & Silver, N. (2015). The seven principles for making marriage work: A practical guide from the country's foremost relationship expert (Rev. ed.). Harmony Books.

Grant, A. M. (2006). A primer on professional and executive coaching: What's in it for clients and practitioners? *The Psychologist, 19*(9), 522–525.

Green, L. S., Oades, L. G., & Grant, A. M. (2006). Cognitive-behavioral, solution-focused life coaching: Enhancing goal striving, well-being, and hope. *The Journal of Positive Psychology, 1*(3), 142–149. https://doi.org/10.1080/17439760600619849

Hudson, F., & McLean, N. (2012). *The coaching manager: Developing top talent in business* (2nd ed.). SAGE Publications.

International Coach Federation. (2021). *ICF code of ethics*. https://coachingfederation.org/ethics

Lavner, J. A., Karney, B. R., & Bradbury, T. N. (2016). Does commitment buffer the negative effects of relationship conflict? A study of newlywed couples. *Journal of Personality and Social Psychology, 110*(6), 818–833. https://doi.org/10.1037/pspi0000041

Linehan, M. M. (1993). *Cognitive-behavioral treatment of borderline personality disorder*. Guilford Press.

Norcross, J. C., & Wampold, B. E. (2011). Evidence-based therapy relationships: Research conclusions and clinical practices. *Psychotherapy, 48*(1), 98–102. https://doi.org/10.1037/a0022161

Parrott, L., & Parrott, L. (2005). *The complete guide to marriage mentoring: Connecting couples to build better marriages*. Zondervan.

Passmore, J. (2015). *Excellence in coaching: The industry guide* (2nd ed.). Kogan Page.

Rogers, C. R. (1951). *Client-centered therapy: Its current practice, implications, and theory*. Houghton Mifflin.

Stanley, S. M., Rhoades, G. K., & Markman, H. J. (2006). Sliding versus deciding: Inertia and the premarital cohabitation effect. *Family Relations, 55*(4), 499–509. https://doi.org/10.1111/j.1741-3729.2006.00418.x

Stober, D. R., & Grant, A. M. (2006). *Evidence-based coaching handbook: Putting best practices to work for your clients*. Wiley.

Chapter 2: Building Trust and Connection with Clients

Ambady, N., & Rosenthal, R. (1993). Half a minute: Predicting teacher evaluations from thin slices of nonverbal behavior and physical attractiveness. *Journal of Personality and Social Psychology, 64*(3), 431–441. https://doi.org/10.1037/0022-3514.64.3.431

Cozolino, L. (2014). *The neuroscience of human relationships: Attachment and the developing social brain* (2nd ed.). W. W. Norton & Company.

Edmondson, A. (1999). Psychological safety and learning behavior in work teams. *Administrative Science Quarterly, 44*(2), 350–383. https://doi.org/10.2307/2666999

Goleman, D. (1995). *Emotional intelligence: Why it can matter more than IQ*. Bantam Books.

Hill, C. E., Knox, S., & Pinto-Coelho, K. G. (2008). Therapist self-disclosure and immediacy: A qualitative study of experienced therapists. *Psychotherapy: Theory, Research, Practice, Training, 45*(4), 419–430. https://doi.org/10.1037/a0014332

Ickes, W. (1997). *Empathic accuracy*. Guilford Press.

Itzchakov, G., & Kluger, A. N. (2018, May 17). The power of listening in helping people change. *Harvard Business Review*. https://hbr.org/2018/05/the-power-of-listening-in-helping-people-change

Parrott, L., & Parrott, L. (2008). *Trading places: The best move you'll ever make in your marriage*. Zondervan.

Rogers, C. R. (1957). The necessary and sufficient conditions of therapeutic personality change. *Journal of Consulting Psychology, 21*(2), 95–103. https://doi.org/10.1037/h0045357

Safran, J. D., & Muran, J. C. (2000). *Negotiating the therapeutic alliance: A relational treatment guide*. Guilford Press.

Singer, T., Seymour, B., O'Doherty, J. P., Kaube, H., Dolan, R. J., & Frith, C. D. (2004). Empathy for pain involves the affective but not sensory components of pain. *Science, 303*(5661), 1157–1162. https://doi.org/10.1126/science.1093535

Chapter 3: Effective Communication Techniques for Coaches

Brooks, D. (2023). *How to know a person: The art of seeing others deeply and being deeply seen*. Random House.

Deci, E. L., & Ryan, R. M. (2000). The "what" and "why" of goal pursuits: Human needs and the self-determination of behavior. *Psychological Inquiry, 11*(4), 227–268. https://doi.org/10.1207/S15327965PLI1104_01

Grant, A. M. (2011). Is it time to REGROW the GROW model? Issues related to teaching coaching session structures. *The Coaching Psychologist, 7*(2), 118–126.

Grant, A. M. (2014). The efficacy of executive coaching in times of organizational change. *Journal of Change Management, 14*(2), 258–280. https://doi.org/10.1080/14697017.2013.805159

Lichtenberg, J. W., Lachmann, F. M., & Fosshage, J. L. (2002). *Developing the reflective self: A psychodynamic approach to psychotherapy*. Routledge.

Rogers, C. R. (1961). *On becoming a person: A therapist's view of psychotherapy*. Houghton Mifflin.

Ryan, R. M., & Deci, E. L. (2000). Intrinsic and extrinsic motivations: Classic definitions and new directions. *Contemporary Educational Psychology, 25*(1), 54–67. https://doi.org/10.1006/ceps.1999.1020

Siegel, D. J. (2010). *The mindful therapist: A clinician's guide to mindsight and neural integration*. W. W. Norton & Company.

Chapter 4: Understanding Relationship Dynamics

Deci, E. L., & Ryan, R. M. (2000). The "what" and "why" of goal pursuits: Human needs and the self-determination of behavior. *Psychological Inquiry, 11*(4), 227–268. https://doi.org/10.1207/S15327965PLI1104_01

Figley, C. R. (2002). *Compassion fatigue: Psychotherapists' chronic lack of self care*. Brunner-Routledge.

Friedman, E. H. (2007). *A failure of nerve: Leadership in the age of the quick fix*. Church Publishing.

Palmer, P. J. (2000). *Let your life speak: Listening for the voice of vocation*. Jossey-Bass.

Ryan, R. M., & Deci, E. L. (2000). Intrinsic and extrinsic motivations: Classic definitions and new directions. *Contemporary Educational Psychology, 25*(1), 54–67. https://doi.org/10.1006/ceps.1999.1020

Siegel, D. J. (2010). *The mindful therapist: A clinician's guide to mindsight and neural integration*. W. W. Norton & Company.

Chapter 5: The Science and Psychology Behind the 5 Love Languages

Aron, E. N., & Aron, A. (1997). Sensory-processing sensitivity and its relation to introversion and emotionality. *Journal of Personality and Social Psychology, 73*(2), 345–68. https://doi.org/10.1037/0022-3514.73.2.345

Asendorpf, J. B., & Wilpers, S. (1998). Personality effects on social relationships. *Journal of Personality and Social Psychology, 74*(6), 1531–44. https://doi.org/10.1037/0022-3514.74.6.1531

Bowlby, J. (1969). *Attachment and loss: Vol. 1. Attachment*. Basic Books.

Burleson, B. R.. The experience and effects of emotional support: What the study of cultural and gender differences can tell us about close relationships, emotion, and interpersonal communication. *Personal Relationships* 10, no. 1 (2003): 1–23. https://doi.org/10.1111/1475-6811.00033

Cacioppo, J. T., Cacioppo, S., Capitanio, J. P., & Cole, S. W. (2015). The neuroendocrinology of social isolation. *Annual Review of Psychology, 66*, 733–67. https://doi.org/10.1146/annurev-psych-010814-015240

Chaplin, T. M., & Aldao, A. (2013). Gender differences in emotion expression in children: A meta-analytic review. *Psychological Bulletin, 139*(4), 735–65. https://doi.org/10.1037/a0030737

Chapman, G. (2024). *The 5 love languages: The secret to love that lasts* (Revised ed.). Northfield Publishing.

Coan, J. A., Schaefer, H. S., & Davidson, R. J. Lending a hand: Social regulation of the neural response to threat. *Psychological Science* 17, no. 12 (2006): 1032–39. https://doi.org/10.1111/j.1467-9280.2006.01832.x

Deci, E. L., & Ryan, R. M. (2000). The "what" and "why" of goal pursuits: Human needs and the self-determination of behavior. *Psychological Inquiry, 11*(4), 227–268. https://doi.org/10.1207/S15327965PLI1104_01

Eisenberger, N. I., & Lieberman, M. D. (2004). Why rejection hurts: A common neural alarm system for physical and social pain. *Trends in Cognitive Sciences, 8*(7), 294–300. https://doi.org/10.1016/j.tics.2004.05.010

Finkel, E. J., Hui, C. M., Carswell, K. L., & Larson, G. M. (2014). The suffocation of marriage: Climbing Mount Maslow without enough oxygen. *Psychological Inquiry, 25*(1), 1–41. https://doi.org/10.1080/1047840X.2014.863723

Glasser, W. (1998). *Choice theory: A new psychology of personal freedom.* Harper Perennial.

Gottman, J. M., & Silver, N. (1999). *The seven principles for making marriage work.* Harmony Books.

Guerrero, L. K., Andersen, P. A., & Afifi, W. A. (2017). *Close encounters: Communication in relationships* (5th ed.). SAGE Publications.

Hazan, C., & Shaver, P. (1987). Romantic love conceptualized as an attachment process. *Journal of Personality and Social Psychology, 52*(3), 511–524. https://doi.org/10.1037/0022-3514.52.3.511

Holt-Lunstad, J., Smith, T. B., & Layton, J. B. (2010). Social relationships and mortality risk: A meta-analytic review. *PLoS Medicine, 7*(7), e1000316. https://doi.org/10.1371/journal.pmed.1000316

Insel, T. R., & Young, L. J. (2001). The neurobiology of attachment. *Nature Reviews Neuroscience, 2*(2), 129–136. https://doi.org/10.1038/35053579

Jensen-Campbell, L. A., & Graziano, W. G. (2001). Agreeableness as a moderator of interpersonal conflict. *Journal of Personality, 69*(2), 323–362. https://doi.org/10.1111/1467-6494.00148

Johnson, S. M. (2008). *Hold me tight: Seven conversations for a lifetime of love.* Little, Brown Spark.

Keely, A. C., & Malouff, J. M. (2022). Love languages as a predictor of relationship satisfaction. *Journal of Social and Personal Relationships, 39*(5), 1263–1283. https://doi.org/10.1177/02654075221074878

Maslow, A. H. (1943). A theory of human motivation. *Psychological Review, 50*(4), 370–396. https://doi.org/10.1037/h0054346

McCrae, R. R., & Costa, P. T. Jr. (1997). Personality trait structure as a human universal. *American Psychologist, 52*(5), 509–516. https://doi.org/10.1037/0003-066X.52.5.509

Mikulincer, M., & Shaver, P. R. (2007). *Attachment in adulthood: Structure, dynamics, and change.* Guilford Press.

Perry, B. D., Pollard, R. A., Blakley, T. L., Baker, W. L., & Vigilante, D. (1995). Childhood trauma, the neurobiology of adaptation, and "use-dependent" development of the brain: How "states" become "traits." *Infant Mental Health Journal, 16*(4), 271–291. https://doi.org/10.1002/1097-0355(199524)16:4<271::AID-IMHJ2280160404>3.0.CO;2-B

Robins, R. W., Caspi, A., & Moffitt, T. E. (2002). It's not just who you're with, it's who you are: Personality and relationship experiences across multiple relationships. *Journal of Personality, 70*(6), 925–964. https://doi.org/10.1111/1467-6494.05028

Ryan, R. M., & Deci, E. L. (2000). Self-determination theory and the facilitation of intrinsic motivation, social development, and well-being. *American Psychologist, 55*(1), 68–78. https://doi.org/10.1037/0003-066X.55.1.68

Simpson, J. A., & Rholes, W. S. (2012). Adult attachment orientations, stress, and romantic relationships. In P. Devine & A. Plant (Eds.), *Advances in Experimental Social Psychology* (Vol. 45, pp. 279–328). Academic Press. https://doi.org/10.1016/B978-0-12-394286-9.00006-8

Skinner, B. F. (1953). *Science and human behavior*. Macmillan.

Chapter 6: Helping Clients Discover Their Primary Love Language

Aron, E. N., & Aron, A. (1997). Sensory-processing sensitivity and its relation to introversion and emotionality. *Journal of Personality and Social Psychology, 73*(2), 345–368. https://doi.org/10.1037/0022-3514.73.2.345

Campbell, J. D., Trapnell, P. D., Heine, S. J., Katz, I. M., Lavallee, L. F., & Lehman, D. R. (2003). Self-concept clarity: Measurement, personality correlates, and cultural boundaries. *Journal of Personality and Social Psychology, 85*(3), 538–556. https://doi.org/10.1037/0022-3514.85.3.538

Feeney, B. C., & Collins, N. L. (2015). A new look at social support: A theoretical perspective on thriving through relationships. *Personality and Social Psychology Review, 19*(2), 113–147. https://doi.org/10.1177/1088868314544222

Gottman, J. M., & Silver, N. (1999). *The seven principles for making marriage work*. New York, NY: Crown Publishers.

Jensen-Campbell, L. A., & Graziano, W. G. (2001). Agreeableness as a moderator of interpersonal conflict. *Journal of Personality, 69*(2), 323–362. https://doi.org/10.1111/1467-6494.00148

Keely, A. C., & Malouff, J. M. (2022). Love languages as a predictor of relationship satisfaction. *Journal of Social and Personal Relationships, 39*(5), 1263–1283. https://doi.org/10.1177/02654075221074878

Mikulincer, M., & Shaver, P. R. (2007). *Attachment in adulthood: Structure, dynamics, and change*. New York, NY: Guilford Press.

Perry, B. D., Pollard, R. A., Blakley, T. L., Baker, W. L., & Vigilante, D. (1995). Childhood trauma, the neurobiology of adaptation, and "use-dependent" development of the brain: How "states" become "traits." *Infant Mental Health Journal, 16*(4), 271–291. https://doi.org/10.1002/1097-0355(199524)16:4<271::AID-IMHJ2280160404>3.0.CO;2-B

Schutte, N. S., Malouff, J. M., Bobik, C., Coston, T. D., Greeson, C., Jedlicka, C., Rhodes, E., & Wendorf, G. (2001). Emotional intelligence and interpersonal relations. *The Journal of Social Psychology, 141*(4), 523–536. https://doi.org/10.1080/00224540109600569

Siegel, D. J. (2012). *The developing mind: How relationships and the brain interact to shape who we are* (2nd ed.). Guilford Press.

Chapter 7: Coaching Words of Affirmation

Brown, B. (2012). *Daring greatly: How the courage to be vulnerable transforms the way we live, love, parent, and lead.* Gotham Books.

Burleson, B. R. (2003). The experience and effects of emotional support: What the study of cultural and gender differences can tell us. *Personal Relationships, 10*(1), 1–23. https://doi.org/10.1111/1475-6811.00033

Chaplin, T. M., & Aldao, A. (2013). Gender differences in emotion expression in children: A meta-analytic review. *Psychological Bulletin, 139*(4), 735–765. https://doi.org/10.1037/a0030737

Guerrero, L. K., Andersen, P. A., & Afifi, W. A. (2017). *Close encounters: Communication in relationships* (5th ed.). Thousand Oaks, CA: SAGE Publications.

Gottman, J. M., & Levenson, R. W. (1992). Marital processes predictive of later dissolution: Behavior, physiology, and health. *Journal of Personality and Social Psychology, 63*(2), 221–233. https://doi.org/10.1037/0022-3514.63.2.221

Gottman, J. M., & Silver, N. (1999). *The seven principles for making marriage work.* Harmony Books.

Jensen-Campbell, L. A., & Graziano, W. G. (2001). Agreeableness as a moderator of interpersonal conflict. *Journal of Personality, 69*(2), 323–362. https://doi.org/10.1111/1467-6494.00148

Keely, A. C., & Malouff, J. M. (2022). Love languages as a predictor of relationship satisfaction. *Journal of Social and Personal Relationships, 39*(5), 1263–1283. https://doi.org/10.1177/02654075221074878

Mikulincer, M., & Shaver, P. R. (2007). *Attachment in adulthood: Structure, dynamics, and change.* Guilford Press.

Rogers, C. R. (1951). *Client-centered therapy: Its current practice, implications, and theory.* Houghton Mifflin.

Siegel, D. J. (2012). *The developing mind: How relationships and the brain interact to shape who we are* (2nd ed.). Guilford Press.

Skinner, B. F. (1953). *Science and human behavior.* Macmillan.

Chapter 8: Coaching Quality Time

Gordon, A. M., & Chen, S. (2016). The role of mindfulness and commitment in predicting responsiveness to relationship partners. *Journal of Experimental Social Psychology, 63*, 18–25. https://doi.org/10.1016/j.jesp.2015.11.004

Mikulincer, M., & Shaver, P. R. (2007). *Attachment in adulthood: Structure, dynamics, and change.* Guilford Press.

Reis, H. T., & Shaver, P. R. (1988). Intimacy as an interpersonal process. In S. Duck (Ed.), *Handbook of personal relationships* (pp. 367–389). Wiley.

Schore, A. N. (2001). The effects of early relational trauma on right brain development, affect regulation, and infant mental health. *Infant Mental Health Journal, 22*(1–2), 201–269. https://doi.org/10.1002/1097-0355(200101/04)22:1<201::AID-IMHJ8>3.0.CO; 2-9

Siegel, D. J. (2012). *The developing mind: How relationships and the brain interact to shape who we are* (2nd ed.). Guilford Press.

Turkle, S. (2015). *Reclaiming conversation: The power of talk in a digital age.* Penguin Press.

Chapter 9: Coaching Receiving Gifts

Belk, R. W. (1979). Gift-giving behavior. *Research in Marketing, 2*, 95–126.

Floyd, K., & Morman, M. T. (2001). Human affection exchange: V. Attributes of the highly affectionate. *Communication Quarterly, 49*(2), 135–153. https://doi.org/10.1080/01463370109385621

Grote, N. K., & Clark, M. S. (2001). Perceiving unfairness in the family: Cause or consequence of marital distress? *Journal of Personality and Social Psychology, 80*(2), 281–293. https://doi.org/10.1037/0022-3514.80.2.281

Sherry, J. F. Jr. (1983). Gift giving in anthropological perspective. *Journal of Consumer Research, 10*(2), 157–168. https://doi.org/10.1086/208956

Solomon, M. R. (1983). The role of products as social stimuli: A symbolic interactionism perspective. *Journal of Consumer Research, 10*(3), 319–329. https://doi.org/10.1086/208971

Chapter 10: Coaching Acts of Service

Algoe, S. B., Gable, S. L., & Maisel, N. C. (2010). It's the little things: Everyday gratitude as a booster shot for romantic relationships. *Personal Relationships, 17*(2), 217–233. https://doi.org/10.1111/j.1475-6811.2010.01273.x

Brown, B. (2012). *Daring greatly: How the courage to be vulnerable transforms the way we live, love, parent, and lead.* Gotham Books.

Cutrona, C. E. (1996). *Social support in couples: Marriage as a resource in times of stress.* Sage.

Feeney, B. C., & Collins, N. L. (2015). A new look at social support: A theoretical perspective on thriving through relationships. *Personality and Social Psychology Review, 19*(2), 113–147. https://doi.org/10.1177/1088868314544222

Gordon, A. M., & Chen, S. (2016). The role of mindfulness and commitment in predicting responsiveness to relationship partners. *Journal of Experimental Social Psychology, 63*, 18–25. https://doi.org/10.1016/j.jesp.2015.11.004

Mikulincer, M., & Shaver, P. R. (2007). *Attachment in adulthood: Structure, dynamics, and change.* Guilford Press.

Offer, S. (2012). The burden of reciprocity: Processes of exclusion and withdrawal in dyadic relationships. *Journal of Marriage and Family, 74*(3), 526–541. https://doi.org/10.1111/j.1741-3737.2012.00974.x

Pepin, J. R., & Cotter, D. A. (2018). Separating spheres? Diverging trends in youth's gender attitudes about work and family. *Journal of Marriage and Family, 80*(1), 7–24. https://doi.org/10.1111/jomf.12433

Reis, H. T., & Clark, M. S. (2013). Responsiveness. In J. A. Simpson & L. Campbell (Eds.), *The Oxford handbook of close relationships* (pp. 400–423). Oxford University Press.

Reis, H. T., Clark, M. S., & Holmes, J. G. (2004). Perceived partner responsiveness as an organizing construct in the study of intimacy and closeness. In D. J. Mashek & A. Aron (Eds.), *Handbook of closeness and intimacy* (pp. 201–225). Lawrence Erlbaum Associates.

Ruppanner, L., Lee, R., & Carlson, D. L. (2021). Fathers, flexibility, and fear: How COVID-19 drives gender inequality. *Gender, Work & Organization, 28*(S1), 725–737. https://doi.org/10.1111/gwao.12508

Shrout, M. R. (2017). Partner support in times of stress: The role of dyadic coping. *Current Opinion in Psychology, 13*, 29–33. https://doi.org/10.1016/j.copsyc.2016.04.014

Chapter 11: Coaching Physical Touch

Chapman, G. (2024). *The 5 love languages: The secret to love that lasts.* Northfield Publishing.

Coan, J. A., Schaefer, H. S., & Davidson, R. J. (2006). Lending a hand: Social regulation of the neural response to threat. *Psychological Science, 17*(12), 1032–1039. https://doi.org/10.1111/j.1467-9280.2006.01832.x

Debrot, A., Schoebi, D., Perrez, M., & Horn, A. B. (2013). Touch as an interpersonal emotion regulation process in couples' daily lives: The mediating role of psychological intimacy. *Personality and Social Psychology Bulletin, 39*(10), 1373–1385. https://doi.org/10.1177/0146167213497592

Field, T. (2010). Touch for socioemotional and physical well-being: A review. *Developmental Review, 30*(4), 367–383. https://doi.org/10.1016/j.dr.2011.01.001

Hertenstein, M. J., Holmes, R., McCullough, M., & Keltner, D. (2006). The communication of emotion via touch. *Emotion, 6*(3), 528–533. https://doi.org/10.1037/1528-3542.6.3.528

Jakubiak, B. K., & Feeney, B. C. (2017). Affectionate touch to promote relational, psychological, and physical well-being in adulthood: A theoretical model and review of the research. *Personality and Social Psychology Review, 21*(3), 228–252. https://doi.org/10.1177/1088868316650307

Morrison, I. (2016). Keep calm and cuddle on: Social touch as a stress buffer. *Adaptive Human Behavior and Physiology, 2*(4), 344–362. https://doi.org/10.1007/s40750-016-0052-x

Trotter, K. S., & Leach, M. M. (2017). The influence of affectionate touch on relationship satisfaction and commitment in romantic couples. *Journal of Social and Personal Relationships, 34*(2), 223–246. https://doi.org/10.1177/0265407516631945

Uvnäs-Moberg, K. (2009). *The oxytocin factor: Tapping the hormone of calm, love, and healing.* Da Capo Press.

Chapter 12: The Value of Assessments in Coaching Relationships

Jarvis, J., Lane, D. A., & Fillery-Travis, A. (2021). *Coaching and mentoring: Theory and practice* (3rd ed.). SAGE Publications.

Kolb, A. Y., & Kolb, D. A. (2018). Eight important things to know about the experiential learning cycle. *Australian Educational Leader, 40*(3), 8–14.

Peterson, C., & Seligman, M. E. P. (2020). *Positive psychotherapy: Clinical tools for promoting well-being.* American Psychological Association.

Ting, S., & Scisco, P. (2006). *The CCL handbook of coaching: A guide for the leader coach.* Jossey-Bass.

Chapter 13: Exploring the 5 Love Languages Premium Assessment

Bodie, G. D. (2011). The active-empathic listening scale (AELS): Conceptualization and evidence of validity within the interpersonal domain. *Communication Quarterly, 59*(3), 277–295. https://doi.org/10.1080/01463373.2011.583495

Chapman, G. (2024). *The 5 love languages: The secret to love that lasts* (Revised ed.). Northfield Publishing.

Goleman, D. (2006). *Social intelligence: The new science of human relationships.* Bantam Books.

Kashdan, T. B., Goodman, F. R., Mallard, T. T., & DeWall, C. N. (2011). Who is most vulnerable to social rejection? The role of emotional intelligence, self-esteem, and emotion regulation. *Personality and Individual Differences, 50*(3), 350–355. https://doi.org/10.1016/j.paid.2010.10.010

McCrae, R. R., & Costa, P. T. Jr. (2008). The five-factor theory of personality. In O. P. John, R. W. Robins, & L. A. Pervin (Eds.), *Handbook of personality: Theory and research* (3rd ed., pp. 159–181). The Guilford Press.

Reis, H. T., & Shaver, P. R. (1988). Intimacy as an interpersonal process. In S. Duck (Ed.), *Handbook of personal relationships* (pp. 367–389). Wiley.

Rogers, C. R. (1959). A theory of therapy, personality, and interpersonal relationships: As developed in the client-centered framework. In S. Koch (Ed.), *Psychology: A study of a science* (Vol. 3, pp. 184–256). McGraw-Hill.

Chapter 14: Walking Through the Assessment Results with Clients

Kashdan, T. B., Goodman, F. R., Mallard, T. T., & DeWall, C. N. (2011). Who is most vulnerable to social rejection? The role of emotional intelligence, self-esteem, and emotion regulation. *Personality and Individual Differences, 50*(3), 350–355. https://doi.org/10.1016/j.paid.2010.10.010

Neff, K. D., & Germer, C. K. (2018). *The mindful self-compassion workbook: A proven way to accept yourself, build inner strength, and thrive.* Guilford Press.

Rogers, C. R. (1959). A theory of therapy, personality, and interpersonal relationships: As developed in the client-centered framework. In S. Koch (Ed.), *Psychology: A study of a science* (Vol. 3, pp. 184–256). McGraw-Hill.

Siegel, D. J. (2010). *The mindful therapist: A clinician's guide to mindsight and neural integration.* W. W. Norton & Company.

Chapter 15: Using the Premium Assessment to Support Growth Over Time

Chapman, G. (2024). *The 5 love languages: The secret to love that lasts* (Revised ed.). Northfield Publishing.

Clark, M. S., & Lemay, E. P. (2010). Close relationships. In S. T. Fiske, D. T. Gilbert, & G. Lindzey (Eds.), *Handbook of social psychology* (5th ed., pp. 898–940). Wiley.

Duhigg, C. (2012). *The power of habit: Why we do what we do in life and business.* Random House.

Fiese, B. H., Tomcho, T. J., Douglas, M., Josephs, K., Poltrock, S., & Baker, T. (2002). A review of 50 years of research on naturally occurring family routines and rituals: Cause for celebration? *Journal of Family Psychology, 16*(4), 381–390. https://doi.org/10.1037/0893-3200.16.4.381

Fogg, B. J. (2020). *Tiny habits: The small changes that change everything.* Houghton Mifflin Harcourt.

Gottman, J. M., & Silver, N. (1999). *The seven principles for making marriage work.* Crown Publishers.

Michie, S., Johnston, M., Francis, J., Hardeman, W., & Eccles, M. (2009). From theory to intervention: Mapping theoretically derived behavioural determinants to behaviour change techniques. *Applied Psychology, 57*(4), 660–680. https://doi.org/10.1111/j.1464-0597.2008.00341.x

Neff, K. D., & Germer, C. K. (2018). *The mindful self-compassion workbook: A proven way to accept yourself, build inner strength, and thrive.* Guilford Press.

Reis, H. T., & Gable, S. L. (2003). Toward a positive psychology of relationships. In C. L. M. Keyes & J. Haidt (Eds.), *Flourishing: Positive psychology and the life well-lived* (pp. 129–159). American Psychological Association. https://doi.org/10.1037/10594-006

Schrodt, P., Witt, P. L., & Messersmith, A. S. (2007). A meta-analytical review of the association between family communication patterns and relational satisfaction. *Communication Monographs, 74*(4), 490–516. https://doi.org/10.1080/03637750701716525

Ward, M. K., & Broniarczyk, S. M. (2016). Ask and you shall (not) receive: Close friends' reactions to gift requests. *Journal of Marketing Research, 53*(6), 1001–1017. https://doi.org/10.1509/jmr.13.0417

Weger Jr., H., Castle, G. R., & Emmett, M. C. (2014). Active listening in peer interviews: The influence of message paraphrasing on perceptions of listening skill. *The International Journal of Listening, 28*(1), 13–31. https://doi.org/10.1080/10904018.2014.861293

Chapter 16: Helping Couples Understand Each Other's Love Language

Driver, J. L., & Gottman, J. M. (2004). Daily marital interactions and positive affect during marital conflict among newlywed couples. *Family Process, 43*(3), 301–314. https://doi.org/10.1111/j.1545-5300.2004.00024.x

Gottman, J. M., & Silver, N. (1999). *The seven principles for making marriage work.* Crown Publishers.

Gottman, J. M., Coan, J., Carrere, S., & Swanson, C. (1998). Predicting marital happiness and stability from newlywed interactions. *Journal of Marriage and the Family, 60*(1), 5–22. https://doi.org/10.2307/353438

Johnson, S. M. (2008). *Hold me tight: Seven conversations for a lifetime of love.* Little, Brown Spark.

Kellas, J. K. (2005). Family ties: Communicating identity through jointly told family stories. *Communication Monographs, 72*(4), 365–389. https://doi.org/10.1080/03637750500322513

Maisel, N. C., & Gable, S. L. (2009). For richer… in good times… and in health: Positive processes in relationships. In E. P. Lemay & J. G. Holmes (Eds.), *The social psychology of relationships* (pp. 269–292). Guilford Press.

Mikulincer, M., & Shaver, P. R. (2007). *Attachment in adulthood: Structure, dynamics, and change.* Guilford Press.

Reis, H. T., Clark, M. S., & Holmes, J. G. (2004). Perceived partner responsiveness as an organizing construct in the study of intimacy and closeness. In D. J. Mashek & A. Aron (Eds.), *Handbook of closeness and intimacy* (pp. 201–225). Lawrence Erlbaum.

Reis, H. T., & Shaver, P. R. (1988). Intimacy as an interpersonal process. In S. Duck (Ed.), *Handbook of personal relationships* (pp. 367–389). Wiley.

Chapter 17: Leveraging the "Love Tank"

Butler, E. A., & Randall, A. K. (2013). Emotional coregulation in close relationships. *Emotion Review, 5*(2), 202–210. https://doi.org/10.1177/1754073912451630

Campbell, R. (1977). *How to really love your child.* Victor Books.

Chapman, G. (2024). *The 5 love languages: The secret to love that lasts* (Revised ed.). Northfield Publishing.

Collins, N. L., & Feeney, B. C. (2004). An attachment theory perspective on closeness and intimacy. In D. J. Mashek & A. Aron (Eds.), *Handbook of closeness and intimacy* (pp. 163–187). Lawrence Erlbaum.

Gable, S. L., Gonzaga, G. C., & Strachman, A. (2006). Will you be there for me when things go right? Supportive responses to positive event disclosures. *Journal of Personality and Social Psychology, 91*(5), 904–917. https://doi.org/10.1037/0022-3514.91.5.904

Galinsky, A. D., Maddux, W. W., Gilin, D., & White, J. B. (2008). Why it pays to get inside the head of your opponent: The differential effects of perspective taking and empathy in negotiations. *Psychological Science, 19*(4), 378–384. https://doi.org/10.1111/j.1467-9280.2008.02096.x

Gordon, A. M., & Chen, S. (2013). Does power help or hurt? The moderating role of self–other focus on power and perspective taking in romantic relationships. *Personality and Social Psychology Bulletin, 39*(8), 1097–1110. https://doi.org/10.1177/0146167213490031

Gottman, J. M., & Silver, N. (1999). *The seven principles for making marriage work.* Crown Publishers.

Greenberg, L. S., & Goldman, R. N. (2008). *Emotion-focused couples therapy: The dynamics of emotion, love, and power.* American Psychological Association.

Reis, H. T., & Clark, M. S. (2013). Responsiveness. In J. A. Simpson & L. Campbell (Eds.), *The Oxford handbook of close relationships* (pp. 400–423). Oxford University Press.

Reis, H. T., & Shaver, P. R. (1988). Intimacy as an interpersonal process. In S. Duck (Ed.), *Handbook of personal relationships* (pp. 367–389). Wiley.

Chapter 18: The Love Language That Matters Most

Algoe, S. B., Fredrickson, B. L., & Gable, S. L. (2013). The social functions of the emotion of gratitude via expression. *Emotion, 13*(4), 605–609. https://doi.org/10.1037/a0032701

Aron, A., Melinat, E., Aron, E. N., Vallone, R. D., & Bator, R. J. (1997). The experimental generation of interpersonal closeness: A procedure and some preliminary findings. *Personality and Social Psychology Bulletin, 23*(4), 363–377. https://doi.org/10.1177/0146167297234003

Chapman, G., Parrott, L., & Parrott, L. (2026). *The love language that matters most.* Northfield Publishing.

Detweiler-Bedell, B., & Whisman, M. A. (2005). The role of homework assignments in cognitive therapy for depression: Potential methods for enhancing adherence and efficacy. *Clinical Psychology: Science and Practice, 12*(4), 376–382. https://doi.org/10.1093/clipsy.bpi048

Gable, S. L., Gonzaga, G. C., & Strachman, A. (2006). Will you be there for me when things go right? Supportive responses to positive event disclosures. *Journal of Personality and Social Psychology, 91*(5), 904–917. https://doi.org/10.1037/0022-3514.91.5.904

Galinsky, A. D., Maddux, W. W., Gilin, D., & White, J. B. (2008). Why it pays to get inside the head of your opponent: The differential effects of perspective taking and empathy in negotiations. *Psychological Science, 19*(4), 378–384. https://doi.org/10.1111/j.1467-9280.2008.02096.x

Gordon, A. M., & Chen, S. (2013). Does power help or hurt? The moderating role of self–other focus on power and perspective taking in romantic relationships. *Personality and Social Psychology Bulletin, 39*(8), 1097–1110. https://doi.org/10.1177/0146167213490031

Gordon, A. M., Impett, E. A., Kogan, A., Oveis, C., & Keltner, D. (2012). To have and to hold: Gratitude promotes relationship maintenance in intimate bonds. *Journal of Personality and Social Psychology, 103*(2), 257–274. https://doi.org/10.1037/a0028723

Kazantzis, N., Deane, F. P., & Ronan, K. R. (2000). Homework assignments in cognitive and behavioral therapy: A meta-analysis. *Clinical Psychology: Science and Practice, 7*(2), 189–202. https://doi.org/10.1093/clipsy.7.2.189

Kashdan, T. B., & Roberts, J. E. (2004). Trait and state curiosity in the genesis of intimacy: Differentiation from related constructs. *Journal of Social and Clinical Psychology, 23*(6), 792–816. https://doi.org/10.1521/jscp.23.6.792.54800

Kashdan, T. B., Sherman, R. A., Yarbro, J., & Funder, D. C. (2011). How are curious people viewed and how do they behave in social situations? From the perspectives of self, friends, parents, and unacquainted observers. *Journal of Personality, 79*(2), 231–256. https://doi.org/10.1111/j.1467-6494.2010.00662.x

Keysar, B., Lin, S., & Barr, D. J. (2003). Limits on theory of mind use in adults. *Psychological Science, 14*(4), 307–311. https://doi.org/10.1111/1467-9280.24454

Laurenceau, J. P., Barrett, L. F., & Pietromonaco, P. R. (1998). Intimacy as an interpersonal process: The importance of self-disclosure, partner disclosure, and perceived partner responsiveness. *Journal of Personality and Social Psychology, 74*(5), 1238–1251. https://doi.org/10.1037/0022-3514.74.5.1238

Lieberman, M. D. (2013). Social: *Why our brains are wired to connect.* New York, NY: Crown Publishers.

Longmire, N. H., & Harrison, D. A. (2018). Seeing their side versus feeling their pain: Differential consequences of perspective-taking and empathy at work. *Journal of Applied Psychology, 103*(8), 894–915. https://doi.org/10.1037/apl0000307

Parrott, L., & Parrott, L. (2008). *Trading places: The best move you'll ever make in your marriage.* Zondervan.

Reis, H. T., Clark, M. S., & Holmes, J. G. (2004). Perceived partner responsiveness as an organizing construct in the study of intimacy and closeness. In D. J. Mashek & A. P. Aron (Eds.), *Handbook of closeness and intimacy* (pp. 201–225). Mahwah, NJ: Lawrence Erlbaum Associates.

Reis, H. T., & Shaver, P. (1988). Intimacy as an interpersonal process. In S. Duck (Ed.), *Handbook of Personal Relationships* (pp. 367–389). Wiley.

Sprecher, S., & Hendrick, S. S. (2004). Self-disclosure in intimate relationships: Associations with individual and relationship characteristics over time. *Journal of Social and Clinical Psychology, 23*(6), 857–877. https://doi.org/10.1521/jscp.23.6.857.54803

Zaki, J., & Ochsner, K. N. (2012). The neuroscience of empathy: Progress, pitfalls and promise. *Nature Neuroscience*, 15(5), 675–680. https://doi.org/10.1038/nn.3085

Chapter 19: Coaching Singles with the 5 Love Languages

Adamczyk, K., & Segrin, C. (2015). Direct and indirect effects of young adults' relationship status on life satisfaction through loneliness and perceived social support. *Psychological Topics, 24*(1), 127–144.

Chapman, G. (2004). *The 5 love languages: Singles edition.* Moody Publishers.

Chopik, W. J. (2017). Associations among relational values, support, health, and well-being across the adult lifespan. *Personal Relationships, 24*(2), 408–422. https://doi.org/10.1111/pere.12187

Dimidjian, S., Barrera, M., Martell, C., Muñoz, R. F., & Lewinsohn, P. M. (2011). The origins and current status of behavioral activation treatments for depression. *Annual Review of Clinical Psychology, 7*, 1–38. https://doi.org/10.1146/annurev-clinpsy-032210-104535

Reis, H. T., & Shaver, P. (1988). Intimacy as an interpersonal process. In S. Duck (Ed.), *Handbook of personal relationships* (pp. 367–389). Wiley.

Chapter 20: Coaching Parents with the 5 Love Languages

Chapman, G. (1992). *The 5 love languages: The secret to love that lasts.* Northfield Publishing.

Chapman, G., & Campbell, R. (2012). *The 5 love languages of children: The secret to loving children effectively.* Northfield Publishing.

Liss, M., Schiffrin, H. H., Mackintosh, V. H., Miles-McLean, H., & Erchull, M. J. (2013). Development and validation of a quantitative measure of intensive parenting attitudes. *Journal of Child and Family Studies, 22*(5), 621–636. https://doi.org/10.1007/s10826-012-9616-y

Reis, H. T., & Shaver, P. (1988). Intimacy as an interpersonal process. In S. Duck (Ed.), *Handbook of personal relationships* (pp. 367–389). Wiley.

Tronick, E. (2007). *The neurobehavioral and social-emotional development of infants and children.* Norton.

Chapter 21: Coaching Love Languages in Crisis and Conflict

Gottman, J. M., & Gottman, J. S. (2015). *10 principles for doing effective couples therapy.* W. W. Norton & Company.

Johnson, S. M. (2008). *Hold me tight: Seven conversations for a lifetime of love.* Little, Brown Spark.

Mikulincer, M., & Shaver, P. R. (2007). *Attachment in adulthood: Structure, dynamics, and change.* Guilford Press.

Porges, S. W. (2011). *The polyvagal theory: Neurophysiological foundations of emotions, attachment, communication, and self-regulation.* W. W. Norton & Company.

Chapter 22: The Business of Love Language Coaching

Bachkirova, T., Cox, E., & Clutterbuck, D. (2014). *The complete handbook of coaching* (2nd ed.). Sage.

International Coaching Federation. (2021). *ICF code of ethics.* Retrieved from https://coachingfederation.org/ethics/code-of-ethics

Jones, R. J., Woods, S. A., & Guillaume, Y. R. F. (2016). The effectiveness of workplace coaching: A meta-analysis of learning and performance outcomes from coaching. *Journal of Occupational and Organizational Psychology, 89*(2), 249–277.

Nagle, T. T., Hogan, J. E., & Zale, J. (2016). *The strategy and tactics of pricing: A guide to growing more profitably* (5th ed.). Routledge.

Chapter 23: Marketing Your Coaching Services

Jiwa, B. (2019). *Marketing: A love story: How to matter to your customers.* Perceptive Press.

Kotler, P., Kartajaya, H., & Setiawan, I. (2017). *Marketing 4.0: Moving from traditional to digital.* Wiley.

Miller, D. (2017). *Building a storybrand: Clarify your message so customers will listen.* HarperCollins Leadership.

Chapter 24: Partnering with Churches and Organizations

American Association for Marriage and Family Therapy. (2015). *Best practices in mental health collaboration.* AAMFT.

Frame, M. W. (2003). *Integrating faith and practice: A professional guide for Christian counselors.* Brooks/Cole.

Olson, D. H., & Olson-Sigg, A. (2000). Empowering churches to build strong marriages and healthy families. *Journal of Psychology and Christianity, 19*(3), 281–289.

Pargament, K. I. (2007). *Spiritually integrated psychotherapy: Understanding and addressing the sacred.* Guilford Press.

Chapter 25: Continuing Education and Growth as a Coach

Rogers, C. R. (1961). *On becoming a person: A therapist's view of psychotherapy.* Houghton Mifflin.

Schön, D. A. (1983). *The reflective practitioner: How professionals think in action.* Basic Books.

Index